HTML, JAVASCRIPT, AND ADVANCED INTERNET TECHNOLOGIES BASICS

D0218893

Karl Barksdale
Technology Consultant, Provo, Utah

E. Shane Turner
Software Engineer, Orem, Utah

THOMSON
★
COURSE TECHNOLOGY™

Australia • Canada • Mexico • Singapore • Spain • United Kingdom • United States

THOMSON

COURSE TECHNOLOGY

HTML, JavaScript, and Advanced Internet Technologies
by Karl Barksdale and E. Shane Turner

Vice President, School Publishing and Marketing
Cheryl Costantini

Product Manager
David Rivera

Editorial Assistant
Justine Brennan

Director of Production
Patty Stephan

Senior Acquisitions Editor
Jane Mazares

Senior Marketing Manager
Kim Ryttel

School Market Specialist
Meagan Putney

Development Editor
Custom Editorial Productions, Inc.

Production Editor
Custom Editorial Productions, Inc.

Compositor
GEX Publishing Services

Printer
Banta—Menasha

COPYRIGHT © 2006 Thomson Course Technology, a division of Thomson Learning, Inc. Thomson Learning™ is a trademark used herein under license.

Printed in the United States of America

1 2 3 4 5 6 7 8 9 BM 04 03 02

For more information, contact Course Technology, 25 Thomson Place, Boston, Massachusetts, 02210.

Or find us on the World Wide Web at: www.course.com

ALL RIGHTS RESERVED. No part of this work covered by the copyright hereon may be reproduced or used in any form or by any means—graphic, electronic, or mechanical, including photocopying, recording, taping, Web distribution, or information storage and retrieval systems—without the written permission of the publisher.

For permission to use material from this text or product, contact us by

Tel (800) 730-2214
Fax (800) 730-2215
www.thomsonrights.com

Disclaimer
Course Technology reserves the right to revise this publication and make changes from time to time in its content without notice.

ISBN 0-619-26627-9

Get Back to the Basics...
With these *exciting new products*

Our exciting new series of short, programming and application suite books will provide everything needed to learn this software. Other books include:

NEW! HTML BASICS, 3ʳᵈ Ed. by Barksdale and Turner
20+ hours of instruction for beginning through intermediate learners

0-619-26626-0	Textbook, softcover
0-619-26628-7	Instructor Resources
0-619-26629-5	Review Pack (Data CD)

NEW! HTML and JavaScript BASICS, 3rd Ed. by Barksdale and Turner
20+ hours of instruction for beginning through intermediate learners

0-619-26625-2	Textbook, softcover
0-619-26628-7	Instructor Resources
0-619-26629-5	Review Pack (Data CD)

Programming BASICS, Using Microsoft Visual Basic, C++, HTML, and Java
by Knowlton & Barksdale
35+ hours of instruction for beginning through intermediate learners

0-619-05803-X	Textbook, hardcover
0-619-05801-3	Textbook, softcover
0-619-05802-1	Instructor Resources
0-619-05800-5	Activities Workbook
0-619-05949-4	Review Pack (Data CD)

Internet BASICS by Barksdale, Rutter, & Teeter
35+ hours of instruction for beginning through intermediate learners

0-619-05905-2	Textbook, softcover, spiral-bound
0-619-05906-0	Instructor Resources

NEW! Microsoft Office 2003 BASICS by Pasewark and Pasewark
35+ hours of instruction for beginning through intermediate learners

0-619-18335-7	Textbook, hardcover, spiral-bound
0-619-18337-3	Instructor Resources
0-619-18336-5	Activities Workbook
0-619-18338-1	Review Pack (Data CD)

Join Us On the Internet **www.course.com**

TABLE OF CONTENTS

UNIT 1 HTML BASICS

UNIT 2 THE EXCITING WORLD OF JAVASCRIPT

UNIT 3 ADVANCED INTERNET TECHNOLOGIES

How to Use This Book

What makes a good text about HTML and JavaScript? Sound instruction and hands-on skill-building and reinforcement. That is what you will find in *HTML, JavaScript, and Advanced Internet Technologies BASICS.* Not only will you find a colorful and inviting layout, but also many features to enhance learning.

Objectives— Objectives are listed at the beginning of each lesson, along with a suggested time for completion of the lesson. This allows you to look ahead to what you will be learning and to pace your work.

Step-by-Step Exercises— Preceded by a short topic discussion, these exercises are the "hands-on practice" part of the lesson. Simply follow the steps to reinforce the skills and concepts you have learned.

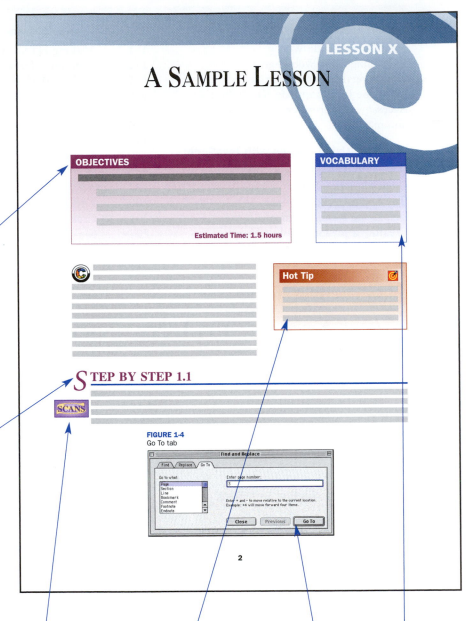

LESSON X

A SAMPLE LESSON

OBJECTIVES

Estimated Time: 1.5 hours

VOCABULARY

Hot Tip

S TEP BY STEP 1.1

SCANS

FIGURE 1-4
Go To tab

2

SCANS (Secretary's Commission on Achieving Necessary Skills)—The U.S. Department of Labor has identified the school-to-careers competencies.

Marginal Boxes— These boxes provide additional information about the topic of the lesson.

Vocabulary— Terms identified in boldface throughout the lesson and summarized at the end.

Enhanced Screen Shots— Screen shots now come to life on each page with color and depth.

How to Use This Book

Special Feature Boxes—These boxes provide interesting additional information about career opportunities, tips on how to create better Web pages, and historical Internet milestones.

Summary—At the end of each lesson, you will find a summary to prepare you to complete the end-of-lesson activities.

Vocabulary/Review Questions—Review material at the end of each lesson and each unit enables you to prepare for assessment of the content presented.

Lesson Projects—Hands-on application of what you have learned in the lesson allows you to apply the techniques and concepts covered.

Critical Thinking Activities—Each lesson gives you an opportunity to apply creative analysis and use the Help system to solve problems.

Command Summary—At the end of each unit, a command summary is provided for quick reference.

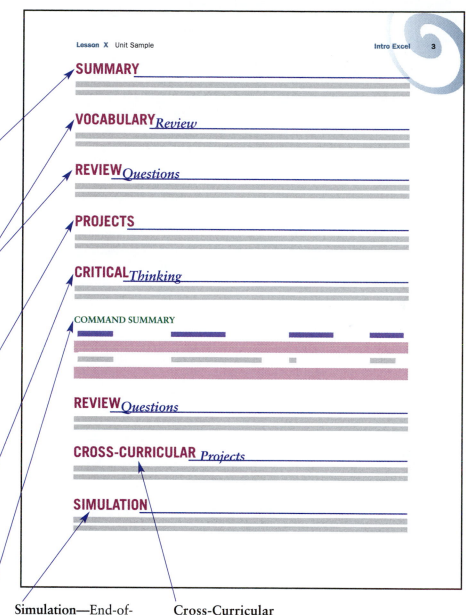

Simulation—End-of-unit hands-on jobs provide opportunity for a comprehensive review and practice for your future.

Cross-Curricular Projects—End-of-unit projects apply Internet concepts to topics across the curriculum.

PREFACE

Everyone knows how popular the Internet is, but very few people know why. The technologies that make the Internet work have been in existence for over three decades. So why did the Web suddenly become an overnight success?

The Internet owes its tremendous growth to Hypertext Markup Language, or HTML, and the open-platform environment that the Web creates. This open HTML platform enables programs, such as those written in JavaScript, to run on Macintosh, Windows, Linux, or any other computer systems connected to the Web. HTML and JavaScript make an unbeatable combination for Web site developers.

HTML is a relatively simple method of making documents and online content look great! HTML gives the Web eye-catching appeal. In 1995, many powerful businesses took notice and realized they could advertise, promote their products, or even sell their products online — and the rush to develop online Web sites began.

Despite its many wonderful qualities, however, HTML is a limited language. There are many useful tasks that simply cannot be accomplished by HTML alone, so many professional Web pages make use of supplemental technology. Although there are several different technologies available that can expand the base functionality of HTML, there is no better choice than JavaScript. Like HTML, JavaScript can be created without the use of complex or expensive development software. In fact, JavaScript source code is entered directly into the appropriate HTML Web page file by means of a standard text editor or word processor. But perhaps the most valuable characteristic of the JavaScript language is that it is built upon solid, object-oriented programming concepts. This means that not only can you acquire impressive programming skills quickly, but you can also apply the skills to several other popular programming languages, such as Java, C++, Visual Basic, or even Pascal.

HTML and JavaScript work together. HTML is the backbone of the World Wide Web. It is the primary mechanism used to distribute data across the Internet. JavaScript adds interactivity and new capacities beyond the HTML language; however, without knowledge of the structure of HTML, writing programs with JavaScript can be confusing. Learning the capabilities and structure of HTML is essential for anyone who would like to create colorful and interactive JavaScript-enabled Web pages like those developed by professional Web designers.

Fortunately, HTML and JavaScript are relatively easy to learn. HTML tags and JavaScript code can be created with a standard text editor or word processor without the purchase of expensive software compilers. These are additional reasons why HTML and JavaScript became popular so quickly.

Things are always changing in the high-tech world of computer software, and this is especially true with Internet technologies. HTML and JavaScript will continue to be the dominant players for years to come, but there are several other advanced Internet technologies that are becoming increasingly popular and prominent in some circles.

XML has gained a strong following among many businesses, and its power and flexibility will help ensure its place in the industry for the foreseeable future. XML has proven its worth in many situations, and it is used across many types of hardware and operating systems. In addition, XML has given rise to other emerging standards that are based on the multi-platform capabilities of XML.

The World Wide Web Consortium (W3C) has declared the HTML standard to be "frozen," and has adopted the XML-based XHTML standard to be the technology of choice going forward. XHTML is, of course, very similar to HTML, but it enforces the syntax rules of XML to help make Web pages more consistent and robust.

Although the use of XML is by no means restricted to the World Wide Web, it has much to offer this environment. But since XML itself does not convey any display information, it is necessary to use a companion technology in order to construct XML-based Web pages that can be viewed by a common browser. That technology is XSL which, interestingly enough, is itself another XML-based standard.

XML/XSL Web pages are virtually identical in appearance to standard HTML Web pages. And since they provide essentially the same functionality, they can also stand to benefit from the interactive capabilities of JavaScript. Learning to identify and utilitize the relative strengths of XML, XSL, and JavaScript together will certainly prove to be extremely valuable to students of Internet technologies.

Course Technology is recognized as a leader in Internet-related instruction. Our mission is to change the way people teach and learn technology. In the last ten years, HTML and supplemental tools such as JavaScript have had the same colossal impact on society as Gutenberg's printing press over 500 years ago. They create a communications environment that you should learn. With this book, you will change how you view the Internet and gain a perspective on how you can contribute in a positive way to the Web.

Organization and Features of the Text

H*TML, JavaScript, and Advanced Internet Technologies BASICS* has been written so that HTML, JavaScript, and advanced Internet technologies skills can be developed quickly and easily. The Step-by-Step sections are fully illustrated and are easy to follow, allowing you to master the basics.

The text is divided into twelve interactive hands-on lessons:

Lesson 1—Quick HTML Know-How introduces the basic structure of HTML and will allow you to create your first basic Web page.

Lesson 2—HTML Organization Techniques teaches you how to format Web pages and gives you the techniques required to create hypertext links.

Lesson 3—HTML Power Techniques teaches you how to insert graphics, integrate tables, and manipulate the size, style, and color of fonts.

Lesson 4—HTML Structural Design Techniques teaches you how you can have several Web pages and navigation systems working together.

Lesson 5—What Is JavaScript? explains the history and purpose of JavaScript and shows how JavaScript is integrated into HTML Web pages. This lesson also defines central JavaScript terms and describes some of the most basic parts of JavaScript syntax, including keywords, operators, objects, and methods.

Lesson 6—Using Images with JavaScript shows you how to use graphic images in conjunction with JavaScript events and functions to add some impressive visual effects to a Web page. These effects include image rollovers, hyperlink rollovers, cycling ad banners, random image displays, and electronic slide shows.

Lesson 7—Creating Forms with JavaScript builds on the introduction to forms presented in Lesson 3. It demonstrates how JavaScript can be used to enhance the functionality of HTML forms. This lesson will teach you how to lay out an electronic form, validate user input data, and provide the user with appropriate feedback.

Lesson 8—Using JavaScript with Frames teaches you how to create a JavaScript function with a parameter list, enable hyperlinks that affect other frames, enable buttons that affect other frames, and create top-level JavaScript functions. This teaches you how you can have several Web page frames interacting together.

Lesson 9—Introduction to XML provides an overview of the purpose, features, and syntax of the eXtensible Markup Language. Students also learn how to use a Web browser to validate the structure of XML documents.

Lesson 10—Introduction to XHTML teaches students about the next-generation language for developing Web pages. XHTML is XML-based and, therefore, enforces the syntax rules of XML. Students are taught how to transition standard HTML documents to an XHTML-compliant format.

Lesson 11—Introduction to XSL shows students how to transform their XML data documents into attractive, organized Web pages. XSL is also XML-based, and enforces the same syntax rules as XHTML. But XSL also includes many basic features of programming language to greatly enhance its capabilities.

Lesson 12—Advanced XSL with JavaScript introduces students to some of the advanced features of XSL, including powerful tags and intrinsic functions. This lesson also shows students how to integrate JavaScript into their XML/XSL Web pages for even greater interactive appeal.

These skills will prove very valuable as you progress to additional Web design tutorials, such as *Web Design BASICS*, or advanced programming tutorials.

HTML, JavaScript, and Advanced Technologies BASICS steps through the basics of HTML, JavaScript, and advanced Internet technologies literacy. Each lesson includes the following:

- Lesson objectives to specify learning goals.

- Estimated time of completion.

- Vocabulary to introduce new terms used in the lesson.

- Step-by-Step exercises that teach the basics you need to know.

- Screen illustrations that provide visual reinforcement of what you're learning.

- Sidebars with Internet tips related to the lesson topics.

- Special features such as Internet Milestone and Netiquette, which provide information about Net history.

- SCANS correlations.

The end-of-lesson exercises focus on the reinforcement of the skills you have learned in the lesson and provide a comprehensive review of ways you can apply your skills. The end-of-lesson features include the following:

- Lesson summary.

- Vocabulary review of the new terms presented in the lesson.

- Review questions to assess your comprehension of what you have studied.

- Projects for applying the concepts learned in the lesson.

- Critical Thinking activities that require you to analyze and express your own ideas on a variety of HTML and JavaScript challenges.

The unit reviews are designed to evaluate your overall comprehension of the lessons. The unit reviews include the following:

- HTML tags and attributes, command summaries, and JavaScript code summaries.

- Review questions.

- Cross-curricular activities that apply HTML skills in the areas of language arts, science, social studies, and math.

- Special SCANS projects to help you master the skills you have learned.

- Career simulation activities that will help you apply your HTML skills to job-related situations.

A glossary is provided at the end of the text to provide you with definitions for those tricky HTML tags and terms we all need to learn.

GUIDE FOR USING THIS BOOK

Software

✔ Internet Explorer or Netscape Navigator to view Web pages.

✔ Windows Notepad or Macintosh SimpleText to create HTML documents.

Each of these tools currently comes installed on nearly all standard computers. You may substitute Notepad or SimpleText for a word processor capable of saving text files as .htm or .html documents.

Instructor Resource Kit CD-ROM

The *Instructor Resource Kit* CD-ROM contains a wealth of instructional support that will help an instructor teach *HTML, JavaScript, and Advanced Internet Technologies BASICS*. Read and access the *Instructor Resource Kit* with Internet Explorer, just as if you were surfing live on the Internet. Simply open the *begin_html_teacher.htm* file using Internet Explorer and click your way through the various sections of the *Instructor Resource Kit*.

These files may be copied from the CD directly to a hard drive on a computer or to a network drive. The resources are also available online at *www.course.com*.

A separate Student Guide can also be accessed online or from the CD. Open the student folder and access the student simulation files by choosing *begin_html_student.htm* using Internet Explorer.

SCANS

The Secretary's Commission on Achieving Necessary Skills (SCANS) from the U.S. Department of Labor was asked to examine the demands of the workplace and whether new learners are capable of meeting those demands. Specifically, the Commission was directed to advise the Secretary on the level of skills required to enter employment.

SCANS workplace competencies and foundation skills have been integrated into *HTML, JavaScript, and Advanced Internet Technologies BASICS*. The workplace competencies are identified as 1) ability to use resources, 2) interpersonal skills, 3) ability to work with information, 4) understanding of systems, and 5) knowledge and understanding of technology. The foundation skills are identified as 1) basic communication skills, 2) thinking skills, and 3) personal qualities.

Exercises in which learners must use a number of these SCANS competencies and foundation skills are marked in the text with the SCANS icon.

ABOUT THE AUTHORS

Mr. Karl Barksdale is an instructor at Farrer Middle School in Provo, Utah. He has written many textbooks for Thomson on topics such as the Internet, Web sites, speech recognition, PDAs, and is a co-author of the text called *DigiTools*. Formerly an employee of WordPerfect Corporation, Mr. Barksdale conducts seminars across the country on new technology. His seminars include topics on speech recognition, handwriting recognition, the use of Tablet PCs, and PDAs; each carefully crafted for the middle and high school student and instructor.

Mr. E. Shane Turner is currently a senior software engineer for a benefits practice management company based in Utah. He has written many textbooks for Thomson as well as numerous software reviews for three online computer magazine publications. Mr. Turner was first introduced to HTML in 1994 while attending classes for his M.S. in Computer Science at Brigham Young University. He has taught Computer Science at both Weaver State University and Colorado Technical University. Besides being a working professional and author in the computer technology sector, Mr. Turner is also an accomplished musician, playing trumpet as a member of the Utah Premiere Brass ensemble. Mr. Turner resides with his wife and nine children in Utah.

Acknowledgments

The authors would like to publicly thank the many individuals for the completion and success of their books.

First and foremost, we would like to thank Cheryl Costantini, Vice President of School Publishing and Marketing; and Jane Mazares, Senior Acquisitions Editor. Their guidance and foresight to capture the market's needs and the ability to work with us is invaluable.

Next, we'd like to thank David Rivera, Product Manager; Kim Ryttel, Senior Marketing Manager; Megan Putney, School Market Specialist; and Justine Brennan, Editorial Assistant/Associate Product Manager. Thanks for all of your help promoting our product and managing the publishing process. We are truly lucky to have you as a part of our publication and know much of our success is due to your efforts.

We would also like to thank the QA team, especially Susan Whalen, for doing an outstanding job of ensuring accuracy and consistency within the text, Step-by-Step activities, and end-of-unit projects.

Finally, we'd like to thank Rose Marie Kuebbing, Developmental Editor; Ericka McIntyre, Production Editor; and Jan Clavey, Supplements Developer from Custom Editorial Productions, Inc. We appreciate all of your efforts ensuring "all of our *i's* were dotted and our *t's* crossed." Thanks for all your patience and your diligent work to ensure our writing reflected the message we were trying to convey. We also appreciate your efforts in getting this book to market.

HTML BASICS

Unit 1

 Estimated Time for Unit: 6 hours

QUICK HTML KNOW-HOW

OBJECTIVES

Upon completion of this lesson, you should be able to:

- Discover HTML tags.
- Enter starting tags.
- Save correctly.
- Integrate levels of headings into Web pages.
- Create unordered, ordered, and embedded lists.

Estimated Time: 1.5 hrs.

VOCABULARY

Angle brackets

Flash

Home page

HTML page

Hypertext Markup Language (HTML)

Internet Explorer

Java

JavaScript

Mosaic

Netscape Navigator

Web browser

Web page

Web site

Welcome page

Communicating on the Web

Every time you go online and begin clicking links, you'll open up one new *Web page* after another. Web pages can be composed of pictures, text, and multimedia effects. Their purpose is to share information with Web visitors. Web pages are displayed by special software programs called *Web browsers* whose job it is to find and display Web information. The two most popular browsers are *Internet Explorer* and the *Netscape Navigator*.

Hypertext Markup Language, or *HTML*, allows you to create Web pages. HTML organizes documents and tells Web browsers how Web pages should look on your computer screen. The colors, pictures, and backgrounds on Web pages are determined by HTML tags.

HTML tags work with any Web browser. If you create a Web page, and do it correctly, your Web browser can read it. In fact, HTML is the official language of the World Wide Web!

There are many other languages used in cyberspace, such as *Java,* a programming language used widely with Internet applications; *Flash,* a high impact multimedia creation tool; and *JavaScript*, a Java-like scripting language used to create miniapplications and multimedia effects. HTML is the most widely used of any of these Web page development tools. HTML creates the foundation upon which these other programs can build.

How HTML Works

HTML tags work everywhere on the Web. HTML tags display Web pages on Macintosh or Windows computers. They work on Linux and UNIX computers. They even work on Web-enabled cell phones, palm-sized devices, and televisions with a Web device.

HTML tags are so simple that anyone can learn a few essential tags quickly. They usually appear in pairs enclosed in *angle brackets*. These brackets can be found on the comma and period keys on your keyboard. Hold the Shift key and press either of these keys to create an angle bracket.

To more clearly understand how HTML tags work, analyze the following example. If you want to center the title of this book on a Web page, all you need to do is key:

<CENTER>HTML and JavaScript BASICS</CENTER>

Notice that there is a starting tag, <CENTER>, and a closing tag, </CENTER>. The only difference between the two tags is a slash (/) following the first angle bracket in the closing tag. <CENTER></CENTER> form a pair of tags, and if you haven't guessed already, these tags are called center tags. Anything between these tags will be centered on the page. Anything outside of these tags will not be affected by the command. It can't get any simpler!

Uncover the Page Beneath the Page

The Web is full of Web pages. Some are very interesting, some are very exciting, some are too busy, and some are dull and boring.

It doesn't matter if a page is interesting or dull; all pages have the same characteristics. Let's see what that means.

For example, all of the words, pictures, and colors that you see in Figure 1-1A are organized and created by the HTML tags you see in Figure 1-1B.

Figures 1-1A and 1-1B are actually the same page viewed in different ways.

FIGURE 1-1A

Course Technology home page at www.course.com

FIGURE 1-1B

HTML tags for the home page shown in Figure 1-1A

Notice that Figure 1-1B isn't very pretty. It shows the HTML tags that create the more exciting page shown in Figure 1-1A. Figure 1-1B shows exactly what the page behind the colorful page really looks like. The Web browser interprets the tags and creates the Web page that the average Web surfer sees.

There are lots of tags and lots of ways to use them. This hint should keep you from getting confused: *The HTML tags are just instructions to the Web browser.* They tell the browser how to display information. Many times you can look at the final Web page and guess what tags created the effect. If you remember this hint, learning HTML will be much easier.

Now it's your turn. The following steps will allow you to open a Web page of your choosing. Viewing the page behind the page is as easy as selecting Source or some similar command, such as Page Source, from the View menu in your browser (see Figures 1-3A and 1-3B).

S TEP-BY-STEP 1.1

1. Open your Web browser by double-clicking its icon, as shown in Figures 1-2A and 1-2B.

FIGURE 1-2A
Internet Explorer icon

FIGURE 1-2B
Netscape Navigator icon

STEP-BY-STEP 1.1 Continued

2. When a page appears, use your mouse to move your pointer over the View menu, as shown in Figures 1-3A and 1-3B.

FIGURE 1-3A
The View Source command in Internet Explorer

FIGURE 1-3B
The View Page Source command in Netscape Navigator

3. Select **View** followed by **Source** in your Internet Explorer (IE) browser, or **View** followed by **Page Source** in your Netscape browser.

4. Examine the tags that appear on the page beneath the colorful page. The tags will look something like the tags you saw in Figure 1-1B.

> **Note**
>
> Different browsers may use different words for this command. Look around; the option will be there.

5. Jump around to three or four other Web pages and View the Source. List seven tags that you keep running into over and over. Guess and record what they do in the table that follows.

TABLE 1-1
Common tags

NUMBER	TAG	THE EFFECT IT CAUSES ON THE WEB
Sample	<CENTER></CENTER>	Centers text on a Web page
1		
2		
3		
4		
5		
6		
7		

6. Exit your software and shut down your computer if you are finished for today. Otherwise, continue to the next section.

 Internet Milestone

Business Discovers the Web

The World Wide Web (WWW) was created in the late 1980s in Europe. It was used limitedly in academic circles for about the next five years. However, it didn't capture the public's imagination until 1994 when a Web browser called *Mosaic* came on the scene. It was the first Web browser that allowed both pictures and text to accompany Web pages.

Excitement grew around this new way to present and share information. Then, Netscape Communications Corp. released its browser called Netscape Navigator. Netscape caught the imagination of businesses in 1995, and everything was different from that point on.

In just a few short years, the World Wide Web became the new advertising and commercial medium that we see today. Billions and billions of dollars were invested by companies and corporations hoping to cash in on this new golden information-sharing system. Suddenly, thousands and thousands of corporate Web page creators began to learn HTML so they could put their business Web pages online.

Enter Your Mystery Tags the Old-Fashioned Way

Before you start entering tags, you need to be aware of the many terms used to describe pages created with HTML tags. The truth is, these names are used so interchangeably that most people are totally unaware that there are slight distinctions in their meanings.

- *Web page*: Also referred to as a Web document, any page created in HTML that can be placed on the World Wide Web.

- *Home page*: The main or primary Web page for a corporation, organization, or for an individual. A personal home page is the first page you see as you start up your Web browser. When you click the Home icon in the browser, you will go directly to your starting home page.

- *Welcome page*: Designed especially for new visitors to a site.

- *HTML page*: Also referred to as an HTML document, any document created in HTML that can be displayed on the World Wide Web.

- *Web site*: Can include a collection of many interconnected Web pages organized by a specific company, organization, college or university, government agency, or individual. Web sites are stored on Web servers. There are many Web sites and thousands of HTML pages on each Web site.

Is it all clear now? Don't let these subtle distinctions get in the way of your understanding of how the Web works.

Creating a Powerful Advantage with Tags

There are many ways to create HTML tags. You can use specialized software, such as FrontPage by Microsoft, GoLive from Adobe, or Dreamweaver from Macromedia, to create super Web pages. These programs help organize your HTML page, enter text, move things around, and create superior Web page effects without ever entering an HTML tag. You can do the same with many of the newer versions of word processing programs, such as Microsoft Word and Corel WordPerfect. These word processors have built-in HTML tags.

You will want to use one of these programs for most of your Web pages. For the following activity, however, you are going to enter HTML tags the old-fashioned way. Learning to enter a few HTML tags in the old-fashioned way will give you a big advantage as you start to learn JavaScript in Unit 2. Let's quickly cover the basics. First, by entering a few tags, you will develop a deeper understanding of how HTML really works. Second, you'll be able to troubleshoot Web pages when picky little errors occur. Third, you'll be able to view other pages and learn how they achieve certain effects. Fourth, you'll understand a little better the file and folder structures found on Web computers. Finally, and most importantly, you'll understand how HTML and JavaScript work together.

What to Use

Almost any word processing program or text editor will work for creating both HTML and JavaScript. This is one of the reasons HTML and JavaScript are so popular. You do not need any specialized software tools in order to create exciting Web pages like you need for Java, Shockwave, or some of the other software-intensive options.

Our recommendation is to use the simplest, most basic tools available. In Windows, you can use Notepad. On a Macintosh, you can use SimpleText. These programs are easy to use and available on nearly every computer on the planet. Use your favorite word processing program, such as Microsoft Word, Corel WordPerfect, or AppleWorks. However, you will need to experiment a little bit with each word processing program to learn its idiosyncrasies. Instructions for Microsoft Word and AppleWorks are provided in this text as examples. Many other word processors have similar HTML creation features. Check the software's help system if you have any difficulties, or revert to Notepad or SimpleText to complete the Step-by-Step activities.

> **Net Tip**
>
> Sophisticated software programs, such as Dreamweaver, GoLive, and FrontPage, really streamline the job of creating classy Web pages quickly. These programs provide options that allow you to see the tags. If you're using one of these programs, select the HTML Source option so you can enter the tags directly.

STEP-BY-STEP 1.2

1. Open Notepad, SimpleText, or your favorite word processing software.

2. Create a new document if necessary.

3. Enter the tags shown in Figure 1-4 in this exact order. Don't leave out any angle bracket (<) or slash (/). Everything is important.

FIGURE 1-4
Enter these tags exactly as shown here

```
<HTML>
<TITLE></TITLE>
<BODY>
<CENTER></CENTER>
<P></P>
<P></P>
<P></P>
<P></P>
<P></P>
</BODY>
</HTML>
```

STEP-BY-STEP 1.2 Continued

4. The tags you just entered are called the basic tags. They include a standard set of tags that appear in most Web pages. But your page will look very sad without some text. Enter the text between the tags, as shown in Figure 1-5. Notice that the new text to be entered is shown in bold.

FIGURE 1-5
Enter the text between the tags exactly as shown here

```
<HTML>
<TITLE>HTML and JavaScript</TITLE>
<BODY>
<CENTER>Creating HTML and JavaScript</CENTER>
<P>Learning to create HTML tags can help you in many ways:</P>
<P>You will develop a deeper understanding of how HTML really works.</P>
<P>You will be able to troubleshoot Web pages when errors occur.</P>
<P>You will be able to view other pages and learn how certain effects were created.</P>
<P>You will understand how HTML and JavaScript work together.</P>
</BODY>
</HTML>
```

5. Leave your text editor open and go on to Step-by-Step 1.3, where you will learn how to save HTML files.

Save and View Your HTML Page

HTML documents are text files. This means that they are saved in the simplest way possible. For the most part, text files only save the letters you see on your keyboard. All of the sophisticated word processing commands are erased, leaving just the letters.

Saving as text allows HTML files to move quickly over the Web. However, the problem with text files is that most people don't know how to save them. Before you save, there are a few things you need to know first.

To tell one kind of file from another, computers often add file extensions to filenames. Sometimes you can see these extensions on your computer and sometimes you can't. Depending on your computer's settings, the extensions may or may not be visible, but the software on your computer knows the kinds of file types it can open.

> **Net Tip**
>
> HTML isn't case sensitive. You can use uppercase <TAGS>, or you can use lowercase <tags>. Uppercase <TAGS> are easier to see. If you're emphasizing the tags, use uppercase <TAGS>. If you would rather emphasize the words in the document, use lowercase <tags>.
>
> You can even mix uppercase <TAGS> and lowercase <tags> together like <Tag> or <TAG></tag>. However, mixing cases is not considered good form.

Extensions are used a lot. For example, in Windows, text files are saved with a .txt ending or extension. If you use a word processor much, you may have seen these popular extensions:

.doc	Microsoft Word document
.rtf	Microsoft's Rich Text Format
.wpd	Corel WordPerfect document

.txt	text file
.html	HTML file
.htm	HTML file on some computer systems

HTML files are text files with an .html or .htm extension. While the format that you need for HTML is called text, the ending or extension must be .html (or .htm if you're using older Windows-based software programs). The .html or .htm extensions signal to the Web browser that this is an HTML text file. The .html extension is like putting up a sign saying, "Hey, browser, read me. I'm an HTML document."

Follow along. We are going to show you how to save with different software programs. Use the software instructions that most closely resemble the software on your computer system. They are Notepad, Microsoft Word, SimpleText, and AppleWorks.

STEP-BY-STEP 1.3

1. Select **Save As** from the **File** menu. (Microsoft Word users beware! DO NOT select Save as Web page from the File menu! Use the regular Save As command.)

2. From the Save As dialog box, create a new folder in which to save your HTML and JavaScript work.

3. For both Notepad in Windows and SimpleText for Macintosh, the steps are very similar. Word and AppleWorks users should skip to Step 5.

4. Select the folder into which you wish to save your files.

5. Name your file one.html as shown in Figure 1-6. Check with your instructor to make sure you save your file properly. Click Save. If everything saved okay, go on to Step 6.

Note ☑

Check with your instructor to see where you should save your work.

Note ☑

Older Windows systems will only accept an .htm extension.

FIGURE 1-6
Name a text file with an .html extension

Name your html file

STEP-BY-STEP 1.3 Continued

In your word processing software, there are a few additional steps. While Notepad and SimpleText automatically save as text only, word processors save in their own unique format. You must select the proper text format from your saving options. Instructions for Word and AppleWorks are provided here to help you to learn this important step. Other word processors may have their own text saving options. Check with your instructor to make sure you are following the steps properly for your software.

If you are a **_Microsoft Word_** user, perform the following steps.

a. Locate the folder in which you want to place your file.

b. Select **Plain Text** as the **Save as type** or format type, as shown in Figure 1-7.

c. Name your file **one.html**.

d. Choose **Save**.

Note

In older Windows programs, the name will be truncated, or shortened, to one.htm.

FIGURE 1-7
Saving text files in Microsoft Word

Name your file one.html

Select Plain Text

If you are an **_AppleWorks_** user, perform the following steps.

a. Locate the folder into which you want to place your file.

b. Select **Plain Text** as the **File Format**.

STEP-BY-STEP 1.3 Continued

   c. Name your file **one.html**, as shown in Figure 1-8.

   d. Choose **Save**.

FIGURE 1-8
Saving text files in AppleWorks

Select Text   **Name your file one.html**

6. Viewing your HTML page in a Web browser is easy. We'll show you how to do this in Netscape and Internet Explorer.

If you are an ***Internet Explorer*** user, perform the following steps.

   a. Open your Web browser.

   b. Select **File**, and then **Open**.

   c. Locate the folder where you saved your file. Choose the **Browse** button to do this.

   d. Select your HTML file in the Open text box, and choose **Open**.

   e. Click **OK**, as shown in Figure 1-9.

FIGURE 1-9
Find your file in IE

Click OK

If you are a ***Netscape Navigator*** user, perform the following steps.

   a. Open your Web browser.

   b. From the **File** menu, choose **Open File**.

   c. Select **All files** under the Files of type option, if necessary.

STEP-BY-STEP 1.3 Continued

d. Browse to the folder where you saved your file.

e. Select your HTML file, and click **Open** as shown in Figure 1-10.

FIGURE 1-10
Find your file in Netscape

7. View your file. It should look like Figure 1-11.

FIGURE 1-11
Congratulations! Your Web page probably looks like this sample!

8. How does your Web page look? Make any corrections necessary, save again, return to your browser, and then click **Reload** or **Refresh** to see the changes you have made.

Using Headings

Most printed documents use headings to help the reader find important portions of text. Think of a report you have written for school. The main heading usually appears at the top and in the center of the page. Subheadings or secondary headings usually appear at the side of the paper. They are often shown in bold.

HTML gives you six standard headings, or title sizes, from which to choose. In later Step-by-Steps, you'll learn of more sophisticated ways to manipulate the size and appearance of text. Nevertheless, the heading tags provide an easy way to control the size of your text, making it stand out so your reader can view the headings clearly.

The heading tags are easy to remember. They use the letter H with a number from 1 to 6 to indicate the level of the heading. Heading numbers indicate the level of importance for marked headings, with 1 being the most prominent and 6 being the least prominent. Look for:

<H1></H1>

<H2></H2>

<H3></H3>

<H4></H4>

<H5></H5>

<H6></H6>

 Internet Milestone

The Browser Wars

In the last few years, Netscape and Internet Explorer have been fighting it out for supremacy in the Web browser world. But this wasn't the first browser battle. In 1994, the dominant browser was called Mosaic. It was freeware out of the National Supercomputing Center at the University of Illinois in Champaign-Urbana. At the time Netscape came on the scene, Mosaic was adding 600,000 new users a month. But things changed in a hurry.

In the first three months of 1995, Netscape's Navigator browser gained a reputation for being a faster browser. By midyear it had captured 50% of browser users, and by the end of the year it commanded a whopping 80% of the browser market.

Netscape's dominance was quickly challenged by rival Microsoft, which came out with its Internet Explorer browser. Microsoft gave away copies of its browser in hopes of cutting into Netscape's lead. Microsoft also had an advantage in that its Windows operating system ran on over 90% of personal computers. By making Windows and Internet Explorer work together, Microsoft created a more user-friendly Web system.

Microsoft's advantage, however, lead to many legal battles. Several antitrust lawsuits argued that Microsoft was using its dominance in Windows to crush Netscape and to eliminate its competition unfairly. Microsoft claimed it was simply adding more value for its customers by making its Internet Explorer browser easier to access.

The browser wars continue today. Although Microsoft's Internet Explorer is still the dominant player in most markets, Netscape's Navigator is still very popular in many circles. In addition, there are other new Web browsers that are making their move into cyberspace. These browsers include Firefox, Camino, Opera, and Safari. Who will win in the end?

Anything inside the heading tags will be made larger or smaller, depending on the number. For example:

<H1>VERY BIG</H1>

<H3>In the Middle</H3>

<H6>Very Small</H6>

In this Step-by-Step, you will open the HTML file you have been working on and add the heading or title tags.

STEP-BY-STEP 1.4

1. Open your text editor.

2. Open your **one.html** or **one.htm** file, if necessary. If you are using Notepad, select **All Files** under the **Files of type** option, as shown in Figure 1-12A. Otherwise, you will not be able to view your .html or .htm file! If you are using Microsoft Word, when you open an .html file, Word may display your Web page as it would appear in a Web browser. In order to view the HTML tags, select **HTML Source** from the **View** menu, as shown in Figure 1-12B.

> **Hot Tip**
>
> When you select HTML Source on the View menu in Word, a dialog box may appear stating that the HTML Source Editor feature is not yet installed. You may need to insert the Office CD and install this feature before you can view the HTML source.

FIGURE 1-12A
Notepad users

Select All Files

FIGURE 1-12B
MS Word users

Select HTML Source

STEP-BY-STEP 1.4 Continued

3. Enter the heading tags shown in bold in Figure 1-13.

FIGURE 1-13
Add the heading tags

```
<HTML>
<TITLE>HTML and JavaScript</TITLE>
<BODY>
<CENTER><H1>Creating HTML and JavaScript</H1></CENTER>
<P><H2>Learning to create HTML tags can help you in many ways: </H2></P>
<P><H3>You will develop a deeper understanding of how HTML really works. </H3></P>
<P><H4>You will be able to troubleshoot Web pages when errors occur. </H4></P>
<P><H5>You will be able to view other pages and learn how certain effects were created.
</H5></P>
<P><H6>You will understand how HTML and JavaScript work together. </H6></P>
</BODY>
</HTML>
```

4. Save your new HTML page as **two.html** or **two.htm**.

5. Open your Web browser. Open your **two.html** or **two.htm** file, and view it. It should look like Figure 1-14. (Navigator users may see the "Pop-Up Block" option turned On and Off. Simply click the button to toggle the current setting.) Heading tags really change the look of a page. In our example in Figure 1-14, however, the heading tags are misused. At best, there are only three levels of information:

<H1></H1> The title at the top

<H2></H2> The introductory line followed by a colon (:)

<H3></H3> The list of the reasons to learn HTML tags

FIGURE 1-14
Headings in a Web page

STEP-BY-STEP 1.4 Continued

6. Return to your document and reorganize the heading tags. Use no more than three <H></H> tags. Think about your tag choices for a second, then make your document comfortable to read, emphasizing the three levels this document dictates. Resave your file to make your changes become effective.

7. Exit your software and shut down your computer if you are finished for today. Otherwise, continue to the next section.

Numbered and Bulleted Lists

In the last Step-by-Step, you were asked to reorganize your two.html file and use the <H> tags in a more consistent manner. In this Step-by-Step, we are going to whip things into shape even further.

One of the most powerful ways to organize information on a Web page is by the use of lists. There are several kinds of lists, including the following:

Unordered (or Bulleted) lists   <UL></UL>

Ordered (or Numbered) lists   <OL></OL>

The unordered lists tags <UL></UL> create bulleted lists. Start your list with the opening <UL> unordered lists tag, mark the items to be listed with the list <LI></LI> tags, and place an </UL> tag at the end of your list. Try it!

STEP-BY-STEP 1.5

1. Open your **two.html** or **two.htm** file for text editing.

STEP-BY-STEP 1.5 Continued

2. Enter the **<UL></UL>** tags at the start and at the end of the list to create an unordered list, as shown in Figure 1-15.

FIGURE 1-15
Enter the unordered list tags

```
<HTML>
<TITLE>HTML and JavaScript</TITLE>
<BODY>
<CENTER><H1>Creating HTML and JavaScript</H1></CENTER>
<P><H2>Learning to create HTML tags can help you in many ways: </H2></P>

<UL>
<LI><H3>You will develop a deeper understanding of how HTML really works.
</H3></LI>
<LI><H3>You will be able to troubleshoot Web pages when errors occur.
</H3></LI>
<LI><H3>You will be able to view other pages and learn how certain effects were
created. </H3></LI>
<LI><H3>You will understand how HTML and JavaScript work together.
</H3></LI>
</UL>

</BODY>
</HTML>
```

3. Replace the **<P>** and **</P>** tags with **<LI>** and **</LI>** tags for each sentence in the list, as shown in Figure 1-15.

4. Save your file as **three.html** or **three.htm**.

STEP-BY-STEP 1.5 Continued

5. View your page in a browser to see how it looks. It should be similar to Figure 1-16.

FIGURE 1-16
An unordered list

6. Open your **three.html** or **three.htm** file for text editing, if necessary.

STEP-BY-STEP 1.5 Continued

7. Change the pair of **\<UL>\</UL>** tags to **\<OL>\</OL>** tags to change your list from an unordered list to an ordered list, as shown in Figure 1-17. No other changes are necessary.

> **Note**
>
> Don't use a zero; use the letter O for ordered.

FIGURE 1-17
Enter the ordered lists tags

```
<HTML>
<TITLE>HTML and JavaScript</TITLE>
<BODY>
<CENTER><H1>Creating HTML and JavaScript</H1></CENTER>
<P><H2>Learning to create HTML tags can help you in many ways: </H2></P>

<OL>
<LI><H3>You will develop a deeper understanding of how HTML really works.
</H3></LI>
<LI><H3>You will be able to troubleshoot Web pages when errors occur.
</H3></LI>
<LI><H3>You will be able to view other pages and learn how certain effects were created.
</H3></LI>
<LI><H3>You will understand how HTML and JavaScript work together.
</H3></LI>
</OL>

</BODY>
</HTML>
```

8. Save your file as **four.html** or **four.htm**.

STEP-BY-STEP 1.5 Continued

9. View your page in a browser to see how it looks. It should look similar to Figure 1-18.

FIGURE 1-18
An ordered or numbered list

10. Open your **four.html** or **four.htm** file for text editing, if necessary.

STEP-BY-STEP 1.5 Continued

11. Add two pairs of **<UL></UL>** tags in the middle of the list, as shown in Figure 1-19.

FIGURE 1-19
Enter the unordered lists tags

```
<HTML>
<TITLE>HTML and JavaScript</TITLE>
<BODY>
<CENTER><H1>Creating HTML and JavaScript</H1></CENTER>
<P><H2>Learning to create HTML tags can help you in many ways: </H2></P>

<OL>
<LI><H3>You will develop a deeper understanding of how HTML really works.
</H3></LI>

<UL>
<LI><H3>You will be able to troubleshoot Web pages when errors occur. </H3></LI>
<UL>
<LI><H3>You will be able to view other pages and learn how certain effects were created.
</H3></LI>
</UL>
</UL>

<LI><H3>You will understand how HTML and JavaScript work together.
</H3></LI>
</OL>
</BODY>
</HTML>
```

12. Save your file as **five.html** or **five.htm**.

STEP-BY-STEP 1.5 Continued

13. View your page to see how it looks. It should look similar to Figure 1-20.

FIGURE 1-20
Embedded and indented lists

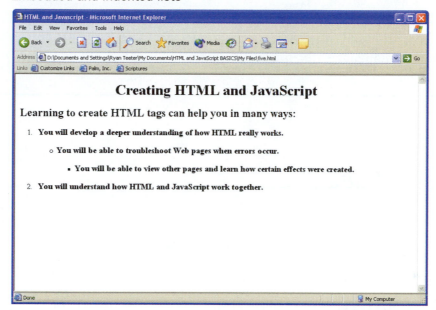

14. Exit your software and shut down your computer if you are finished for today. Otherwise, continue to the Summary section.

SUMMARY

In this lesson, you learned:

■ You can identify HTML tags.

■ You can enter your starting tags.

■ You can save your HTML file correctly.

■ You can integrate levels of headings into Web pages.

■ You can create unordered, ordered, and embedded lists.

VOCABULARY *Review*

Define the following terms:

Angle brackets	Internet Explorer	Web browser
Flash	Java	Web page
Home page	JavaScript	Web site
HTML page	Mosaic	Welcome page
Hypertext Markup Language (HTML)	Netscape Navigator	

REVIEW *Questions*

TRUE/FALSE

Circle T if the statement is true or F if the statement is false.

T   F   **1.** The <LI> tag defines a list item.

T   F   **2.** The <OL> tag creates a bulleted list.

T   F   **3.** The <CENTER> tag formats text so that it is centered on the page.

T   F   **4.** Learning HTML is very difficult.

T   F   **5.** The <UL> tag creates a list with no particular order.

FILL IN THE BLANK

Complete the following sentences by writing the correct word or words in the blanks provided.

1. An unordered or _____ list shows items in no particular order.

2. An ordered or _____ list shows items in a numerical order.

3. File _____ are three-letter suffixes that tell what type of file a file is.

4. _____ was the first Web browser that Netscape competed against.

5. HTML is made up of _____, which are commands enclosed in angle brackets (< >).

WRITTEN QUESTIONS

Write a short answer to each of the following questions:

1. Think of a way to explain how HTML tags work to people who have never created a Web page before in their lives. How can you explain how HTML works to a novice?

2. Explain the process of viewing the HTML source code for an HTML Web page.

3. Explain how you must save HTML text pages.

4. What are filename extensions? Give examples.

5. What are Mosaic, Netscape Navigator, and Internet Explorer? What has each contributed to the growth of the Web?

PROJECTS

 PROJECT 1-1

You have just been hired as the Webmaster for GreatApplications, Inc., a major software and Web site developer, but your HTML skills are limited. You need to find some good HTML information fast! What do you do?

The answer is obvious. Hit the Web. Pick a search portal, such as Yahoo!, Excite, Lycos, or some other search site, and enter the search words:

Hypertext Markup Language

HTML

HTML Guides

Learning HTML

Use the following table to record the titles and URLs or Web addresses and write a brief summary of the helpful HTML Web pages you find:

TABLE 1-2
Helpful Web pages

TITLE THAT APPEARS IN THE TITLE BAR	WEB ADDRESS OR URL	DESCRIPTION

 TEAMWORK PROJECT

GreatApplications, Inc. is looking for design ideas for their new Web site welcome page. In a team of three or four, create a list of your favorite Web pages. Find seven great Web pages and discuss what makes them so cool. Vote, and make your vote count as you rank the seven welcome pages from Number 1 to Number 7. List your team's choices below for future reference.

TABLE 1-3
Well-designed Web pages

RANKING	TITLE AS IT APPEARS IN THE TITLE BAR	WEB ADDRESS OR URL
1.		
2.		
3.		
4.		
5.		
6.		
7.		

WEB PROJECT

Web sites are important for many companies, groups, and individuals. We all know that many corporations would go out of business without their quality Web sites. But just how important are great-looking Web sites for noncommercial organizations and government agencies?

List reasons why these organizations need Web sites:

Government agencies:

Nonprofit organizations:

Universities:

CRITICAL*Thinking*

Prepare a 100- to 250-word answer to each of the following questions.

 ACTIVITY 1-1

The World Wide Web is a large web of computer networks that share HTML files. You can visit a new Web page every minute of every day for the rest of your life and never come close to reading a fraction of the available Web pages. How many millions or billions of Web pages exist in cyberspace? While HTML has allowed people to share Web pages easily, has HTML also contributed to information overload? If so, how?

 ACTIVITY 1-2

There is an error in the following set of tags and you are to find it and fix it. What will the current tags do to your page? What does it look like after you make the correction?

<OL>

<LI>Item A</LI>

<UL>

<LI>Item A1</LI>

<LI>Item A2</LI>

</UL>

<LI>Item B</LI>

<UL>

<LI>Item B1</LI>

<LI>Item B2</LI>

</UL>

</UL>

 ACTIVITY 1-3

How can you create a sophisticated outline in HTML (you know, the kind you had to do for your last research paper)? In what ways can your research paper be enhanced online in HTML?

SUMMARY*Project*

All good authors know that before starting a big writing project it is often a good idea to create an outline of the information they wish to present. Outlines can be very effective in helping writers organize their thoughts, and to make sure their writing follows a logical flow of ideas. Use the HTML skills you have learned in this lesson to create an outline for a book which is composed of units, chapters, and sections. Figure 1-21 below will give you an idea of how your completed outline should look.

FIGURE 1-21
A sample book outline

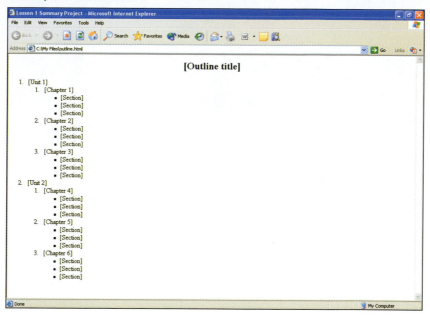

Project Requirements

- Your outline must have a title that is centered at the top of the page.

- Your outline must contain at least two units in an ordered list.

- Your outline must contain at least three chapters per unit, also ordered.

- You outline must contain at least three sections per chapter – not ordered.

HTML ORGANIZATION TECHNIQUES

OBJECTIVES

Upon completion of this lesson, you should be able to:

■ Organize page information with single and double spacing.

■ Organize page information with lines.

■ Implement attributes and values.

■ Change Web page color defaults by altering attributes and values.

■ Alter Web page text colors.

■ Create a hyperlink to another spot within a Web page.

■ Create a hyperlink to an URL or Web page anywhere on the WWW.

■ Create a hyperlink to another Web page on your own computer.

Estimated Time: 1.5 hours

VOCABULARY

Attribute

Fonts

Hexadecimal

Hyperlinks

Hypertext links

Hypertext Transfer Protocol (HTTP)

Uniform Resource Locator (URL)

Value

Creating Better Web Pages

The World Wide Web is a creation of hundreds of thousands of people who are constantly creating, improving, and posting exciting Web pages. The Web is a place to be totally creative. All you need to join in the fun is a little knowledge of HTML and JavaScript. With these tools in your bag of tricks, you will be limited only by your imagination.

As you have surfed the Web, you have seen wonderfully exciting Web pages, and you have seen other pages that fall flat. The main difference between a great and a dull page comes down to the little things—the choice of lettering colors, pictures, and the selection of elements that help with the overall organization of the pages.

You can use many HTML techniques to make your pages perfectly presentable. These are single and double spacing techniques and other specialized organizing tags that can make any Web page easy to read. For example, Web pages can be made more appealing by adding space between paragraphs or by placing lines between different sections of the Web page. Changing the colors of your text and page background can also make an HTML document more appealing. Color choices are extremely important. There is nothing uglier in cyberspace than a Web page that mixes all the wrong colors. Use just the right colors, and your page will be fabulous.

Fonts, or the style of lettering, can be altered. Every font has a style all its own. Here are some samples of the most common fonts:

This is Times New Roman.

This is Arial.

This is Courier.

Hypertext links help make Web pages interesting and easy to navigate. *Hyperlinks*, as they are often called, allow users to click and zoom off to another place on the Web, to another page users have created, or to a spot within the current document. If you have a lot of information on a single page, creating an index can help your reader hyper-jump to the exact information for which they are looking.

As you learn the new HTML elements taught in this lesson, you will be introduced to new ideas on how to organize your Web pages.

Single and Double Spacing

Most early Web pages, before 1995, are best described as long, boring collections of words. Early versions of HTML supplied only the simplest ways to break text into readable sections.

That has changed. There is no longer any reason to create a boring, hard-to-read Web page. In the following Step-by-Step, you'll see firsthand how to improve the readability and organization of your page.

S TEP-BY-STEP 2.1

1. Open Notepad, SimpleText, or your word processing software.

STEP-BY-STEP 2.1 Continued

2. Key the HTML Web page information exactly as shown in Figure 2-1.

Note

If you are using Notepad, select the **Word Wrap** option from the **Format** menu before you enter the text.

FIGURE 2-1
Enter these tags and words exactly as shown

```
<HTML>
<TITLE>HTML and JavaScript</TITLE>

<BODY>
<CENTER><H1>Organizing Tags</H1></CENTER>

There are many ways to organize a Web page. This Web page will organize text,
hypertext links, colors, and fonts. You'll also demonstrate single spacing, double spacing,
and the use of line breaks.

This Web page will display how to organize Web pages in a number of ways using:

Powerful Lines
Hyperlinks to HTML and JavaScript Sources
Hyperlinks to Previously Created Web Pages
Fancy Fonts
Perfect Pictures
Orderly Tables
Extraordinary Extras

</BODY>
</HTML>
```

3. Save the file as you learned to save in Step-by-Step 1.3 with the name **six.html** or **six.htm.**

STEP-BY-STEP 2.1 Continued

4. Open your Web browser and view your page. It should look messy, as in Figure 2-2. (Refer back to Step-by-Step 1.3 if you need a reminder on how to view an HTML file in your Web browser.) Notice that while the page may have looked organized when you entered it in HTML, the organization of the page falls apart on the Web without a few organizing tags. The use of a few selected tags can really clean up a page. The two easiest tags you can use to organize a page are the <P></P>, or paragraph, tags, and the <BR>, or break tag. The <P></P> tags create a double space around the text. The <BR> tag creates a single-spaced break.

FIGURE 2-2
An unorganized Web page

5. Open your **six.html** or **six.htm** file, if necessary, in your word processor, Notepad, or SimpleText.

Note ☑

If you are using Notepad, select the **Word Wrap** option from the **Format** menu when you open the file so that you can see all of the text on your screen.

STEP-BY-STEP 2.1 Continued

6. Add the <P></P> and <BR> tags, as marked in bold in Figure 2-3.

FIGURE 2-3
Enter the <P></P> and <BR> tags.

```
<HTML>
<TITLE>HTML and JavaScript</TITLE>

<BODY>
<CENTER><H1>Organizing Tags</H1></CENTER>

<P>There are many ways to organize a Web page. This Web page will organize text,
hypertext links, colors, and fonts. You'll also demonstrate single spacing, double spacing,
and the use of line breaks. </P>

<P>This Web page will display how to organize Web pages in a number of ways using: </P>

<BR>Powerful Lines
<BR>Hyperlinks to HTML and JavaScript Sources
<BR>Hyperlinks to Previously Created Web Pages
<BR>Fancy Fonts
<BR>Perfect Pictures
<BR>Orderly Tables
<BR>Extraordinary Extras

</BODY>
</HTML>
```

7. Use the **Save As** option to save your reorganized file as **seven.html** or **seven.htm**.

STEP-BY-STEP 2.1 Continued

8. Review your work. It should look much better this time, similar to Figure 2-4.

FIGURE 2-4
<P></P> and <BR> tags clean up a Web page

9. Continue to the next section, or close your software and shut down your computer if you're finished for the day.

Lines and Background Colors

HTML tags can be enhanced. Take the <BODY> tag, for instance. You can add commands to the body tag that will dramatically change the look of your Web page. For example, to change the background color of your Web page, you can add the background *attribute* (or special quality) and give the tag a color *value* (or a definition of the attribute), as shown in Figure 2-5.

Attributes and values are powerful tools to help you organize your Web pages. One of the most widely used tags is the <HR> or Horizontal Rule. This tag simply creates a horizontal line across the page. You can add attributes to change the size and shape of the horizontal rule as well.

FIGURE 2-5
Changing background colors

STEP-BY-STEP 2.2

1. Open your **seven.html** or **seven.htm** file for text editing, if necessary.

2. Enter **BGCOLOR=YELLOW** inside the BODY tag near the top of your Web page, as shown in bold in Figure 2-5.

3. Save your work as **eight.html** or **eight.htm**.

4. View these changes in your Web browser. Your page should turn yellow.

5. Experiment. Change the background color value to **BLUE, GREEN, RED, WHITE**, or another color of your choice.

STEP-BY-STEP 2.2 Continued

6. Switch back to your **eight.html** or **eight.htm** file. Enter the various <HR> tags, attributes, and values as marked in bold in Figure 2-6 near the bottom of the page before the </BODY> tag.

FIGURE 2-6
Adding background colors and lines

```
<HTML>
<TITLE>HTML and JavaScript</TITLE>

<BODY BGCOLOR=YELLOW>
<CENTER><H1>Organizing Tags</H1></CENTER>

<P>There are many ways to organize a Web page. This Web page will organize text,
hypertext links, colors, and fonts. You'll also demonstrate single spacing, double spac-
ing, and the use of line breaks. </P>

<P>This Web page will display how to organize Web pages in a number of ways using: </P>

<BR>Powerful Lines
<BR>Hyperlinks to HTML and JavaScript Sources
<BR>Hyperlinks to Previously Created Web Pages
<BR>Fancy Fonts
<BR>Perfect Pictures
<BR>Orderly Tables
<BR>Extraordinary Extras
<HR>

<P><H2>Powerful Lines</H2></P>

A Horizontal Rule tag 50% wide and 10 pixels high.
<HR WIDTH=50% SIZE=10>

A Horizontal Rule tag 25% wide and 20 pixels high.
<HR WIDTH=25% SIZE=20>

A Horizontal Rule tag 10% wide and 30 pixels high.
<HR WIDTH=10% SIZE=30>

A Horizontal Rule tag without attributes and values.
<HR>

</BODY>
</HTML>
```

7. Save your file as **nine.html** or **nine.htm**.

STEP-BY-STEP 2.2 Continued

8. View the horizontal lines in your Web browser. Your page should look like Figure 2-7.

FIGURE 2-7
Powerful lines

9. Continue to the next section, or close your software and shut down your computer if you're finished for the day.

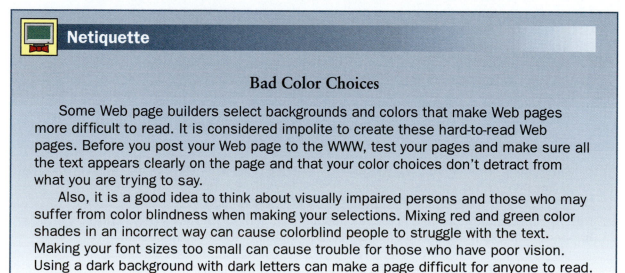

Netiquette

Bad Color Choices

Some Web page builders select backgrounds and colors that make Web pages more difficult to read. It is considered impolite to create these hard-to-read Web pages. Before you post your Web page to the WWW, test your pages and make sure all the text appears clearly on the page and that your color choices don't detract from what you are trying to say.

Also, it is a good idea to think about visually impaired persons and those who may suffer from color blindness when making your selections. Mixing red and green color shades in an incorrect way can cause colorblind people to struggle with the text. Making your font sizes too small can cause trouble for those who have poor vision. Using a dark background with dark letters can make a page difficult for anyone to read.

Hyperlinks Inside Your Document

Web pages became popular because they could link easily to other pages or to various sections inside a document at the speed of an electron. Hyperlinks are easy to use but a little difficult to understand at first.

To use a hyperlink, just click on the link. Links may be pictures or words that are underlined and appear in a different color, as shown in Figure 2-8.

 Internet Milestone

Hexadecimal Colors

Computers speak only in numbers. Values are expressed as numbers that the computer understands. Color values can be carefully controlled and changed to match virtually every color in the rainbow by using special numerical or **hexadecimal** values for certain colors. The invention of hexadecimal is one of the greatest advances in computing. Hexadecimal digits operate on a base-16 number system rather than the base-10 number system we humans normally use. Hexadecimal numbers use the letters A, B, C, D, E, and F along with the numbers 0 to 9 to create 16 different digits. For example, look at the following color values expressed as numbers:

White   =#FFFFFF
Green   =#00FF00
Black   =#000000
Blue   =#0000FF
Red   =#FF0000
Yellow   =#FFFF00

Shades of these colors are created by changing the numbers. For example, a really great sky blue can be created on your HTML page with the hexadecimal number 00CCFF. Do you want a nice light purple? Try FF95FF. An ugly green can be created with AAFF00. Substitute text color values with numbers in your Web page and see what happens. For example, try this in the <BODY> tag and see what happens:

BGCOLOR=#AAFF00 VLINK=#FF95FF TEXT=#00CCFF LINK=#FFFF00

FIGURE 2-8
A hyperlink text

Hyperlinks are created with special tags called anchor tags. The tag has several parts. The opening and closing tags are called the anchor or link tags and look like this:

<A HREF="insert location of file"></A>

Link or anchor tags are fairly useless unless you define the place to which you are linking. There are several ways to use anchor tags. You can:

- Link to another spot within your own document.

- Link to an URL or Web page anywhere on the WWW.

- Link to another Web page on your own computer.

In Step-by-Step 2.4, you will link to the WWW, and in Step-by-Step 2.5, you will create hyperlinks to all the Web pages you have created so far. In this activity, we will start linking within your HTML page.

These internal hyperlinks help users navigate between important parts of your Web page. The first <A> tag you insert will create a hypertext link to a location within your document. You will create the tag in Step 3. The attribute is HREF= and the value is "#POWERFUL". The quotation marks are necessary, as is the #, or pound sign.

The second anchor tag will identify the exact location in your Web page to which you want to link. In Step 4, you will create a tag with the attribute NAME= and a value called "POWERFUL" with quotation marks.

STEP-BY-STEP 2.3

1. Open your **nine.html** or **nine.htm** file for text editing, if necessary.

2. Change the background color back to white by changing the **BGCOLOR** attribute from **YELLOW** to **WHITE**.

3. Add the following anchor **<A></A>** tags before and after the first Powerful Lines list item, as shown in Figure 2-9.

<A HREF="#POWERFUL">Powerful Lines**</A>**

4. Insert the following anchor **<A></A>** tags around the second Powerful Lines list item, as shown here and marked in bold in Figure 2-9.

<P><H2>**<A NAME="POWERFUL">**Powerful Lines**</A>**</H2></P>

5. Save your new file as **ten.html** or **ten.htm**.

Note

The pound sign # can be created by holding the Shift key down and pressing the number 3. The quotation marks (") are created by holding down Shift and pressing the single quote (') key.

Net Ethics

Respect the WWW

What you write in a Web page shouldn't be offensive to others. You're responsible for what you create and post on the WWW. RESPECT the Web. When creating your Web pages, consider these guidelines:

R = Responsibility: Assume personal responsibility and create only ethical and appropriate pages.

E = Everybody: Try to create Web pages that everybody can enjoy, appreciate, and consider of value.

S = Simplicity: Make your Web pages easy to navigate. Make information simple to find.

P = Purpose: Have a clear purpose for every Web page you put on the Web. Don't post unnecessary pages.

E = Ethical: Make sure all the content of every Web page you post corresponds to your values and has a beneficial purpose.

C = Correct: Make sure all the words on your page are spelled correctly, all the sentences are written correctly, and all the hyperlinks work.

T = Totally worth visiting: Try to create pages that others will think are totally worth their time to visit.

STEP-BY-STEP 2.3 Continued

6. View the changes in your Web browser. Your link should look like the sample in Figure 2-8. When you click this link, you should jump down the page to the Powerful Lines heading in your document.

7. Continue to the next section, or close your software and shut down your computer if you're finished for the day.

FIGURE 2-9

Insert background color and internal linking tags

```
<HTML>
<TITLE>HTML and JavaScript</TITLE>

<BODY BGCOLOR=WHITE>
<CENTER><H1>Organizing Tags</H1></CENTER>

<P>There are many ways to organize a Web page. This Web page will organize text,
hypertext links, colors, and fonts. You'll also demonstrate single spacing, double spac-
ing, and the use of line breaks. </P>

<P>This Web page will display how to organize Web pages in a number of ways using: </P>

<BR><A HREF="#POWERFUL">Powerful Lines</A>
<BR>Hyperlinks to HTML and JavaScript Sources
<BR>Hyperlinks to Previously Created Web Pages
<BR>Fancy Fonts
<BR>Perfect Pictures
<BR>Orderly Tables
<BR>Extraordinary Extras
<HR>

<P><H2><A NAME="POWERFUL">Powerful Lines</A></H2></P>

A Horizontal Rule tag 50% wide and 10 pixels high.
<HR WIDTH=50% SIZE=10>

A Horizontal Rule tag 25% wide and 20 pixels high.
<HR WIDTH=25% SIZE=20>

A Horizontal Rule tag 10% wide and 30 pixels high.
<HR WIDTH=10% SIZE=30>

A Horizontal Rule tag without attributes and values.
<HR>

</BODY>
</HTML>
```

Creating Hypertext Links to the Web

The thing that first made the WWW popular was the ability to jump from one page to another anywhere in the world. Before you can do this, however, you must know all about URLs. *URL* stands for *Uniform Resource Locator*. URLs allow a Web browser to pinpoint an exact file on the Web. The concept is really quite simple. Have you ever seen an URL similar to this sample?

http://www.course.com/webpagefolder/anotherfolder/afile.html

When you enter an URL into your HTML Web page, you're identifying a path to a specific HTML file located somewhere online. This file may be on your local computer or somewhere on the Web.

You often can see the name of the file at the end of an URL. Look at the end of our sample URL. The filename *afile.html* is the name of an HTML file (afile). The .html extension identifies the file as an HTML document that your Web browser can display.

However, before you can get to *afile.html*, you need to know the path or the way to this file-name. The key to finding the filename's path is by looking at its URL or Web address. Let's see what this means by breaking down the sample URL into its various parts.

In some URLs, you may see the letters *http* followed by a colon and a couple of slashes. The *http://* tells your network how to transfer or move the files you are requesting. *HTTP* stands for *Hypertext Transfer Protocol*. A protocol is a communication system that is used to transfer data over networks. It is like a secret digital language that Web servers use to communicate with Web browsers.

The second part of the address, *www.course.com*, is the actual name of the server (or Web computer) that hosts the Web page for which you are looking. The *www* stands for World Wide Web. The www tells you that the server uses Web technology. The *.course* part is the name of the company that maintains the Web server. In this case, course is short for Course Technology. The *.com* says that this is a commercial or business site. You may see other addresses that are marked as *.edu* for education, *.gov* for government Web sites, or *.biz* for business sites.

The slashes and names in the rest of the URL (*/webpagefolder/anotherfolder/*) represent folders on the Web server. These are also called subdirectories. You have subdirectories on your computer also. Figure 2-10 shows how folders are organized on a Windows computer. All computers use some sort of folder system to organize files. If you want to find a file on a computer, you need to know the path through the many possible folders in which the file is stored. Knowing the path is the key to finding the Web page you want.

FIGURE 2-10
A Windows folder or directory organization

Before you can find a Web site's welcome page, you need to know the URL. In this Step-by-Step, you'll enter URLs for some of the most important companies in the race to create a better, more exciting Web. Many of the sites have information on HTML, JavaScript, and other important Web tools. They include:

http://www.microsoft.com

http://www.sun.com

http://home.netscape.com

http://www.oracle.com

S TEP-BY-STEP 2.4

1. Open your **ten.html** or **ten.htm** file for text editing, if necessary.

2. Create a hypertext link (as shown here and in bold in Figure 2-11) from the list near the top of the page to the new section you are creating.

<A HREF="#HYPERLINKS">Hyperlinks to HTML and JavaScript Sources**</A>**

STEP-BY-STEP 2.4 Continued

3. Add a new level 2 heading with the words **Hyperlinks to HTML and JavaScript Sources** just below the last <HR> tag of your Web page and just before the </BODY> tag as shown here and in Figure 2-11. Include the <A NAME> tag so that you can create an internal hypertext link from the link you created in Step 2.

```
<P><H2><A NAME="HYPERLINKS">Hyperlinks to HTML and JavaScript Sources</A></H2></P>
```

4. Below your new heading and before the </BODY> tag, create the following hypertext links exactly as shown here and in bold in Figure 2-11.

```
<BR><A HREF="http://www.microsoft.com">Microsoft</A>
<BR><A HREF="http://home.netscape.com">Netscape</A>
<BR><A HREF="http://www.sun.com">Sun</A>
<BR><A HREF="http://www.oracle.com">Oracle</A>
<HR>
```

STEP-BY-STEP 2.4 Continued

FIGURE 2-11
Hypertext linking tags

```
<HTML>
<TITLE>HTML and JavaScript</TITLE>

<BODY BGCOLOR=WHITE>
<CENTER><H1>Organizing Tags</H1></CENTER>

<P>There are many ways to organize a Web page. This Web page will organize text,
hypertext links, colors, and fonts. You'll also demonstrate single spacing, double spac-
ing, and the use of line breaks. </P>

<P>This Web page will display how to organize Web pages in a number of ways using: </P>

<BR><A HREF="#POWERFUL">Powerful Lines</A>
<BR><A HREF="#HYPERLINKS">Hyperlinks to HTML and JavaScript Sources</A>
<BR>Hyperlinks to Previously Created Web Pages
<BR>Fancy Fonts
<BR>Perfect Pictures
<BR>Orderly Tables
<BR>Extraordinary Extras
<HR>

<P><H2><A NAME="POWERFUL">Powerful Lines</A></H2></P>

A Horizontal Rule tag 50% wide and 10 pixels high.
<HR WIDTH=50% SIZE=10>

A Horizontal Rule tag 25% wide and 20 pixels high.
<HR WIDTH=25% SIZE=20>

A Horizontal Rule tag 10% wide and 30 pixels high.
<HR WIDTH=10% SIZE=30>

A Horizontal Rule tag without attributes and values.
<HR>

<P><H2><A NAME="HYPERLINKS">Hyperlinks to HTML and JavaScript Sources
</A></H2></P>

<BR><A HREF="http://www.microsoft.com">Microsoft</A>
<BR><A HREF="http://home.netscape.com">Netscape</A>
<BR><A HREF="http://www.sun.com">Sun</A>
<BR><A HREF="http://www.oracle.com">Oracle</A>
<HR>

</BODY>
</HTML>
```

STEP-BY-STEP 2.4 Continued

5. Your entire page of tags should appear like those in Figure 2-11. Save your work as **eleven.html** or **eleven.htm**.

6. View your work in your Web browser. Your new links should look like Figure 2-12.

FIGURE 2-12
Hyperlinks in your Web browser

7. If you have a live connection to the Web, try your links and see if they work! If your links don't work properly, carefully review your tags and make any necessary corrections. Save your work again. Then reload or refresh your page in your Web browser and try again.

8. Continue to the next section or close your software and shut down your computer if you're finished for the day.

Net Tip

Your browser won't look for your newly corrected Web page unless you tell it to. You can do this in a couple of ways. You can open the page again, or simply click the **Reload** or **Refresh** buttons to load an updated copy of your Web page into your browser.

Linking to Pages You Have Already Created

In this Step-by-Step, you'll link to the first 11 HTML pages you have created in this book. Keeping track of all your pages in this way will help you quickly review the progress you have made.

S TEP-BY-STEP 2.5

1. Open your **eleven.html** or **eleven.htm** file, if necessary.

2. Create a hypertext link from your list near the top of the page to the new section you are creating. The text to be entered is shown below and in bold in Figure 2-13.

<A HREF="#PREVIOUS">Hyperlinks to Previously Created Web Pages**</A>**

3. As shown in Figure 2-13, add a new level 2 heading called **Hyperlinks to Previously Created Web Pages** just below the HR tag you added in the previous exercise, and just before the </BODY> tag. Include the <A NAME> tag so you can link to this exact spot from the tag you created in Step 3.

<P><H2><A NAME="PREVIOUS">Hyperlinks to Previously Created Web Pages </A></H2></P>

4. Below the new heading near the end of your document, create the hypertext links exactly as shown here and in bold in Figure 2-13.

**
<A HREF="one.html">one</A>**
**
<A HREF="two.html">two</A>**
**
<A HREF="three.html">three</A>**
**
<A HREF="four.html">four</A>**
**
<A HREF="five.html">five</A>**
**
<A HREF="six.html">six</A>**
**
<A HREF="seven.html">seven</A>**
**
<A HREF="eight.html">eight</A>**
**
<A HREF="nine.html">nine</A>**
**
<A HREF="ten.html">ten</A>**
**
<A HREF="eleven.html">eleven</A>**
<HR>

STEP-BY-STEP 2.5 Continued

5. Your entire page of tags should now appear like those in Figure 2-13. Save your work as **twelve.html** or **twelve.htm**.

FIGURE 2-13
Creating links to Web pages you have created

```
<HTML>
<TITLE>HTML and JavaScript</TITLE>

<BODY BGCOLOR=WHITE>
<CENTER><H1>Organizing Tags</H1></CENTER>

<P>There are many ways to organize a Web page. This Web page will organize text,
hypertext links, colors, and fonts. You'll also demonstrate single spacing, double spac-
ing, and the use of line breaks. </P>

<P>This Web page will display how to organize Web pages in a number of ways using: </P>

<BR><A HREF="#POWERFUL">Powerful Lines</A>
<BR><A HREF="#HYPERLINKS">Hyperlinks to HTML and JavaScript Sources</A>
<BR><A HREF="#PREVIOUS">Hyperlinks to Previously Created Web Pages</A>
<BR>Fancy Fonts
<BR>Perfect Pictures
<BR>Orderly Tables
<BR>Extraordinary Extras
<HR>

<P><H2><A NAME="POWERFUL">Powerful Lines</A></H2></P>

A Horizontal Rule tag 50% wide and 10 pixels high.
<HR WIDTH=50% SIZE=10>

A Horizontal Rule tag 25% wide and 20 pixels high.
<HR WIDTH=25% SIZE=20>

A Horizontal Rule tag 10% wide and 30 pixels high.
<HR WIDTH=10% SIZE=30>

A Horizontal Rule tag without attributes and values.
<HR>

<P><H2><A NAME="HYPERLINKS">Hyperlinks to HTML and JavaScript Sources
</A></H2></P>

<BR><A HREF="http://www.microsoft.com">Microsoft</A>
<BR><A HREF="http://home.netscape.com">Netscape</A>
<BR><A HREF="http://www.sun.com">Sun</A>
<BR><A HREF="http://www.oracle.com">Oracle</A>
```

STEP-BY-STEP 2.5 Continued

FIGURE 2-13 (Continued)
Creating links to Web pages you have created

```
<HR>

<P><H2><A NAME="PREVIOUS">Hyperlinks to Previously Created Web Pages
</A></H2></P>

<BR><A HREF="one.html">one</A>
<BR><A HREF="two.html"">two</A>
<BR><A HREF="three.html">three</A>
<BR><A HREF="four.html">four</A>
<BR><A HREF="five.html">five</A>
<BR><A HREF="six.html">six</A>
<BR><A HREF="seven.html">seven</A>
<BR><A HREF="eight.html">eight</A>
<BR><A HREF="nine.html">nine</A>
<BR><A HREF="ten.html">ten</A>
<BR><A HREF="eleven.html">eleven</A>
<HR>

</BODY>
</HTML>
```

STEP-BY-STEP 2.5 Continued

6. View your work in your Web browser. Your new links should look like Figure 2-14. Test each link and make sure they all work. Make any corrections that are necessary.

> **Note** ☑️
>
> All of your HTML files must be located in the same folder in order for the hyperlinks to work correctly.

FIGURE 2-14
Links to previously created Web pages

7. Continue to the next section or close your software and shut down your computer if you're finished for the day.

Coloring Text

While surfing the Web, have you noticed that the text colors often change from page to page? In Step-by-Step 2.1, you changed the background color of your Web page by inserting the YELLOW value into the BGCOLOR= attribute in the <BODY> tag. Then you changed the background to several other colors. Changing text color is just as easy.

Table 2-1 shows the three basic types of text color you can change.

TABLE 2-1
Text color

TYPE OF TEXT	ATTRIBUTE
1. The text itself	TEXT=
2. The hypertext link color	LINK=
3. The visited link color (or the links you have already selected)	VLINK=

STEP-BY-STEP 2.6

1. Open your **twelve.html** or **twelve.htm** file, if necessary.

2. In the body tag at the beginning of the Web page, leave the BGCOLOR as WHITE, but insert **TEXT=BLUE**, **LINK=RED**, and **VLINK=GREEN**, as shown in Figure 2-15.

FIGURE 2-15
Changing the text color on a Web page

```
<HTML>
<TITLE> HTML and JavaScript </TITLE>

<BODY BGCOLOR=WHITE TEXT=BLUE LINK=RED VLINK=GREEN>
```

3. Save your work as **thirteen.html** or **thirteen.htm**. View your work in your Web browser. Your page should appear with blue text, red hyperlinks, and green visited links on a white background as seen in Figure 2-16.

4. Continue to the Summary section or close your software and shut down your computer if you're finished for the day.

FIGURE 2-16
Changing text colors

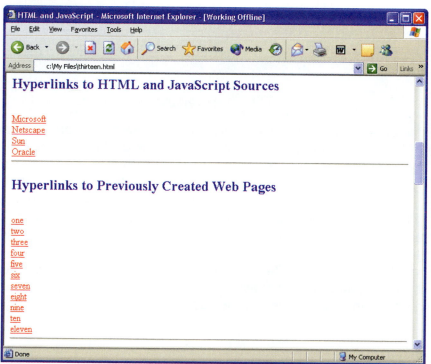

Perfect Proofreading Tips

Proofreading HTML tags can be difficult. Even the slightest error can drastically change the look of a Web page. Here are some common errors to look for:

- Make sure all your angle brackets < > are facing in the proper direction.

- Often, Web page writers misuse the shift key when making angle brackets or creating a slash. This results in a comma, a period, or a question mark where the slash or angle brackets should appear.

- If all the text appears centered, perhaps you forgot to use the close </CENTER> tag.

- If you want a double space instead of a single space, use a <P></P> tag instead of a <BR> tag.

- If bullets appear long after a list, perhaps you forgot the close unordered list tag </UL>.

Net Fun

Another fun tag is the marquee tag. Anything you put between the marquee tags, <MARQUEE> </MARQUEE>, will scroll across the screen like a stock market ticker. The tag was designed for the Internet Explorer browser by Microsoft, and doesn't work on every browser. Experiment, and see what happens!

 Internet Milestone

HTML Standards

HTML is a powerful tool because it allows all kinds of computers to display Web pages. With HTML, it doesn't matter if you're running a Macintosh or a Windows machine. You can even be on a Linux or UNIX workstation or some other type of computer. The reason HTML Web pages can be viewed by all types of computers is because there are standards that all Web browsers understand. New standards and new HTML tags and commands are being added all the time. Each new tag is submitted to a standards committee for review. Every now and then enough new commands are added to HTML for a new version of HTML to be developed. These versions are marked by numbers: HTML 1, HTML 2, HTML 3, HTML 4, and so on. You can learn more about HTML standards and receive help expanding your HTML skills online. Go to your search portal and try these search words:

HTML
HTML Standards
HTML Standards Committee
HTML Learning
HTML Guides

SUMMARY

In this lesson, you learned:

- You can organize page information with single and double spacing.
- You can organize page information with lines.
- You can use attributes and values to improve Web page design.
- You can change color defaults, attributes, and values.
- You can create hypertext links to a spot in a Web document.
- You can create hypertext links to another page on the World Wide Web.
- You can create hypertext links to Web pages on your own computer.

VOCABULARY *Review*

Define the following terms:

Attribute	Hypertext links	Uniform Resource Locator
Fonts	Hypertext Transfer Protocol	(URL)
Hexadecimal	(HTTP)	Value
Hyperlinks		

REVIEW *Questions*

TRUE/FALSE

Circle T if the statement is true or F if the statement is false.

T   F   **1.** Hexadecimal numbers operate on a base-10 number system.

T   F   **2.** The <BR> tag creates a double-space around the text.

T   F   **3.** HREF is an attribute to the <A></A> anchor tag.

T   F   **4.** You can change the color of just about any text on your Web page.

T   F   **5.** The <HR> tag creates a single-space break.

FILL IN THE BLANK

Complete the following sentences by writing the correct word or words in the blanks provided.

1. The _____ tag creates text that scrolls across the screen.

2. You can _____ space in an HTML document with the <P> tag.

3. A(n) _____ is a communications system that is used to transfer data over networks.

4. A(n) _____ number lets you define a color with numbers and letters.

5. The _____ attribute changes a Web page's background color.

WRITTEN QUESTIONS

Write a brief answer to the following questions.

1. What tag allows text to scroll across the screen repeatedly?

2. What hexadecimal value will create the color yellow?

3. Which tag(s) do you know of that do not require a closing tag in order to work effectively?

4. What are three common HTML errors?

5. Why are there different versions of HTML?

PROJECTS

PROJECT 2-1

In the Teamwork activity from Lesson 1, you identified the greatest Web pages you could find. In this Project, GreatApplications, Inc., wants you to identify the five worst pages you can find. These are to be used in a training seminar to help new employees learn how to create high-quality Web pages. Your managers suggested that you surf the Web and find five examples of hard-to-read, unorganized, or boring Web pages to show new interns exactly what not to do.

Surf the Web looking for awful Web page examples. Record the title and URL of each page and list a few reasons why these pages are horrible!

TABLE 2-2
Examples of unorganized Web pages

TITLE THAT APPEARS IN THE TITLE BAR	WEB ADDRESS OR URL	REASONS WHY THIS PAGE IS BAD
1.		
2.		
3.		
4.		
5.		

  ### TEAMWORK PROJECT

GreatApplications, Inc., is holding a design contest to see who can build the most informative and organized Web pages. Specifically, they are looking for a team that can create Web pages to introduce new products to customers over the Web.

The contest gives teams of three to five people two hours to create an informative Web page about a product of their choice. Form your team and brainstorm a new product to introduce. It could be a new DVD or a new computer game. It could be a new fashion or a new car. For the purpose of this contest, it doesn't really matter what product you pick, so don't take up too much of your time deciding what product you will use.

Create your team's Web page contest entry. Divide the writing responsibilities. Have one person enter the basic tags and serve as Webmaster. Each team member must research and write a portion of the Web page. Collaborate by editing and revising each other's writing and HTML tags. Use the techniques you have learned in this lesson to organize the information you wish to present.

WEB PROJECT

We all know that teamwork is important. However, are there times when teamwork is harder than working alone? Answer the following questions about teams creating Web pages together.

1. As you worked together on the Teamwork Project, what problems did you encounter?

2. How did you organize your team? How did you divide the work? Which team members were responsible for which activities?

3. Did teamwork create a better Web page? If so, how?

4. What advice would you give to other teams that are trying to create Web pages?

CRITICAL *Thinking*

Prepare a 100- to 250-word answer to each of the following questions.

 ACTIVITY 2-1

Can you figure out how to create an internal hyperlink that will allow you to move from the bottom of your document to the very top? Use the steps you learned in Step-by-Step 2.3 to create a link just before the </BODY> tag that will link you to the top of the page. Your link should look like this: <u>Top of Page</u>. Why do you think a link back to the top of a page would be valuable?

 ACTIVITY 2-2

What are your top 10 most important Web sites? What makes them important to you? Create a new HTML page that indexes and lists your most important personal Web pages. Call the page **My Web Resources**. Keep adding to your Web resources page as you work through this text.

SUMMARY *Project*

No matter what career you may choose for yourself later in life, it is very important to develop good communication skills. For example, everyone can benefit from learning how to write a well-formatted business letter. Use the HTML text formatting skills you learned in this lesson to develop a business letter to your teacher. When you are finished, your letter should have the general appearance of the sample letter shown in Figure 2-17.

FIGURE 2-17
A sample business letter

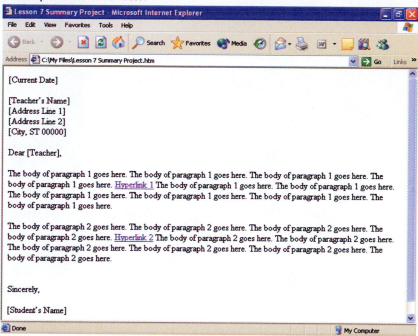

Project Requirements

- Your letter should have a date at the top of the page.

- The date should be followed by an address and a salutation.

- The main body of your letter must contain at least two full paragraphs.

- Your letter should end with a closing phrase and your own name.

- You must include at least one hyperlink per paragraph in your letter.

- The text should display in blue, and the hyperlinks should be red.

- Make sure that your letter maintains its formatting when you resize your browser window. (The spacing between paragraphs should remain consistent.)

HTML POWER TECHNIQUES

OBJECTIVES

Upon completion of this lesson, you should be able to:

■ Control the size, style, and color of fonts.

■ Download pictures from the Web.

■ Insert pictures into your Web page.

■ Change the size of graphics.

■ Use tables to organize information.

■ Turn pictures into hyperlinks.

■ Insert a variety of data input options into a Web page.

Estimated Time: 1.5 hours

VOCABULARY

.gif

.jpg or .jpeg

Graphics Interchange Format

Joint Photographic Experts Group

Table cells

The Exciting Web

The Web is full of pictures, sounds, and movies that add interest to Web pages. Generally, there are two kinds of pictures, called graphics or images, on the World Wide Web. They include .gif files (Graphics Interchange Format) and .jpg or .jpeg (Joint Photographic Experts Group) files. The extensions .gif and .jpg help tell your browser that these files are pictures, not .html text files, and require special handling. We will discuss and define these files in more detail later in the lesson.

The more you learn about HTML, the more you can add exciting new effects and styles to your Web pages. As we mentioned in Lesson 2, fonts, or the style of letters, can be changed. Every font has a style all its own.

By using the <FONT> tag's many attributes and values, you can manipulate fonts in unlimited ways, as you will soon experience in this lesson.

Tables allow the parts of a Web page to be divided up, creating special spaces for each new element or piece of information you may want to include.

Tables, fonts, and pictures can add power to your pages. In this lesson, you will learn to manipulate the special HTML features. You'll also learn about some extraordinary input tags that will allow visitors to your Web page to interact with your Web page.

Font Attributes and Values

When you change text colors in the <BODY> tag, as you did in Step-by-Step 2.6 in Lesson 2, you change the color of your words for the entire page. If you want to have more control (that is, if you want to change the size, color, or style of a single paragraph, a single sentence, or even a single word) use the <FONT> tag.

Use <FONT> tag attributes to control:

- The size of words with the SIZE attribute <FONT SIZE=#>

- The style of words with the FACE attribute <FONT FACE=#>

- The color of words with the COLOR attribute <FONT COLOR=#>

STEP-BY-STEP 3.1

1. Open your **thirteen.html** or **thirteen.htm** file (from Lesson 2) for text editing.

2. Create a hypertext link in the list near the top of the page that will hyperlink to the new section you'll be creating in this Step-by-Step. The text to be entered is shown in bold here and in Figure 3-1.

<A HREF="#FONTS">Fancy Fonts</A>

3. As shown in Figure 3-1, add a new level 2 heading called **Fancy Fonts** just below the <HR> tag you created at the end of Step-by-Step 2.6 from Lesson 2 and just before the </BODY> tag. This will finish the internal hypertext link you started in step 2 of this Step-by-Step.

<P><H2><A NAME="FONTS">Fancy Fonts</A></H2></P>

4. Below the new heading, near the end of your document, enter the font tags, attributes, and values exactly as shown here and in bold in Figure 3-1.

**
<FONT FACE=HELVETICA SIZE=4 COLOR=RED>This is the Helvetica font at Size 4</FONT>**
**
<FONT FACE=TIMES SIZE=6 COLOR=GREEN>This is the Times font at Size 6</FONT>**
**
<FONT FACE=ARIAL SIZE=8 COLOR=ORANGE>This is the Arial font at Size 8</FONT>**
**
<FONT FACE=COURIER SIZE=2 COLOR=BLACK>This is the Courier font at Size 2</FONT>**
<HR>

STEP-BY-STEP 3.1 Continued

5. Your tags should appear like those in Figure 3-1. Save your work as **fourteen.html** or **fourteen.htm**.

FIGURE 3-1
Applying font styles, sizes, and colors

```
<HTML>
<TITLE> HTML and JavaScript </TITLE>

<BODY BGCOLOR=WHITE TEXT=BLUE LINK=RED VLINK=GREEN>
<CENTER><H1>Organizing Tags</H1></CENTER>

<P>There are many ways to organize a Web page. This Web page will organize text,
hypertext links, colors, and fonts. You'll also demonstrate single spacing, double spac-
ing, and the use of line breaks. </P>

<P>This Web page will display how to organize Web pages in a number of ways using: </P>

<BR><A HREF="#POWERFUL">Powerful Lines</A>
<BR><A HREF="#HYPERLINKS">Hyperlinks to HTML and JavaScript Sources</A>
<BR><A HREF="#PREVIOUS">Hyperlinks to Previously Created Web Pages</A>
<BR><A HREF="#FONTS">Fancy Fonts</A>
<BR>Perfect Pictures
<BR>Orderly Tables
<BR>Extraordinary Extras

<HR>
<P><H2><A NAME="POWERFUL">Powerful Lines</A></H2></P>

A Horizontal Rule tag 50% wide and 10 pixels high.
<HR WIDTH=50% SIZE=10>

A Horizontal Rule tag 25% wide and 20 pixels high.
<HR WIDTH=25% SIZE=20>

A Horizontal Rule tag 10% wide and 30 pixels high.
<HR WIDTH=10% SIZE=30>

A Horizontal Rule tag without attributes and values.
<HR>

<P><H2><A NAME="HYPERLINKS">Hyperlinks to HTML and JavaScript Sources
</A></H2></P>

<BR><A HREF="http://www.microsoft.com">Microsoft</A>
<BR><A HREF="http://home.netscape.com">Netscape</A>
<BR><A HREF="http://www.sun.com">Sun</A>
<BR><A HREF="http://www.oracle.com">Oracle</A>
<HR>
```

STEP-BY-STEP 3.1 Continued

FIGURE 3-1 (Continued)
Applying font styles, sizes, and colors

```
<P><H2><A NAME="PREVIOUS">Hyperlinks to Previously Created Web Pages
</A></H2></P>

<BR><A HREF="one.html">one</A>
<BR><A HREF="two.html">two</A>
<BR><A HREF="three.html">three</A>
<BR><A HREF="four.html">four</A>
<BR><A HREF="five.html">five</A>
<BR><A HREF="six.html">six</A>
<BR><A HREF="seven.html">seven</A>
<BR><A HREF="eight.html">eight</A>
<BR><A HREF="nine.html">nine</A>
<BR><A HREF="ten.html">ten</A>
<BR><A HREF="eleven.html">eleven</A>
<HR>

<P><H2><A NAME="FONTS">Fancy Fonts</A></H2></P>

<BR><FONT FACE=HELVETICA SIZE=4 COLOR=RED>This is the Helvetica font at
Size 4</FONT>
<BR><FONT FACE=TIMES SIZE=6 COLOR=GREEN>This is the Times font at Size 6
</FONT>
<BR><FONT FACE=ARIAL SIZE=8 COLOR=ORANGE>This is the Arial font at Size 8
</FONT>
<BR><FONT FACE=COURIER SIZE=2 COLOR=BLACK>This is the Courier font at
Size 2 </FONT>
<HR>

</BODY>
</HTML>
```

STEP-BY-STEP 3.1 Continued

6. View your work in your Web browser. Your changes should look like Figure 3-2. Make any corrections that appear necessary.

FIGURE 3-2
Various font styles, sizes, and colors

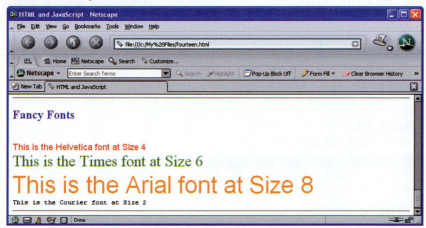

7. Continue to the next section or close your software and shut down your computer if you're finished for the day.

Downloading and Inserting Graphics

Pictures can be found in many places. You can find pictures in your clip art collection, scan pictures into your computer with a scanner, draw your own pictures, or copy them from the Web. However, before you can easily use pictures in your Web pages, you need to convert them into one of the acceptable Web formats. The common formats are .gif and .jpg or .jpeg.

Net Tip

There are other ways to change the look of text. Try these tags around certain words and see what effects they create. Can you guess what they do?
<B></B>
<EM></EM>
<STRONG></STRONG>
<I></I>

The first type of graphics or image format, *.gif*, was originally created by one of the first online companies, CompuServe, to provide a compressed graphics format that could transfer easily over low-speed modems. The *Graphics Interchange Format* is usually abbreviated as GIF. There is some debate on how to say GIF. In some parts of the country it is pronounced with a hard *g* as in Kathie Lee GIFford. In other parts of the country it is pronounced with a soft *g* as in JIFfy Peanut Butter. Either pronunciation works. After all, the pronunciation doesn't change the file format in the least.

The second commonly used format is *.jpg* or *.jpeg*. It is pronounced *J-Peg* by Web artists in-the-know. JPEG is short for *Joint Photographic Experts Group*. This format adheres to an international set of graphics standards. JPEG graphics, like GIF pictures, are compact enough for Internet use.

Other graphic file formats are emerging. But if you know how to work with these two formats, you'll know how to work with any other picture format on the World Wide Web.

STEP-BY-STEP 3.2

1. Open your Web browser.

2. Enter the URL **www.course.com** in your Web browser.

3. Click in the Search For box as shown in Figure 3-3 and enter the ISBN of this book.

Net Tip

To copy and download the graphics you need for this lesson, go to *www.course.com*, search for the ISBN of this book, and follow the rest of the steps outlined in Step-by-Step 3.2. (The ISBN can be found on the back cover of the book.)

FIGURE 3-3
Visit *www.course.com*

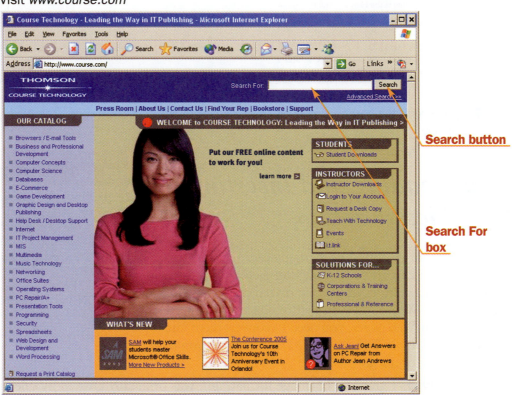

4. Choose **Search** and wait for the results to appear.

5. Click on the title of this book, then choose the link called Student Online Companion.

6. Click the **Lesson 3** link and choose the **Data Files & Graphics** link from the list that appears. Scroll down until you see a dragon.

STEP-BY-STEP 3.2 Continued

7. If you're on a Windows computer, click the right mouse button on the dragon's nose, pictured in Figure 3-4. If you're using a Macintosh, click and hold your mouse button on the dragon's nose.

FIGURE 3-4
Copy and save the graphic

Right click in Windows

Click and hold in Macintosh

8. Choose the **Save Image As...** or **Save Picture As...** command from the list that appears, as shown in Figures 3-5A and 3-5B. (*Note:* The command on your browser may be worded differently. Keep trying the various commands that appear until you find the correct command.)

FIGURE 3-5A
With Netscape, select
Save Image

FIGURE 3-5B
With Internet Explorer, select Save
Picture As

9. Save your file (called *levy.gif*) in the exact same folder where you have been saving your Web pages.

STEP-BY-STEP 3.2 Continued

10. Open your **fourteen.html** or **fourteen.htm** Web page in your word processor or text editor.

11. Create a hypertext link in the list near the top of the page that will hyperlink to the new section you will be creating. The text to be entered is shown in bold here and in Figure 3-6.

```
<BR><A HREF="#PICTURES">Perfect Pictures</A>
```

12. As shown in Figure 3-6, add a new level 2 heading called **Perfect Pictures** just below the last <HR> tag you created previously and just before the </BODY> tag. Include the <A NAME> tag so you can finish the internal hypertext link you started in step 11.

```
<P><H2><A NAME="PICTURES">Perfect Pictures</A></H2></P>
```

13. Below your new heading, near the end of your document, enter an Image Source <IMG SRC> tag, as shown here and in Figure 3-6. Notice that the name of the file you just downloaded appears between quotation marks.

```
<IMG SRC="levy.gif">
<HR>
```

14. Your tags should now appear like those in Figure 3-6. If everything looks correct, save your work as **fifteen.html** or **fifteen.htm**.

FIGURE 3-6
Inserting a graphic or image file

```
<HTML>
<TITLE> HTML and JavaScript </TITLE>

<BODY BGCOLOR=WHITE TEXT=BLUE LINK=RED VLINK=GREEN>
<CENTER><H1>Organizing Tags</H1></CENTER>

<P>There are many ways to organize a Web page. This Web page will organize text,
hypertext links, colors, and fonts. You'll also demonstrate single spacing, double spac-
ing, and the use of line breaks. </P>

<P>This Web page will display how to organize Web pages in a number of ways using: </P>

<BR><A HREF="#POWERFUL">Powerful Lines</A>
<BR><A HREF="#HYPERLINKS">Hyperlinks to HTML and JavaScript Sources</A>
<BR><A HREF="#PREVIOUS">Hyperlinks to Previously Created Web Pages</A>
<BR><A HREF="#FONTS">Fancy Fonts</A>
<BR><A HREF="#PICTURES">Perfect Pictures</A>
<BR>Orderly Tables
<BR>Extraordinary Extras

<HR>
<P><H2><A NAME="POWERFUL">Powerful Lines</A></H2></P>
A Horizontal Rule tag 50% wide and 10 pixels high.
<HR WIDTH=50% SIZE=10>
```

STEP-BY-STEP 3.2 Continued

FIGURE 3-6 (Continued)
Inserting a graphic or image file

```
A Horizontal Rule tag 25% wide and 20 pixels high.
<HR WIDTH=25% SIZE=20>

A Horizontal Rule tag 10% wide and 30 pixels high.
<HR WIDTH=10% SIZE=30>

A Horizontal Rule tag without attributes and values.
<HR>

<P><H2><A NAME="HYPERLINKS">Hyperlinks to HTML and JavaScript Sources
</A></H2></P>

<BR><A HREF="http://www.microsoft.com">Microsoft</A>
<BR><A HREF="http://home.netscape.com">Netscape</A>
<BR><A HREF="http://www.sun.com">Sun</A>
<BR><A HREF="http://www.oracle.com">Oracle</A>
<HR>

<P><H2><A NAME="PREVIOUS">Hyperlinks to Previously Created Web Pages
</A></H2></P>

<BR><A HREF="one.html">one</A>
<BR><A HREF="two.html">two</A>
<BR><A HREF="three.html">three</A>
<BR><A HREF="four.html">four</A>
<BR><A HREF="five.html">five</A>
<BR><A HREF="six.html">six</A>
<BR><A HREF="seven.html">seven</A>
<BR><A HREF="eight.html">eight</A>
<BR><A HREF="nine.html">nine</A>
<BR><A HREF="ten.html">ten</A>
<BR><A HREF="eleven.html">eleven</A>
<HR>

<P><H2><A NAME="FONTS">Fancy Fonts</A></H2></P>

<BR><FONT FACE=HELVETICA SIZE=4 COLOR=RED>This is the Helvetica font at
Size 4</FONT>
<BR><FONT FACE=TIMES SIZE=6 COLOR=GREEN>This is the Times font at Size 6
</FONT>
<BR><FONT FACE=ARIAL SIZE=8 COLOR=ORANGE>This is the Arial font at Size 8
</FONT>
<BR><FONT FACE=COURIER SIZE=2 COLOR=BLACK>This is the Courier font at
Size 2 </FONT>
<HR>
```

STEP-BY-STEP 3.2 Continued

FIGURE 3-6 (Continued)
Inserting a graphic or image file

```
<P><H2><A NAME="PICTURES">Perfect Pictures</A></H2></P>

<IMG SRC="levy.gif">
<HR>

</BODY>
</HTML>
```

15. View your work in your Web browser. Your picture should look like Figure 3-7, but it may appear larger or smaller in your browser.

FIGURE 3-7
Your GIF image as seen in a browser

16. Continue to the next section or close your software and shut down your computer if you're finished for the day.

Pictures of All Sizes

Pictures can be altered in a variety of ways by changing a tag's values. Pictures can be used as wallpaper to cover the entire background of a Web page. They can be aligned in the center, to the left side, or to the right side of a page. They can be made bigger or smaller, depending on your needs.

You can also change the size of the picture by using the HEIGHT and WIDTH attributes. Controlling the exact size of a picture can be very helpful in making a page look sharp and interesting.

In the first part of Step-by-Step 3.3, you'll align your picture to the right of the page and make it small. In the second section, you'll align three dragons of varying sizes across the page, and then you'll place three dragons vertically on the Web page by manipulating a few tags.

Net Tip

A common error is created by transposing the R and the C in the <IMG SRC> tag. Think of this as the IMaGe SouRCe tag and you won't forget to place the letters in the right order.

Net Tip

An easy way to allow your Web page visitors to e-mail you with one click is to create the following tag:
<A HREF=mailto:your_email @address>Your Name</A>.

STEP-BY-STEP 3.3

1. Open your **fifteen.html** or **fifteen.htm** file for text editing.

2. Near the end of your document, add the following information to your <IMG SRC> tag as shown in bold here and in Figure 3-8.

`<P><IMG SRC="levy.gif" ALIGN=RIGHT HEIGHT=50 WIDTH=50></P>`

 Technology Careers

Artists on the Web

Artists are in great demand among Web site development companies. There was a time when a Web page would be made entirely of words or text. Today, pictures dominate Web pages, attracting a greater number of visitors than ever before.

If you are considering an artistic career, consider the Web. You may find that much of your artwork will end up on the Web. Big corporations with Web sites and Web site developers are always on the lookout for great artists.

You can create your art using any medium or method you like. Scanners can convert your pictures into digital images. Digital files can be converted into formats that will work on the Web such as .gif or .jpg. You can also use a variety of art software to create your works of art or to improve any art you have scanned into Web images.

The best training for a Web artist would be to take as many art classes as you can. The graphics tools you need to use to convert your artwork are easily learned. The skills of an artist will take much more time to develop.

STEP-BY-STEP 3.3 Continued

3. Save your changes as **sixteen.html** or **sixteen.htm**.

4. View your changes in your Web browser. The dragon should appear smaller and right-aligned as shown in Figure 3-9.

5. Next, create three images that appear across the screen, with each graphic appearing as a different size. To do so, enter the following tags below your first IMG SRC tag, as shown here and in Figure 3-8.

```
<IMG SRC="levy.gif" HEIGHT=100 WIDTH=100>
<IMG SRC="levy.gif" HEIGHT=150 WIDTH=150>
<IMG SRC="levy.gif" HEIGHT=200 WIDTH=200>
```

6. Resave your changes using the same **sixteen.html** or **sixteen.htm** filename and view your additions in your Web browser. Your changes should appear similar to the three images shown in Figure 3-9. If your graphics don't appear, make any necessary corrections, resave, and view again.

7. Just below the three tags you entered in the previous step, add two more IMG SRC tags, using <P> tags to cause several graphics to appear vertically. Enter these tags exactly as shown here and in Figure 3-8.

```
<P><IMG SRC="levy.gif" HEIGHT=150 WIDTH=150></P>
<P><IMG SRC="levy.gif" HEIGHT=200 WIDTH=200></P>
```

8. Save your changes again as **sixteen.html** or **sixteen.htm**, and view the result in your Web browser. Check Figures 3-8 and 3-9 to evaluate how the tags and graphics should appear. Make corrections where necessary, and review any changes in your browser.

9. Continue to the next section or close your software and shut down your computer if you're finished for the day.

FIGURE 3-8
Dragons everywhere

```
<HTML>
<TITLE> HTML and JavaScript </TITLE>

<BODY BGCOLOR=WHITE TEXT=BLUE LINK=RED VLINK=GREEN>
<CENTER><H1>Organizing Tags</H1></CENTER>

<P>There are many ways to organize a Web page. This Web page will organize text,
hypertext links, colors, and fonts. You'll also demonstrate single spacing, double spacing,
and the use of line breaks. </P>

<P>This Web page will display how to organize Web pages in a number of ways using: </P>

<BR><A HREF="#POWERFUL">Powerful Lines</A>
<BR><A HREF="#HYPERLINKS">Hyperlinks to HTML and JavaScript Sources</A>
```

STEP-BY-STEP 3.3 Continued

FIGURE 3-8 (Continued)
Dragons everywhere

```
<BR><A HREF="#PREVIOUS">Hyperlinks to Previously Created Web Pages</A>
<BR><A HREF="#FONTS">Fancy Fonts</A>
<BR><A HREF="#PICTURES">Perfect Pictures</A>
<BR>Orderly Tables
<BR>Extraordinary Extras

<HR>
<P><H2><A NAME="POWERFUL">Powerful Lines</A></H2></P>

A Horizontal Rule tag 50% wide and 10 pixels high.
<HR WIDTH=50% SIZE=10>

A Horizontal Rule tag 25% wide and 20 pixels high.
<HR WIDTH=25% SIZE=20>

A Horizontal Rule tag 10% wide and 30 pixels high.
<HR WIDTH=10% SIZE=30>

A Horizontal Rule tag without attributes and values.
<HR>

<P><H2><A NAME="HYPERLINKS">Hyperlinks to HTML and JavaScript Sources
</A></H2></P>

<BR><A HREF="http://www.microsoft.com">Microsoft</A>
<BR><A HREF="http://home.netscape.com">Netscape</A>
<BR><A HREF="http://www.sun.com">Sun</A>
<BR><A HREF="http://www.oracle.com">Oracle</A>
<HR>

<P><H2><A NAME="PREVIOUS">Hyperlinks to Previously Created Web Pages
</A></H2></P>

<BR><A HREF="one.html">one</A>
<BR><A HREF="two.html">two</A>
<BR><A HREF="three.html">three</A>
<BR><A HREF="four.html">four</A>
<BR><A HREF="five.html">five</A>
<BR><A HREF="six.html">six</A>
<BR><A HREF="seven.html">seven</A>
<BR><A HREF="eight.html">eight</A>
<BR><A HREF="nine.html">nine</A>
<BR><A HREF="ten.html">ten</A>
<BR><A HREF="eleven.html">eleven</A>
<HR>
```

STEP-BY-STEP 3.3 Continued

FIGURE 3-8 (Continued)
Dragons everywhere

```
<P><H2><A NAME="FONTS">Fancy Fonts</A></H2></P>

<BR><FONT FACE=HELVETICA SIZE=4 COLOR=RED>This is the Helvetica font
at Size 4</FONT>
<BR><FONT FACE=TIMES SIZE=6 COLOR=GREEN>This is the Times font at Size 6
</FONT>
<BR><FONT FACE=ARIAL SIZE=8 COLOR=ORANGE>This is the Arial font at Size 8
</FONT>
<BR><FONT FACE=COURIER SIZE=2 COLOR=BLACK>This is the Courier font at
Size 2 </FONT>
<HR>

<P><H2><A NAME="PICTURES">Perfect Pictures</A></H2></P>

<P><IMG SRC="levy.gif" ALIGN=RIGHT HEIGHT=50 WIDTH=50></P>

<IMG SRC="levy.gif" HEIGHT=100 WIDTH=100>
<IMG SRC="levy.gif" HEIGHT=150 WIDTH=150>
<IMG SRC="levy.gif" HEIGHT=200 WIDTH=200>

<P><IMG SRC="levy.gif" HEIGHT=150 WIDTH=150></P>
<P><IMG SRC="levy.gif" HEIGHT=200 WIDTH=200></P>
<HR>

</BODY>
</HTML>
```

 Net Ethics

Picture Piracy

One of the big problems on the Web is picture piracy. Since it is so easy to pull pictures off the Web, many people do so without permission. Many pictures are copyrighted; that is, someone owns them. To use them, you need to obtain permission or pay the owner or the artist.

For instance, Disney has many copyrighted images. They have taken legal action against Web site creators who grab and illegally use or alter Disney's copyrighted images.

Consider which pictures you download and use from the Web. Are they free for you to use? Many places allow the free download of images. For instance, the images you borrowed from the Web site for this book are authorized for your use.

STEP-BY-STEP 3.3 Continued

FIGURE 3-9
Your GIF images after changing their attributes and values

Net Tip

To turn a picture into a hyper-link, try this series of tags, attributes, and values!

<A HREF="http:
//www.course.com"><IMG
SRC="levy.gif" HEIGHT=50
WIDTH=50></A>

Net Tip

To have a picture become your background, insert the BACK-GROUND attribute in the <BODY> tag like this:

<BODY BACKGROUND="levy.gif">

Orderly Tables

When you think of a dining room table, well-set and ready for a big holiday dinner, you think of how organized everything is. All the place settings, plates, cups, and silverware are well ordered and in just the right spots.

Electronic tables are like that. Tables create little boxes in which you can place things to keep them organized. In Step-by-Step 3.4, you will create a table and then insert many of the tags you have already learned into little boxes called *table cells*.

Creating a table is so easy with the <TABLE> tag. A cell can have a border by adding a BORDER attribute and a number value. You can also make cells appear larger around pictures and text with the CELLPADDING attribute. Within cells, you can align pictures and text to the center, left, or right.

S TEP-BY-STEP 3.4

1. Open your **sixteen.html** or **sixteen.htm** file, if necessary.

2. Create a hypertext link in your listing at the top of the page that will hyperlink to the new section you are creating. The text to be entered is shown in bold here and in Figure 3-10.

<A HREF="#TABLES">Orderly Tables</A>

3. As shown in Figure 3-10, add a new level 2 heading called **Orderly Tables** just below the <HR> tag you created in the previous Step-by-Step and just before the </BODY> tag. Include the <A NAME> tag so you can complete the internal hyperlinks you started in Step 2.

<P><H2><A NAME="TABLES">Orderly Tables</A></H2></P>

4. Below the new heading, near the end of your document, enter the <TABLE> tags, attributes, and values, exactly as shown here and in bold in Figure 3-10.

```
<TABLE BORDER=5 CELLPADDING=10 ALIGN=CENTER>
<TR>
        <TH>Dragons</TH>
        <TH>Colors</TH>
        <TH>Fonts</TH>
</TR>
<TR>
        <TD><IMG SRC="LEVY.GIF" HEIGHT=50 WIDTH=50></TD>
        <TD BGCOLOR=RED ALIGN=CENTER>Red</TD>
        <TD ALIGN=CENTER><FONT FACE=TIMES SIZE=7 COLOR=GREEN>Times</TD>
</TR>
<TR>
        <TD><IMG SRC="LEVY.GIF" HEIGHT=75 WIDTH=50></TD>
        <TD BGCOLOR=GREEN ALIGN=CENTER>Green</TD>
        <TD ALIGN=CENTER><FONT FACE=COURIER SIZE=10 COLOR=GREEN>Courier</TD>
</TR>
</TABLE>
<HR>
```

STEP-BY-STEP 3.4 Continued

5. Your tags should now appear like those in Figure 3-10. Save your work as **seventeen.html** or **seventeen.htm**.

FIGURE 3-10

Creating a table in HTML

```
<HTML>
<TITLE> HTML and JavaScript </TITLE>

<BODY BGCOLOR=WHITE TEXT=BLUE LINK=RED VLINK=GREEN>
<CENTER><H1>Organizing Tags</H1></CENTER>

<P>There are many ways to organize a Web page.  This Web page will organize text,
hypertext links, colors, and fonts.  You'll also demonstrate single spacing, double spac-
ing, and the use of line breaks. </P>

<P>This Web page will display how to organize Web pages in a number of ways using: </P>

<BR><A HREF="#POWERFUL">Powerful Lines</A>
<BR><A HREF="#HYPERLINKS">Hyperlinks to HTML and JavaScript Sources</A>
<BR><A HREF="#PREVIOUS">Hyperlinks to Previously Created Web Pages</A>
<BR><A HREF="#FONTS">Fancy Fonts</A>
<BR><A HREF="#PICTURES">Perfect Pictures</A>
<BR><A HREF="#TABLES">Orderly Tables</A>
<BR>Extraordinary Extras

<HR>
<P><H2><A NAME="POWERFUL">Powerful Lines</A></H2></P>

A Horizontal Rule tag 50% wide and 10 pixels high.
<HR WIDTH=50% SIZE=10>

A Horizontal Rule tag 25% wide and 20 pixels high.
<HR WIDTH=25% SIZE=20>

A Horizontal Rule tag 10% wide and 30 pixels high.
<HR WIDTH=10% SIZE=30>

A Horizontal Rule tag without attributes and values.
<HR>

<P><H2><A NAME="HYPERLINKS">Hyperlinks to HTML and JavaScript Sources
</A></H2></P>

<BR><A HREF="http://www.microsoft.com">Microsoft</A>
<BR><A HREF="http://home.netscape.com">Netscape</A>
<BR><A HREF="http://www.sun.com">Sun</A>
```

STEP-BY-STEP 3.4 Continued

FIGURE 3-10 (Continued)
Creating a table in HTML

```
<BR><A HREF="http://www.oracle.com">Oracle</A>
<HR>

<P><H2><A NAME="PREVIOUS">Hyperlinks to Previously Created Web Pages
</A></H2></P>

<BR><A HREF="one.html">one</A>
<BR><A HREF="two.html">two</A>
<BR><A HREF="three.html">three</A>
<BR><A HREF="four.html">four</A>
<BR><A HREF="five.html">five</A>
<BR><A HREF="six.html">six</A>
<BR><A HREF="seven.html">seven</A>
<BR><A HREF="eight.html">eight</A>
<BR><A HREF="nine.html">nine</A>
<BR><A HREF="ten.html">ten</A>
<BR><A HREF="eleven.html">eleven</A>
<HR>

<P><H2><A NAME="FONTS">Fancy Fonts</A></H2></P>

<BR><FONT FACE=HELVETICA SIZE=4 COLOR=RED>This is the Helvetica font at
Size 4</FONT>
<BR><FONT FACE=TIMES SIZE=6 COLOR=GREEN>This is the Times font at Size 6
</FONT>
<BR><FONT FACE=ARIAL SIZE=8 COLOR=ORANGE>This is the Arial font at Size 8
</FONT>
<BR><FONT FACE=COURIER SIZE=2 COLOR=BLACK>This is the Courier font at
Size 2 </FONT>
<HR>

<P><H2><A NAME="PICTURES">Perfect Pictures</A></H2></P>

<P><IMG SRC="levy.gif" ALIGN=RIGHT HEIGHT=50 WIDTH=50></P>

<IMG SRC="levy.gif" HEIGHT=100 WIDTH=100>
<IMG SRC="levy.gif" HEIGHT=150 WIDTH=150>
<IMG SRC="levy.gif" HEIGHT=200 WIDTH=200>

<P><IMG SRC="levy.gif" HEIGHT=150 WIDTH=150></P>
<P><IMG SRC="levy.gif" HEIGHT=200 WIDTH=200></P>
<HR>

<P><H2><A NAME="TABLES">Orderly Tables</A></H2></P>
```

STEP-BY-STEP 3.4 Continued

FIGURE 3-10 (Continued)
Creating a table in HTML

```
<TABLE BORDER=5 CELLPADDING=10 ALIGN=CENTER>
<TR>
        <TH>Dragons</TH>
        <TH>Colors</TH>
        <TH>Fonts</TH>
</TR>
<TR>
        <TD><IMG SRC="LEVY.GIF" HEIGHT=50 WIDTH=50></TD>
        <TD BGCOLOR=RED ALIGN=CENTER>Red</TD>
        <TD ALIGN=CENTER><FONT FACE=TIMES SIZE=7
        COLOR=GREEN>Times</TD>
</TR>
<TR>
        <TD><IMG SRC="LEVY.GIF" HEIGHT=75 WIDTH=50></TD>
        <TD BGCOLOR=GREEN ALIGN=CENTER>Green</TD>
        <TD ALIGN=CENTER><FONT FACE=COURIER SIZE=10
        COLOR=GREEN>Courier</TD>
</TR>
</TABLE>
<HR>

</BODY>
</HTML>
```

STEP-BY-STEP 3.4 Continued

6. View your work in your Web browser. Your new page should look like Figure 3-11. Make any corrections that are necessary.

FIGURE 3-11
An HTML table as seen in your browser

7. Continue to the next section or close your software and shut down your computer if you're finished for the day.

Internet Milestone

Business on the Web

For many years, the Web was a tough place to make a living. The truth is, it took many years before the commercial potential of the Web was realized. Some of the first Web companies to start making a considerable profit online were America Online, Yahoo!, and Amazon.com.

Some succeeded online by daring to go where no one else dared to go. Many said that the Web would never replace bookstores. The people of Amazon.com took exception to that theory and began selling books on the Web. They sold so many books that other book companies quickly realized that they had to go online or give away a big portion of their business to Amazon.com. Barnes & Noble was one of the first major booksellers to join Amazon.com on the WWW.

Sony discovered that the Web was a great place to sell music CDs. Egghead.com, a leading electronics company, found the Web a great place to sell software. What other kinds of things can you think of that could become big sellers online? Can you set up a cyberbusiness and make lots of money from the Web?

Extraordinary Extras

In Step-by-Step 3.5, you'll learn a few extra tags that add extraordinary power to your Web pages. These tags will allow those who visit your Web page to interact with the document.

Many data input or <FORM> tag options have been added to HTML. These options give you many ways to ask questions of visitors to your Web page. These tags give extra functionality to your Web page and can make your Web page more exciting and extraordinary.

You will use the following four basic input tags throughout these lessons:

■ *Text box* – A box where Web site visitors can dictate or key responses.

■ *Drop-down list* – Displays an option and a special arrow symbol that allows users to view other possible responses.

■ *Radio button* – Sometimes referred to as an option button, allows you to choose one option from a group of options.

■ *Check box* – A box that places a check mark in its center when a user selects an option from a group.

As you work through this last Step-by-Step activity of this lesson, think about how you should integrate the new tags into your Web page. Don't worry; you'll pass with flying font colors! If you have any questions, review the steps in previous activities. Figure 3-12 on the next page displays the new tags you will be adding to your Web page.

FIGURE 3-12
A variety of data input tags

```
<FORM>

Enter your first name:
<INPUT TYPE="TEXT" SIZE="25">
<BR>
Enter your last name:
<INPUT TYPE="TEXT" SIZE="25">
<P>

<SELECT>
<OPTION SELECTED>Pick your favorite team from the list:
<OPTION>Chicago Bulls
<OPTION>Utah Jazz
<OPTION>Los Angeles Lakers
<OPTION>Indiana Pacers
<OPTION>New Jersey Nets
<OPTION>Phoenix Suns
</SELECT>
<P>

The best place to eat is:
<BR>
<INPUT TYPE="RADIO" NAME="BEST">Wendy's<BR>
<INPUT TYPE="RADIO" NAME="BEST">McDonald's<BR>
<INPUT TYPE="RADIO" NAME="BEST">Taco Bell<BR>
<INPUT TYPE="RADIO" NAME="BEST">Burger King<BR>
<INPUT TYPE="RADIO" NAME="BEST">Kentucky Fried Chicken<BR>
<P>

I like to eat:
<BR>
<INPUT TYPE="CHECKBOX">Hamburgers<BR>
<INPUT TYPE="CHECKBOX">Tacos<BR>
<INPUT TYPE="CHECKBOX">Chicken Strips<BR>
<INPUT TYPE="CHECKBOX">Fries<BR>
<INPUT TYPE="CHECKBOX">Hot Dogs<BR>
<P>

</FORM>
<HR>
```

STEP-BY-STEP 3.5

1. Open your **seventeen.html** or **seventeen.htm** file, if necessary.

2. Create a section near the end of your Web page called **Extraordinary Extras**.

3. Create an internal hypertext link in the index list near the top of your Web page that will link to the new section you are creating. Call this link **Extraordinary Extras**.

4. Change the color, font size, and font face of the title of your new section in any way you see fit.

5. Enter the tags shown in Figure 3-12 in your new Extraordinary Extras section, just after the last <HR> tag and before the </BODY> tag at the bottom of the page.

6. Save your work as **eighteen.html** or **eighteen.htm**.

7. Open your Web browser and try all the input options. They should appear like those found in Figure 3-13. Which ones work? Correct any errors you find, resave, and try them again.

FIGURE 3-13
Extraordinary Extras created with Forms

8. Modify your form options. Return to your Web page and change all the selection items.

9. Save your work as **eighteen-2.html** or **eighteen-2.htm** and test your changes. How did they work?

10. Continue to the Summary section, or close your software and shut down your computer if you're finished for the day.

SUMMARY

In this lesson, you learned:

- You can control the size, style, and color of fonts.
- You can download pictures from the Web.
- You can insert pictures into your Web pages.
- You can change the size of graphics.
- You can use tables to organize information.
- You can turn pictures into hyperlinks.
- You can insert a variety of data input options into a Web page.

> **Net Tip**
>
> It is considered impolite to download pictures to your school network that you don't intend to use. Graphics take up a great deal of space on a computer. Downloading hundreds and hundreds of pictures and not using them is a waste of network server drive space. Consider deleting any pictures you aren't actually using.

VOCABULARY *Review*

Define the following terms:

.gif   Graphics Interchange Format   Table cells
.jpg or .jpeg   Joint Photographic Experts
                          Group

REVIEW *Questions*

TRUE/FALSE

Circle T if the statement is true or F if the statement is false.

T   F   **1.** You can only change the color of a font with attributes and values placed in the <BODY> tag.

T   F   **2.** You can make an image as big or small as you like.

T   F   **3.** GIF stands for Greater Image Format.

T   F   **4.** All images are available for you to use free over the Internet.

T   F   **5.** The CELLPADDING attribute makes the area between your table cells larger or smaller.

FILL IN THE BLANK

Complete the following sentences by writing the correct word or words in the blanks provided.

1. You can use _____ tags to place pictures and text in an orderly fashion on a Web page.

2. _____ tags allow you to collect information about people who visit your site.

3. The _____ image format was created by CompuServe.

4. The _____ tag creates an item in a drop-down list in a form.

5. The _____ image format is an international standard.

WRITTEN QUESTIONS

Write a brief answer to the following questions.

1. Why are artists in such demand on the WWW?

2. When is it illegal to take pictures off the Web?

3. Why is it important not to download pictures to your school or workplace network if you do not plan to use them?

4. How and why would you use the following tags or attributes?

   <B></B>

   <EM></EM>

<STRONG></STRONG>

<I></I>

<ALIGN=CENTER>

5. What tags would you use to insert a graphic or a hyperlink?

PROJECTS

 PROJECT 3-1

GreatApplications, Inc., wants to enter the online videogame business. However, before it starts programming the next great online videogame, it wants to survey potential customers to see what kinds of online games they want to play and buy.

Brainstorm 10 questions that will help GreatApplications, Inc., learn what its customers want in a videogame program. Using your <FORM> tag skills, create an online survey to gather information from potential customers, such as the respondents' names and e-mail addresses. Ask questions that utilize drop-down lists, radio selection items, and check boxes.

  TEAMWORK PROJECT

GreatApplications, Inc., is asking your team to plan a world tour to demonstrate its new software videogames to people in five major cities. Your team has been asked to create a calendar of events for the tour using <TABLE> tags. The tour must be conducted during a single month and should involve five major cities.

When you create your calendar, create links to tourist information about the cities that you will be visiting on the tour. Use cellpadding and cell borders to make the table interesting. You can even put pictures in the cells to illustrate the five cities you have selected for the software rollout.

WEB PROJECT

How fast can you substitute the levy.gif graphic for another graphic? Think about another graphic you like. How could you manipulate the attributes and values to display your new graphic in a variety of sizes? Go for it! Make the changes! Save your changed file as **web-project.html** or **web-project.htm**.

CRITICAL *Thinking*

 ACTIVITY 3-1

Prepare a 100- to 250-word answer to each of the following questions.

1. How important is the WWW and HTML to the world's economy? What makes them so important?

2. How can the Web benefit small businesses, such as a family-owned flower shop, a local antique store, or a fancy hair salon?

3. Over 500 years ago, Johannes Gutenberg invented movable type, which lead to an explosion in the amount of printed material available to common people and changed the history of the world. But what about 500 years from now? How will people look back on the invention of HTML?

 ACTIVITY 3-2

Prepare a 100- to 250-word answer to each of the following questions.

1. Other than changing font size, what can you do with fonts to make your Web pages more interesting?

2. How can tables be used to display information in your HTML pages? What kinds of things can you create with table tags?

3. What extra features or tags would you like to see added to HTML? What tags do you think should be added to give more power to HTML?

 ACTIVITY 3-3

Each of these extraordinary input boxes asks the user to supply a different kind of information. What kinds of responses would you expect from the following FORM attributes?

TEXT

OPTION

RADIO

CHECKBOX

SUMMARY *Project*

The local city zoo has hired you to create a Web page that describes some of the animals they currently have on display. They want your Web page to be well organized they also want you to include images of the animals along with a short descriptive paragraph about each. Use the information you learned in this lesson about tables, fonts, and images to complete this assignment. When you are finished, your Web page should look something like the one shown in Figure 3-14 below.

FIGURE 3-14
A sample Web page for the local city zoo

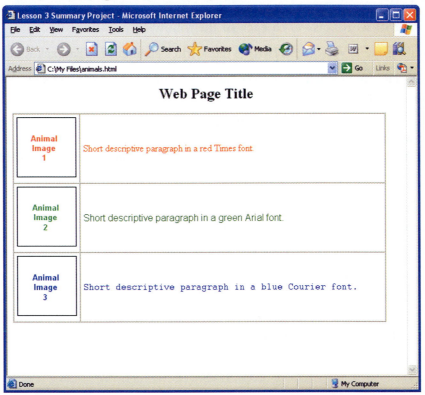

Project Requirements

- Your Web page should have an appropriate title at the top.

- Your animal images should be kept to an appropriate size within the Web page.

- The descriptive paragraph for each animal should be displayed in a variety of font faces and colors.

- The paragraphs should be about 500 pixels wide.

- Your table should have a visible border that separates each cell.

Net Tip

Probably the best way for you to find animal images to use in your page is to surf the Web. Once you have found an animal picture that you want to use, follow the instructions in this lesson to download the image to your workstation. Keep in mind, however, that it is inappropriate for you to download copyrighted images from the Web. Please avoid using any image that displays a copyright message on it or on the Web page where it is located.

HTML STRUCTURAL DESIGN TECHNIQUES

OBJECTIVES

Upon completion of this lesson, you should be able to:

■ Create a frame set.

■ Add a navigation bar.

■ Make a welcome page.

■ Create a nested frame set.

■ Include a title bar frame and page.

■ Utilize frame and frame set options.

Estimated Time: 1.5 hrs.

VOCABULARY

Frames

Frame set tag

Left-hand navigation

Navigation bar

Nested frame set

Pixel

Title bar

Creating an HTML Frame Set

In Lesson 2 you learned how to make your Web browser link from one Web page to another page through the use of hyperlinks. Now it is time to learn how to make your Web browser display two or more Web pages on the screen at the same time! The HTML tags that will help you accomplish this are the <FRAMESET> tag and the <FRAME> tag.

As its name implies, the *frame set tag* allows you to define a set of rectangular areas on your screen called *frames* (see Figure 4-1). Each frame is capable of displaying a different Web page. In a way, you can make your Web browser behave as though you had multiple browsers running on your computer at the same time. However, a frame set allows a Web page in one frame to communicate with a page in a different frame. You'll learn more about this concept later in this lesson.

FIGURE 4-1
Three frames on a Web page

When you create your first HTML frame set file you will notice that it has many things in common with the other HTML pages you created in the previous lessons. However, you should also recognize an important difference. Specifically, you will see that a frame set page does not contain the familiar <BODY> and </BODY> tags that are such an important part of standard Web pages. Instead, the frame set page will contain <FRAMESET> and </FRAMESET> tags that mark the beginning and the end of the frame definition.

In addition, the frame set tag can contain a ROWS attribute or a COLS attribute. The purpose of the ROWS attribute is to give you the means to define horizontal frames, and to specify the height of each frame. Similarly, the COLS attribute allows you to create vertical frames, and to designate the width of each frame. Since you can define only horizontal or vertical frames within any given frame set, the <FRAMESET> tag may contain a ROWS attribute or a COLS attribute, but not both.

As you will see in the following Step-by-Step, the frame set tags will encapsulate two or more <FRAME> tags. In turn, the <FRAME> tags will contain at least two important attributes called NAME and SRC that allow you to give each frame a name, and to specify the source Web page that you wish to have displayed in each frame, respectively. The purpose of the SRC (source) attribute is quite obvious, but the function of the NAME attribute is not immediately apparent. Don't worry. You will learn more about this attribute in Step-by-Step 4.4.

S TEP-BY-STEP 4.1

1. Open Notepad, SimpleText, or your favorite text editor.

2. Enter the HTML text exactly as shown in Figure 4-2.

Important

As you have already learned, you can save files with either an .htm or .html extension. Be careful! If you have used the .htm extension, you must change all the file names in Figure 4-2 accordingly. For example, change navbar.html to navbar.htm in the frame set file.

Note

The asterisk (*) means "whatever's left."

FIGURE 4-2
Name a text file with an .html extension

```
<HTML>
<TITLE>HTML and JavaScript</TITLE>

<FRAMESET COLS="180,*">
<FRAME NAME="LeftFrame" SRC="navbar.html">
<FRAME NAME="RightFrame" SRC="welcome.html">
</FRAMESET>
</HTML>
```

3. Save your newly created file as **frameset-1.html** or **frameset-1.htm**. Proceed to the next Step-by-Step section or close down your system if you are finished for today.

Important

The numbers that accompany the ROWS and COLS attributes can be absolute *pixel* values or percentage values. A pixel is an individual tiny dot of light inside a computer monitor or screen. In step 2 you made the frame set column 180 pixels of light wide. There are thousands of pixels on a typical computer screen, too many to count. Therefore, it's sometimes easier to calculate the percentage values of a screen instead of counting pixels. A percentage value will automatically calculate the 5%, 10%, 50% or more of a screen when deciding how much of the screen to dedicate to a frame. For example, <FRAMESET COLS="20%,*">.

Creating a Navigation Bar

One design that is very commonly used by professional Web designers is to place a Web page in a narrow left-hand frame that contains many hyperlinks. When the user clicks on any of these links, the appropriate Web page is displayed in the larger right-hand frame. This design technique is often referred to as *left-hand navigation*, and the Web page containing the hyperlinks is called a navigation bar. A *navigation bar* is a series of hyperlinks, usually organized horizontally or vertically on a Web page or in a frame. It is used to navigate a Web site. Figure 4-3 shows an example of a Web page with a navigation bar.

FIGURE 4-3
Two frames and a navigation bar on a Web page

At this point in the lesson, we will show you how to create your own navigation bar and to make use of the previous eighteen Web pages you created in Lessons 1, 2, and 3. Your navigation bar will contain an unordered list of eighteen hyperlinks, and these links will refer to the Web pages you previously saved as one.html, two.html, three.html, etc.

The HTML tags you will use to create your navigation bar are not anything special. In fact, they are all tags that you have already used in previous lessons. However, you will see a new attribute in the <A> tag that defines the hyperlinks to the Web pages that will be displayed in the right-hand frame. This attribute is called TARGET, and its purpose is to tell the browser which frame it should use to display the target Web page. You should also take note of the fact that the TARGET attribute uses the frame name that you defined with the NAME attribute in the <FRAME> tag in Step-by-Step 4.1.

STEP-BY-STEP 4.2

1. Open Notepad, SimpleText, or your favorite text editor if it is not already open.

2. Enter the HTML text exactly as shown in Figure 4-4.

FIGURE 4-4
Navigation tags in a frames page

```
<HTML>
<TITLE>HTML and JavaScript</TITLE>

<BODY>
<CENTER><B>Web Pages</B></CENTER>
<UL>
<LI><A HREF="one.html" TARGET="RightFrame">one.html</A></LI>
<LI><A HREF="two.html" TARGET="RightFrame">two.html</A></LI>
<LI><A HREF="three.html" TARGET="RightFrame">three.html</A></LI>
<LI><A HREF="four.html" TARGET="RightFrame">four.html</A></LI>
<LI><A HREF="five.html" TARGET="RightFrame">five.html</A></LI>
<LI><A HREF="six.html" TARGET="RightFrame">six.html</A></LI>
<LI><A HREF="seven.html" TARGET="RightFrame">seven.html</A></LI>
<LI><A HREF="eight.html" TARGET="RightFrame">eight.html</A></LI>
<LI><A HREF="nine.html" TARGET="RightFrame">nine.html</A></LI>
<LI><A HREF="ten.html" TARGET="RightFrame">ten.html</A></LI>
<LI><A HREF="eleven.html" TARGET="RightFrame">eleven.html</A></LI>
<LI><A HREF="twelve.html" TARGET="RightFrame">twelve.html</A></LI>
<LI><A HREF="thirteen.html" TARGET="RightFrame">thirteen.html</A></LI>
<LI><A HREF="fourteen.html" TARGET="RightFrame">fourteen.html</A></LI>
<LI><A HREF="fifteen.html" TARGET="RightFrame">fifteen.html</A></LI>
<LI><A HREF="sixteen.html" TARGET="RightFrame">sixteen.html</A></LI>
<LI><A HREF="seventeen.html" TARGET="RightFrame">seventeen.html</A></LI>
<LI><A HREF="eighteen.html" TARGET="RightFrame">eighteen.html</A></LI>
</UL>
</BODY>

</HTML>
```

3. Save your newly created file as **navbar.html** or **navbar.htm**.

4. Proceed to the next Step-by-Step section in order to learn how to create a Web site welcome page or close down your system if your are finished for today.

Net Tip

Normally when a user clicks on a hyperlink, the target Web page will be loaded into the same frame as the link. The TARGET attribute overrides this behavior and sends the proper Web page to the "target" frame.

Creating a Web Site Welcome Page

Normally a professional Web site developer will create a welcome page that users will see when they first access the site. As you learned in Lesson 1, the primary purpose of the welcome page is simply to give users a good first impression of the site, and to ensure that they recognize the purpose of the site. For example, a company that wants to sell books, music, or other products over the Web wants to create a fancy welcome page that will catch the users' eyes, emphasize the company name, and allow easy access to the various parts of the Web site.

In this next Step-by-Step section you will create a very simple welcome page. In fact, there will be no HTML tags in this page that you have not already seen in earlier lessons. But you should recognize the fact that this page has a particular purpose, and could be enhanced dramatically to liven up your Web site and give the user a memorable experience. One of the primary goals of commercial Web sites is to give users a reason to return to the site again and again.

STEP-BY-STEP 4.3

1. Open Notepad, SimpleText, or your favorite text editor if it is not already open.

2. Enter the HTML text exactly as shown in Figure 4-5.

FIGURE 4-5
Create a simple welcome page

```
<HTML>
<TITLE>HTML and JavaScript</TITLE>

<BODY>
<CENTER><FONT SIZE=6><B>Welcome</B></FONT></CENTER>
<BR>
<CENTER><FONT SIZE=5><B>to</B></FONT></CENTER>
<BR>
<CENTER><FONT SIZE=6><B>HTML and JavaScript</B></FONT></CENTER>
</BODY>

</HTML>
```

3. Save your newly created file as **welcome.html** or **welcome.htm**.

STEP-BY-STEP 4.3 Continued

4. Open your Web browser and view the frameset-1.html document you created in Step-by-Step 4.1. You should see something much like Figure 4-6.

Note ☑

Remember that the files you created in previous Step-by-Steps (one.html, two.html, etc.) must be located in the same folder as the files you created in this Step-by-Step. If they are not in the same folder your hyperlinks will not function correctly.

FIGURE 4-6
A welcome page with a navigation bar

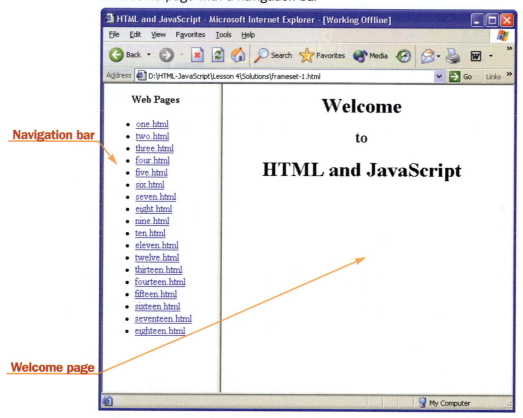

5. Proceed to the next Step-by-Step section in order to learn how to create a nested frame set, or close down your system if you are finished for today.

Creating a Nested Frame Set

There are times when it is desirable to place a third frame into your frame set that will cause the browser to display a horizontal frame across the top of your browser window. You may then place a new Web page into this new frame that could function as a constant title for your Web site.

If you were paying close attention to the material in the first part of this lesson, you should be asking yourself an important question about now. To be specific, we stated early on that it is only possible for a frame set to contain horizontal frames or vertical frames, but not both. So how are you supposed to create a horizontal frame in which to display your title page if you already have vertical frames defined in your existing frame set?

A *nested frame set* solves this problem. The term *nested* is a word that programmers and Web developers use to describe a structure, keyword, or tag that contains one or more additional instances of the same item. In this case, you will use a <FRAMESET> tag inside of another <FRAMESET> tag in order to create both vertical and horizontal frames.

STEP-BY-STEP 4.4

1. Open Notepad, SimpleText, or your favorite text editor if it is not already open.

2. Retrieve the **frameset-1.html** or **frameset-1.htm** file you created in Step-by-Step 4.1.

3. Modify the HTML document by adding the text in bold shown in Figure 4-7 below.

FIGURE 4-7
Name a text file with an .html extension

```
<HTML>
<TITLE>HTML and JavaScript</TITLE>

<FRAMESET ROWS="60,*">
<FRAME NAME="UpperFrame" SRC="title.html">

<FRAMESET COLS="180,*">
<FRAME NAME="LeftFrame" SRC="navbar.html">
<FRAME NAME="RightFrame" SRC="welcome.html">
</FRAMESET>


</FRAMESET>
</HTML>
```

4. Save your newly created file as **frameset-2.html** or **frameset-2.htm**.

5. Proceed to the next section to create a title page for your nested page, or close your system if you are finished for today.

Creating a Title Bar

Just as the Web page you created in Step-by-Step 4.2 is referred to as a navigation bar, a page that has the specific purpose of displaying a constant title for a Web site is commonly called a *title bar*. In this section you will create a title bar to be displayed in the new frame you defined in the previous exercise. Figure 4-8 shows an example of a Web page with a title bar.

FIGURE 4-8
Three frames with a navigation bar, title bar, and welcome page

Like the welcome.html or welcome.htm page you created in Step-by-Step 4.3, this title bar Web page will not contain any new HTML tags. But, as with welcome pages, professional Web developers will typically go to great lengths to create a title bar that will be eye-catching and memorable. Yours, however, will be very simple so that you can more easily grasp this new concept.

STEP-BY-STEP 4.5

1. Open Notepad, SimpleText, or your favorite text editor if it is not already open.

STEP-BY-STEP 4.5 Continued

2. Enter the HTML text exactly as shown in Figure 4-9.

FIGURE 4-9
Tags for a title page

```
<HTML>
<TITLE>HTML and JavaScript</TITLE>

<BODY>
<CENTER><FONT SIZE=5><B>HTML and JavaScript</B></FONT></CENTER>
</BODY>

</HTML>
```

3. Save your newly created file as **title.html** or **title.htm**.

4. Open your Web browser and view the **frameset-2.html** or **frameset-2.htm** document you created in Step-by-Step 4.4. You should see a page like Figure 4-10.

STEP-BY-STEP 4.5 Continued

5. Frame pages can be customized by the user. Slowly roll your mouse over the bars (called frame separators) between the frames as marked in Figure 4-10. When a double arrow appears, click and drag the bar to the left or right or up and down.

FIGURE 4-10
Drag frame separators to customize a page

6. Proceed to the next section or close your system if you are finished for today.

Net Tip

Frames are a great way to learn how Web pages can be organized into sections or parts. Tables provide another way to split a page into sections for artistic and organizational purposes.

Using Advanced HTML Options

Let's take a minute to make a couple of observations about the frames and frame sets you have created so far. First of all, your Web browser is displaying frame separators that make it abundantly obvious where one frame ends and where another frame begins. Secondly, if you position your mouse cursor directly over any one of these frame separators, you will see your mouse pointer change shape to indicate that the frame separator may be moved. This means the user can change the appearance of your Web pages simply by clicking and dragging a frame separator to a different position, as you experienced in the previous exercise.

The frame and frame set characteristics we have just described may be desirable in some situations. However, there are many occasions when professional Web developers do not want the browser to display frame separators, nor would they want the user to be able to change the layout of the screen at will. This is especially true when the developer includes custom-made graphic images in their Web pages. Such images are frequently designed to be a specific size and to fit within a frame of an exact size. If the browser displays frame separators, or if the user were to change the size of the frames, the entire layout of the page could be disrupted, and the resulting clutter of images would be very unappealing.

Fortunately, two important HTML attributes may be used with the <FRAMESET> and <FRAME> tags to address these issues as seen in Figure 4-11. First, you may use the BORDER attribute within the FRAMESET tag to adjust the appearance of the frame separators. In addition, you may also use the NORESIZE attribute within the <FRAME> tags to instruct the browser that the user should not be able to change the size of the frames. These two attributes may be used separately or together to get the appearance and behavior you want.

FIGURE 4-11
Eliminate frame separators on a page

STEP-BY-STEP 4.6

1. Open Notepad, SimpleText, or your favorite text editor if it is not already open.

2. Retrieve the **frameset-2.html** or **frameset-2.htm** file you created in Step-by-Step 4.4.

STEP-BY-STEP 4.6 Continued

3. Modify the HTML document by adding the bold text shown in Figure 4-12 below.

FIGURE 4-12
Adding to a text file with an .html extension

```
<HTML>
<TITLE>HTML and JavaScript</TITLE>

<FRAMESET BORDER=0 ROWS="60,*">
<FRAME NAME="UpperFrame" NORESIZE  SRC="title.html">

<FRAMESET BORDER=0 COLS="180,*">
<FRAME NAME="LeftFrame" NORESIZE SRC="navbar.html">
<FRAME NAME="RightFrame" NORESIZE SRC="welcome.html">
</FRAMESET>

</FRAMESET>
</HTML>
```

4. Save your newly created file as **frameset-3.html** or **frameset-3.htm**.

5. Open your Web browser and view the frameset-3.html document you just saved. You should see something much like Figure 4-11.

6. Proceed to the Summary section or close your system if you are finished for today.

FIGURE 4-13

HTML tags in Dreamweaver

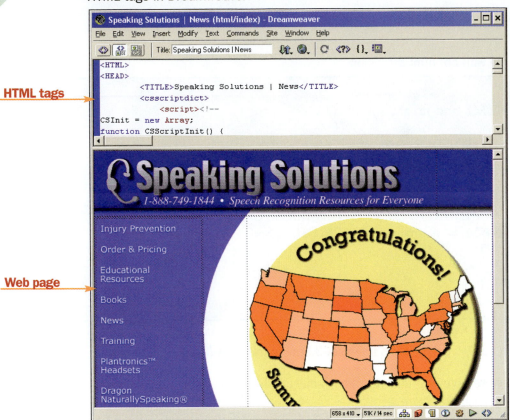

HTML tags →

Web page →

Internet Milestone

HTML Creation Tools

HTML is powerful, but it can take forever to enter all the tags by hand. Someone finally asked, "Is there any way to make HTML simpler to create?" A few years after HTML became the standard way of communicating online, enterprising programmers created software tools that take the pain out of typing in all of the angle brackets and tags. Some of the most popular Web page development tools include Macromedia Dreamweaver, Adobe GoLive, and Microsoft FrontPage. Each of these tools helps you create Web pages in much the same way professionals create documents in word processing or desktop publishing software.

In a program like Dreamweaver, most of the tags will be created for you automatically as you design a page. However, don't believe for a minute that you won't need to know HTML tags to use these powerful and exciting Web page creation tools! There will be times when you will need to edit or make corrections to the tags created by these products. A tag view is always available.

For instance, Figure 4-13 shows a Web page being created using Dreamweaver. Notice that in the bottom portion of the screen you can see the Web page much as it will appear online. However, in the top portion of the Dreamweaver tool you can still view the tags. Knowing how the tags work will help you become an expert Dreamweaver Web page developer and editor.

SUMMARY

In this lesson, you learned:

- You can create a frame set.
- You can interpret frame set attributes and values.
- You can create a navigation bar in a frame.
- You can make a simple welcome page for a frames page.
- You can insert nested tags and attributes.
- You can insert a title bar frame on a Web page.

VOCABULARY *Review*

Define the following terms:

Frames	Navigation bar	Pixel
Frame set tag	Nested frame set	Title bar
Left-hand navigation		

REVIEW *Questions*

TRUE/FALSE

Circle T if the statement is true or F if the statement is false.

T   F   **1.** A frame set can display either rows or columns.

T   F   **2.** The <BODY> tag can be omitted from a frame set page.

T   F   **3.** You must hand-key tags when you use programs like FrontPage, Dreamweaver, or GoLive.

T   F   **4.** The only way to calculate the width of a frame is to count pixels.

T   F   **5.** The TARGET attribute makes frame separators disappear.

FILL IN THE BLANK

Complete the following sentences by writing the correct word or words in the blanks provided.

1. The _____ attribute points a Web page to display in a specific frame.

2. The _____ attribute creates vertically separated frames.

3. The _____ attribute creates horizontally separated frames.

4. The _____ =0 attribute makes frame separators disappear.

5. The _____ attribute prevents viewers of a Web page from changing the size of frames.

WRITTEN QUESTIONS

Write a brief answer to the following questions.

1. What is the purpose of a welcome page as described in this lesson?

2. What is left-hand navigation? Explain how to create a left-hand navigation bar.

3. What is nesting from a programmer's perspective as described in this lesson?

4. What are pixel values and percentage values, and how are they defined in terms of a frame set?

5. Why would a Web site developer want to prevent visitors to the Web site from adjusting the row and column separators on a frames page?

PROJECTS

 PROJECT 4-1

In Project 1-1, you used your Web searching skills to locate information on HTML, HTML guides, and about learning HTML. Your manager has asked that you organize the information you collected into a new frames Web page using two columns only.

GreatApplications, Inc. has asked you to create a Web site with left-hand navigation that will organize the information you collected in Project 1-1 and Table 1-2. This way these helpful Web pages can be made available to everyone in the company online. Create a navigation frame on the left-hand side of your frame set page, and have the information you are linking to appear in the right-hand frame. You can do all of this with tags you have learned in this text.

 ## TEAMWORK PROJECT

In this teamwork project, you are to conduct a survey. To complete the survey you and your team members must visit at least 100 different Web sites. With teamwork, this won't be as difficult as it may first appear. In the Teamwork Project in Lesson 1, you identified the greatest Web pages you could find. In Critical Thinking Activity 2-2, you organized pages you like for easy reference in a Web page that you saved as My Web Resources. In PROJECT 2-1 you identified the five worst pages you could find on the Web. Between all the members of your team you must have already visited over 100 sites.

As a team, revisit both the best and the worst pages you have listed. Visit other sites if necessary. You must, as a team, survey exactly 100 sites, collecting data as you go. Divide the task with each member taking a certain percentage of the sites to view while recording the results of applying the following questions to each Web site.

Survey Questions

1. Investigate. Viewing the source HTML code of your 100 Web pages, how many use frame tags or some type of frame organization to organize their Web pages?

2. Calculate. Viewing the source of your Web pages, how many of these pages use table tags to organize their Web pages?

3. Tabulate. What percentage of these good and bad sites use left-hand navigation systems?

4. Record. How many of the sites use navigation systems at the top of the Web page?

5. How many of these Web sites use an attractive graphic or logo in the title bar area at the top of the Web page?

6. What percentage of the Web sites visited, in the opinion of your team members, have effective welcome pages?

  ## WEB PROJECT

In Project 4-1, you created a left-hand navigation system that will allow you to share with your colleagues at GreatApplications, Inc. information about HTML. In this Web Project, challenge yourself. Change the Web page you created in Project 4-1 to a site that navigates from the top bar of the page. Create two rows in your frame set. In the top frame, create your navigation system using 20 percent of the screen. In the bottom frame, display the information. Save this project as WebProject-4.html or WebProject-4.htm.

CRITICAL *Thinking*

SCANS ACTIVITY 4-1

In your opinion, what are the top ten most important things you have learned about HTML and creating Web pages while completing the previous four lessons? Prepare a 100–250-word report explaining why each of these top ten items have been placed on your list. Save your answer as **Activity 4-1**.

SCANS ACTIVITY 4-2

As you conclude your studies of HTML think about the top three weaknesses that you see in HTML. What are the top three things you would change about HTML? What are the weaknesses or things that you feel can be improved? Explain thoroughly in a 100–250-word report how you would like to see HTML become better, easier to use, and more helpful to you as a Web site developer. Save your answer as **Activity 4-2**.

SCANS SUMMARY *Project*

Professional Web designers often need to understand and utilize the flexibility of HTML frames to give Web sites the desired appearance. For example, some commercial Web sites are designed with top, bottom, or right-hand navigation bars rather than the left-hand oriented navigation bar presented in this lesson. Using what you learned about frames and frame sets, reorganize the Web site shown in Figure 4-10 so that it illustrates the use of right-hand navigation. Also change the structure of the Web site frames so that the navigation bar spans the full height of the browser window, and the title bar does not span the full width. Your reorganized Web page should look something like Figure 4-14.

FIGURE 4-14
A sample Web site with right-hand navigation

Project Requirements

■ You may use the **title.html, welcome.html** and **navbar.html** files you created in this lesson to provide the content for your new frame set.

■ The upper (title) frame should be about 60 pixels high, and the right (navigation) frame should be about 180 pixels wide.

■ Each frame should be separated by a frame border that is <u>not</u> resizable.

■ You may want to use concepts from previous lessons (such as fonts and images) to improve the appearance of your title page and welcome page.

HTML BASICS

HTML TAG AND ATTRIBUTE SUMMARY

TAGS OR ATTRIBUTES	RESULT	LESSON
<A> </A>	Creates an anchor tag that is used to create hyperlinks	2
<B> </B>	Bolds text	3
<BODY> </BODY>	Marks text to appear in the body section of the Web browser	1
 	Creates a line or single-spaced break between text	2
<CENTER> </CENTER>	Centers text or graphics on a Web page	1
<EM> </EM>	Emphasizes or bolds text	3
<FONT> </FONT>	Changes the size, font face, and color of Web page text	3
<FORM> </FORM>	Inserts a form set into a Web page	3
<FRAME> </FRAME>	Defines frames within a frame set on a Web page	4
<FRAMESET> </FRAMESET>	Marks the beginning and the end of a frame set	4
<H1> </H1>	Marks text to appear in the largest heading font size	1
<H2> </H2>	Marks text to appear in the second largest heading font size	1
<H3> </H3>	Marks text to appear in the third largest heading font size	1
<H4> </H4>	Marks text to appear in the third smallest heading font size	1
<H5> </H5>	Marks text to appear in the second smallest heading font size	1
<H6> </H6>	Marks text to appear in the smallest heading font size	1
<HR>	Creates a horizontal line between sections of a Web page	2
<HTML> </HTML>	Indicates the beginning and end of a Web page	1
<I> </I>	Italicizes text	3
<IMG>	Displays an image in a Web page	3
<INPUT> </INPUT>	Defines an input control for a form. For example, radio button, check box, text field, etc.	3
<MARQUEE> </MARQUEE>	Creates a scrolling stock market-like ticker	2
<OL> <LI> <LI> </OL>	Marks text for ordered or numbered (1, 2, 3) lists	1
<OPTION SELECTED>	Allows Web developers to define which of a list of options should be selected by default.	3
<OPTION>	Defines an option in a selection list	3

TAGS OR ATTRIBUTES	RESULT	LESSON
<P> </P>	Creates a paragraph or double-spaced break between text	1
<SELECT> </SELECT>	Defines a list of selection options in a form	3
<STRONG> </STRONG>	Emphasizes or bolds text	3
<TABLE> </TABLE>	Used to define tables and table cells in a Web page	3
<TITLE> </TITLE>	Marks text to appear in the title bar of the Web browser	1
<TR> </TR>	Defines a row in a table	3
<UL> <LI> <LI> </UL>	Marks text for unordered or bulleted (•) lists	1
ALIGN=	Aligns text and graphics to the left, right, and center of a Web page	3
BACKGROUND=	Inputs a graphic as a background for a Web page	3
BGCOLOR=	Defines the background color of the Web page	2
BORDER=	Creates a border around the cells in a table	3
CELLPADDING=	Determines the width of the lines separating cells in a table	3
COLOR=	Changes the color of Web page text	3
COLS=	Defines the number of columns in a frame set	4
FACE=	Changes the style or face of the font being displayed. For example, Times New Roman, Arial, or Helvetica	3
HEIGHT=	Changes the height of a graphic	3
HREF=	The hypertext reference attribute. Defines the path or location to a Web page, Internet location, or other online resource	2
LINK=	Changes the color of hypertext links	2
NAME=	The hypertext reference attribute that defines a location on a page, or gives each frame a name	2, 4
NORESIZE	Turns off the option for the user to resize frames	4
ROWS=	Defines the number of rows in a frame set	4
SIZE=	Changes the height of horizontal lines or the size of fonts	2, 3
SRC=	Specifies the source of a resource, like an image to insert into a Web page, or to specify the source Web page to be displayed in a frame	3, 4
TARGET=	Points a Web page or graphic to a specific frame in a frame set	4
TEXT=	Changes the color of text on a Web page	2
TYPE=	Defines the type of input used by a form	3
VLINK=	Changes the color of hypertext links that have been visited or selected	2
WIDTH=	Changes the width of horizontal lines, the width of graphics, or the width of table cells	2, 3

REVIEW *Questions*

MATCHING

Match the correct term in the right column to its description in the left column.

___ 1. The specialized Web language used to instruct Web browsers how Web elements should appear.

___ 2. A Java-like scripting language used to create miniapplications and multimedia effects.

___ 3. Usually appear in pairs enclosed in angle brackets.

___ 4. Operating in base-16, this system uses letters as well as numbers to express values.

___ 5. The definition of attribute.

___ 6. A protocol used to transfer data from Web servers to Web browsers.

___ 7. Graphical format that adheres to international standards; compact enough for Internet use.

___ 8. Graphical format created by a company called CompuServe. The format compresses graphics to transfer over low-speed modems.

___ 9. Term used by programmers that describes a structure, keyword, or tag that contains one or more additional instances of the same item.

___ 10. Software program that makes it possible to avoid having to manually enter every single tag.

A. Dreamweaver

B. gif

C. HTML

D. HTTP

E. Hexadecimal

F. Tags

G. Nested

H. Value

I. jpeg

J. JavaScript

WRITTEN QUESTIONS

Compose a brief answer to each of the following questions. Save the answers in a single file named HTML Unit Summary.

1. List and explain the function of six tags that you believe can be found on most Web pages.

2. List and explain the origin of each of the following file formats. In your explanation, indicate which formats are used for Web pages.
   A. .doc
   B. .rtf
   C. .wpd
   D. .txt
   E. .htm
   F. .html

3. Explain at least two ways in which font size can be increased or decreased. In addition, describe at least two other ways that fonts can be changed.

4. Explain how the anchor tag is used and written to create hyperlinks to sites on the Web and to individual Web pages on your personal computer. In your explanation, indicate how graphics can be turned into hyperlinks.

5. Explain how frame sets work and how Web pages can be targeted to appear in different frames.

 CROSS-CURRICULAR *Projects*

In this exercise you will demonstrate a practical use for HTML. You're going to design a frames page that will help you organize excellent sources of information in at least five academic subject areas. The four required areas are Language Arts, Science, Social Studies, and Math. Pick another subject area of your own choosing, such as Foreign Language, Music, Art, Physical Education, or Technology. Use Web search tools such as *www.yahoo.com* or *www.google.com* to find legitimate academic resources in these subject areas. Choose sites that you will want to return to again and again for information.

This will take some careful thinking and planning on your part. Here's the trick—create a left-hand navigation bar that will access these resource pages for each of these subject areas. Invent your own filenames for your frame set and navigation bar pages. The title bar page is optional. Test all of the links to make sure each one works.

LANGUAGE ARTS 1

Find five Web sites related to the study of Language Arts and place them on a target page that will appear in the right frame of your cross-curricular frames page. Name this file **la-1.html** or **la-1.htm**.

SCIENCE 1

Find five Web sites related to the study of Science and place them on a target page that will appear in the right frame of your cross-curricular frames page. Name this file **sci-1.html** or **sci-1.htm**.

SOCIAL STUDIES 1

Find five Web sites related to the study of Social Studies and place them on a target page that will appear in the right frame of your cross-curricular frames page. Name this file **ss-1.html** or **ss-1.htm**.

MATH 1

Find five Web sites related to the study of Math and place them on a target page that will appear in the right frame of your cross-curricular frames page. Name this file **m-1.html** or **m-1.htm**.

YOUR CHOICE OF SUBJECT 1

Find five Web sites related to the study of a subject of your choice and place them on a target page that will appear in the right frame of your cross-curricular frames page. Name this file **mychoice-1.html** or **mychoice-1.htm**.

 REVIEW *Projects*

PROJECT 1-1

You've probably been thinking, I have created dozens of Web pages, but when can I branch out and create a Web site entirely of my own? Well, now is your chance to harness all of your Web design creativity.

Pick an appropriate topic or theme for your Web site. Using all of the skills you learned in this unit, create an awesome Web site. Invent your own HTML filenames.

PROJECT 1-2

By now, you probably think your Web page is the most awesome site on the Web. And it probably is! However, it's time to find out if that's true! Team up in groups of three or four. Share your Web pages from both the Cross-Curricular Projects and Project 1-1 with your teammates. If any team member is having problems making elements of his or her pages work, solve these problems as a group. Give each other suggestions on how pages can be improved.

SIMULATION

JOB 1-1

Imagine you have just become the lead Web page designer and Web development Team Manager responsible for the GreatApplications, Inc. Web site. To sharpen your team's skills in cutting-edge technology, you have decided to create a Web page cataloging sites that will help your team members learn more about HTML, JavaScript, Flash, and other Web page creation tools such as Dreamweaver, FrontPage, or GoLive. Look at pages you worked on in this unit involving cataloging the HTML learning sites. Add these to your new Web site. Then, reference some of the dominant Web site development companies online, including Macromedia, creator of Dreamweaver and Flash; Microsoft, creator of FrontPage; Adobe, creator of GoLive and other online multimedia tools. Use Net search engines such as *www.yahoo.com* or *www.google.com* to find the resources you need. Invent your own filenames.

JOB 1-2

Do you want a career in the high-tech online industry? If you do, you'd first better find out what types of jobs are available and whether they are to your liking.

Go online and visit some of the major career Web sites such as *www.flipdog.com* or *www.monster.com* and search for ten jobs related to Web page development. If you have trouble finding these types of jobs on these sites, try entering **Online Job Search** into your search engine.

Create a short report that lists all ten of the jobs you have found and explains a little bit about the qualifications you would need in order to take these jobs in the high-tech Web design industry. Save your work as **Job 1-2**.

SUMMARY *Project*

This is your opportunity to demonstrate that you have mastered all of the major concepts in this unit. Consider the information in Table U1-1. This table summarizes the various HTML topics that were presented in the first three lessons.

Your job is to organize this information into a Web page that is laid out as shown in Figure U1-1. Frame A will contain a list of hyperlinks that represent the first three lessons in the book. Frame B will contain its own list of hyperlinks that correspond to the topics covered in one of the lessons. Frame B will be updated each time the user clicks a hyperlink in Frame A. Frame C will contain a Web page that illustrates one of the topics listed in Frame B, and the Web page will change when a user clicks a different link in Frame B. Figure U1-2 shows an example of how the completed Web page might look if the user clicks on Lesson 1 in Frame A, and Headings in Frame B.

TABLE U1-1

LESSON NUMBER	TOPICS COVERED
1	Headings
	Ordered Lists
	Unordered Lists
2	Horizontal Lines
	Background Colors
	Hyperlinks
	Text/Hyperlink Colors
3	Fonts
	Images
	Tables
	Input Controls

FIGURE U1-1
A Web page containing three frames

layout

FIGURE U1-2
An example Web page with Lesson 1 and Headings selected

PROJECT REQUIREMENTS

- You must use a nested frame set to create the proper Web page layout.

- Make the two left frames about 25% of the screen width.

- The two frames on the left side should each use about 50% of the screen height.

- Name your main frame set page **unit1.html**.

- You will need to create three Web pages for your topic lists. Name your three files **topics1.html, topics2.html** and **topics3.html**.

- You will need to create eleven Web pages for your example pages. Name your files **example1.html, example2.html, example3.html**, etc.

PORTFOLIO *Checklist*

Include the following files from this unit in your student portfolio:

____ HTML Unit Summary Questions

____ Language Arts 1

____ Science 1

____ Social Studies 1

____ Math 1

____ Your Choice of Subject 1

____ Project 1-1

____ Project 1-2

____ Job 1-1

____ Job 1-2

THE EXCITING WORLD OF JAVASCRIPT

Unit 2

 Estimated Time for Unit: 7 hours

WHAT IS JAVASCRIPT?

OBJECTIVES

Upon completion of this lesson, you should be able to:

- Understand the purpose of JavaScript.
- Use the <SCRIPT> and </SCRIPT> tags.
- Use JavaScript objects.
- Use JavaScript methods.
- Understand JavaScript syntax.

Estimated Time: 1.5 hours

VOCABULARY

<SCRIPT> and </SCRIPT> tags

Binary code

Compiler

Condition

Interpretation

Keywords

Methods

Objects

Operators

Parameter list

Programming language

Properties

Scripting language

Status line

Syntax

Token

Hello World Wide Web

JavaScript is sometimes referred to as a *programming language*, but it is really more accurate to call it a *scripting language*. The difference between a programming language and a scripting language is subtle, but important to understand. Both types of languages must be converted from a human-readable form to a machine-readable form.

For programming languages this process is performed before the program runs by a highly specialized piece of software called a *compiler*. The programmer controls this conversion process.

With a scripting language, however, there is no need for the programmer to explicitly initiate the code conversion process. It happens automatically when the source code is processed by the target program. To be more specific, an HTML document must be written by a human and then processed by a Web browser. When that document contains embedded JavaScript code, that code is interpreted by the browser, and converted into its machine-readable form "on-the-fly." *Interpretation* is the term programmers use to describe this line-by-line conversion process that occurs automatically at run time.

Under normal conditions, the output of a JavaScript function will be nothing more than one or perhaps several strings of text that are inserted into the host Web page. The resulting HTML page is then processed by the browser just as it would be if it had been keyed into the source document by a human.

The real power of embedding JavaScript code into Web pages comes from the fact that the resulting text can change from one day to the next, or even from one minute to the next. It is entirely possible for one person to enter a particular URL into his Web browser and see a Web page that is completely different from the page that is seen by another person who enters the exact same URL. These different looking Web pages could be the result of differences in time, differences in location, or even differences in Web browsers. JavaScript is capable of detecting various conditions in the current operating environment, and reacting accordingly. This concept is explored in greater detail in Step-by-Step 5.3.

It is easy for a Web browser to detect if a particular HTML page contains embedded JavaScript code or not. All that is required is for the person who creates the document to use the *<SCRIPT>* tag to mark the beginning of a JavaScript section, and the *</SCRIPT>* tag to indicate the end of that section. The Web browser will interpret everything between these two tags as JavaScript source code rather than standard HTML text. The browser will then convert the script (via the interpretation process) into its equivalent machine-readable form called *binary code*. This binary code will then be executed, and its output (if any) will be inserted into the HTML text stream and displayed as if it had been typed into the original HTML document by a human.

It is important for you to understand that the scripts you will be embedding between the <SCRIPT> and </SCRIPT> tags cannot be just any old text you care to put in there. On the contrary, the text must conform to certain rules, or the Web browser will display an unpleasant error message on the screen when you try to view your page. This is precisely why JavaScript is called a scripting language—because it must adhere to specific rules of grammar known as program *syntax*. In this lesson you will learn about JavaScript objects and methods, as well as JavaScript keywords and operators. Once you have mastered these basic programming elements you will be able to start building big, sophisticated scripts in no time.

The primary purpose of JavaScript is to generate text that will be inserted into the standard HTML text stream. JavaScript is essentially made up of a number of invisible entities called *objects* that contain a well-defined set of capabilities. In order for JavaScript programmers to make use of these capabilities, they must call upon the services of one or more specialized functions known as *methods* within those objects. The programmer invokes the services of these methods by keying the name of the object, followed by a period (the . character), followed by the method name.

Method names are always followed by a *parameter list*, even though the list is sometimes empty. Perhaps the best way to understand method parameters is to visualize a list of ingredients for a recipe. The parameter list simply provides the method with the information it needs to perform its function correctly. The syntax of the parameter list consists of an opening parenthesis, zero or more parameter items, and a closing parenthesis. For example, if you want to invoke the "write" method of the JavaScript object called "document," you key the following line of code:

```
document.write("A string of text.");
```

Now that you've seen a simple example of JavaScript coding, let's give you a chance to incorporate this concept in an actual HTML document with embedded JavaScript.

> ## Important
>
> If your version of Windows XP has Service Pack 2 installed, you may experience various warning messages as you try to work through the following JavaScript activities. If you receive such a warning, simply click the option to enable JavaScript. None of the activities in this book are capable of damaging your system in any way.

STEP-BY-STEP 5.1

1. Open Notepad, SimpleText, or your favorite text editor.

2. Enter the HTML and JavaScript text exactly as shown in Figure 5-1.

FIGURE 5-1
An HTML file with embedded JavaScript

```
<HTML>
<HEAD>
<TITLE>HTML and JavaScript</TITLE>
</HEAD>
<BODY>
<SCRIPT>
   document.write("Hello World Wide Web!");
</SCRIPT>
</BODY>
</HTML>
```

3. Save your newly created file as **js-one.html** or **js-one.htm**.

4. View your work in your Web browser. The resulting Web page should look like Figure 5-2. Continue to the next section, or shut down your computer if you are finished for the day.

FIGURE 5-2
Your first page created with JavaScript

```
Hello World Wide Web!
```

Important

If you are a Windows XP user with Service Pack 2 installed, your browser may display a warning message about blocking active content. If this occurs, click on the warning and follow the subsequent prompts to enable JavaScript. You may also want to disable the active content warning so that you do not have to do this for every activity.

Analyzing the Code You Have Just Entered

At this point you may be thinking that this Web page doesn't look all that impressive. But don't give up on JavaScript yet because we are just getting started. By the time you have worked through a few more Step-by-Steps you will begin to see that JavaScript is capable of much more than this simple Web page demonstrates.

Enhancing Your Web Page

As we mentioned earlier in this chapter, the JavaScript method called document.write() simply inserts a stream of characters into the standard HTML text stream. Another way to think of it is that after the browser has finished processing the HTML document, the end result is that the <SCRIPT> tag, the </SCRIPT> tag, and everything in between the two will be stripped out of the page and replaced by whatever string appears as the parameter of the write() method. This means that any HTML formatting tags you put before or after the script tags will be processed just as they would be in a page without any embedded JavaScript code. To illustrate this point more clearly, let's modify the Web page we created in Step-by-Step 5.1. Let's add some HTML formatting tags so that our Hello World Wide Web! message looks a little more appealing on the screen. Let's also add a second message to the page to make sure you understand the interaction between HTML and JavaScript.

 Netiquette

Mind Your Braces!

One of the characteristics of the JavaScript language that novice programmers tend to struggle with is the use of curly braces. The opening brace ({) indicates the beginning of a statement block, and the closing brace (}) marks the end of that block.

Although the rules of JavaScript syntax are somewhat flexible when it comes to the placement of these braces, we strongly recommend that you follow the style shown in this book. If you start getting sloppy or inconsistent with the way you place your braces, it is very easy to cause yourself some serious problems. When the number of opening braces does not correspond to the number of closing braces, your Web browser will report a syntax error. However, it is also possible for braces to be placed in such a way that no syntax error occurs, but the script will not execute correctly.

The bottom line is that you can save yourself a lot of headaches by following a few simple rules:

1. Always place the opening brace directly below the keyword to which it belongs.

2. Always indent the statements contained within the statement block.

3. Always place the closing brace so that it is vertically aligned with its corresponding opening brace.

STEP-BY-STEP 5.2

1. Open Notepad, SimpleText, or your favorite text editor (if it is not already open).

2. Retrieve the **js-one.html** or **js-one.htm** file you created in Step-by-Step 5.1. Add the bolded HTML and JavaScript code exactly as shown in Figure 5-3.

FIGURE 5-3
HTML page with two embedded JavaScript codes

```
<HTML>
<HEAD>
<TITLE>HTML and JavaScript</TITLE>
</HEAD>
<BODY>
<CENTER>
<H1>
<SCRIPT>
    document.write("Hello World Wide Web!");
</SCRIPT>
</H1>
<H3>
<SCRIPT>
    document.write("Welcome to the exciting world of JavaScript");
</SCRIPT>
</H3>
</CENTER>
</BODY>
</HTML>
```

3. Save your newly created file as **js-two.html** or **js-two.htm**.

4. View your work in your Web browser. The resulting Web page should look like Figure 5-4. Continue to the next section, or shut down your computer if you are finished for the day.

FIGURE 5-4
A nicely formatted JavaScript Web page

Hello World Wide Web!

Welcome to the exciting world of JavaScript

Analyzing the Code You Have Just Entered

If you attained a clear understanding of the HTML material presented in Lesson 1, you should be comfortable with the purpose of the center and heading tags we added to this document. You should also understand that the output string generated by the first occurrence of the document.write() method will be inserted into the HTML text stream between the <CENTER> and </CENTER> tags, as well as between the <H1> and </H1> tags. Likewise, the output string produced by the second call to document.write() will appear between the <CENTER> and </CENTER> tags and the <H3> and </H3> tags.

In other words, the <H1></H1> tag pair will affect only the appearance of the first output string, and the <H3></H3> tag pair will affect only the second string. But the <CENTER> and </CENTER> tags will affect the display position of both strings. Do you understand?

WARNING: You may be tempted to place HTML formatting tags (such as <CENTER>, <H1>, <H3>, etc.) inside of the <SCRIPT> and </SCRIPT> tags, but don't do it! You need to remember that the Web browser will interpret everything you key between the script tags as JavaScript source code. Even though these formatting tags are valid in an HTML context, they are not valid JavaScript statements. If you make the mistake of keying HTML tags within a JavaScript code block, your browser will respond with an unpleasant error message.

Conditional Statements in JavaScript

The astute student may look at the previous two Step-by-Steps and ask, "Why are we even using JavaScript to display text messages on the screen? Wouldn't it be easier to just type the text into the HTML document and eliminate the calls to the document.write() method?"

Well, the honest answer is yes! It would be easier to do it that way. In fact, the Web browser would display the results slightly faster if we eliminated the script tags because it wouldn't have to invoke the JavaScript interpreter. However, don't forget that JavaScript is capable of performing a lot more functions than simply writing text to the screen.

In the next Step-by-Step, you will use one of the most powerful features of the JavaScript language, the conditional statement. Every programming language possesses the ability to make decisions. Or to put it in more technical terms, every language gives programmers the ability to evaluate a specific *condition* and then perform different actions depending on the results of that evaluation.

 Programming Skills

What's with Those Troublesome Semicolons?

If you were to study the source code for many different JavaScript-enabled Web pages on the Internet you would discover that many of them have semicolons (;) after each statement, while many others do not. All of the source listings for the JavaScript Step-by-Step exercises in this lesson include semicolons, but they are not necessary. If you were to go through each exercise one by one and remove the terminating semicolons, all of the scripts would still function correctly. So you may be asking yourself why they are there. The answer is that it is a matter of personal preference—at least in these examples. More importantly, if you were to move from JavaScript coding to some other programming languages (including Pascal, C++, and Java), you would find that the semicolons are no longer optional. Each of these languages will display an error message if you forget to put in a required semicolon, so it is a good idea to get used to them. After all, it is usually much easier to learn a good habit than to unlearn a bad one.

Watch Your Syntax!

The syntax of the conditional statement in JavaScript is very important. The statement begins with the keyword *if*, and then a condition is specified within a pair of parentheses. A **keyword** is recognized as part of the language definition. It is reserved by the language and cannot be used as a variable. Some examples of keywords are *if*, *else*, and *return*.

The condition is followed by a statement block that consists of an opening brace ({), one or more JavaScript statements, and then a closing brace (}). The shell of a JavaScript conditional statement is shown below:

```
if ( <condition> )
{
    statement 1;
    statement 2;
    statement 3;
        .
        .
        .
    statement N;
}
```

The JavaScript *if* statement also supports an optional *else* clause, which defines the action to take if the specified condition is not true. The *else* keyword appears immediately after the statement of the *if* clause, and it is accompanied by a statement block of its own. An example of a JavaScript conditional statement that includes the optional *else* clause is as follows:

```
if ( <condition> )
{
    statement i1;
    statement i2;
    statement i3;
        .
        .
        .
    statement iN;
}
else
{
    statement e1;
    statement e2;
    statement e3;
        .
        .
        .
    statement eN;
}
```

Now that you know the basic structure of JavaScript *if* and *if-else* statements, let's talk a little about the condition part of the syntax (shown as *<condition>* in the JavaScript examples above). A JavaScript condition will always consist of two **tokens** separated by a relational *operator*. A token can be either a variable name (such as *x* or *count*), or it can be a literal constant (like *10* or *"Hello"*). The relational operator may be any one of the following symbols:

OPERATOR	MEANING
==	is equal to
!=	is not equal to
<	is less than
>	is greater than
<=	is less than or equal to
>=	is greater than or equal to

Now that you have learned how to create conditional statements in JavaScript, let's put that knowledge to work in an actual program. In the next Step-by-Step we will include a simple conditional statement in a Web document and teach you a useful programming technique in the process. It is fairly common for Internet content developers to want to perform different tasks

Note

Make sure you use two equal signs to test for equality. If you forget and use only one equal sign, your Web browser will reprimand you with an error message.

 Internet Milestone

Scripting Languages

When Netscape Communications Corporation introduced JavaScript to the world in 1995, they were not the first company to provide Web content developers with a new technology to enhance the capabilities of HTML. However, they were the first to provide a full-featured scripting language, and it didn't take long for other companies to recognize the advantages of this technology.

While scripting does not provide all of the features of a complete programming language, it also does not require the use of complex or expensive compiler software. This makes it an ideal choice for novice programmers, educational institutions, or other organizations with limited financial resources.

So in 1996, Microsoft Corporation quickly joined the scripting initiative by offering both JScript and VBScript as alternatives to the industry-standard JavaScript. These scripting languages are roughly equivalent to JavaScript in terms of the capabilities they provide, but they also offer a few extra features to those users who run Microsoft's Internet Explorer on the Windows platform. Like JavaScript, JScript is based on the syntax of the Java programming language, while VBScript is based on the programming syntax of Visual Basic.

The scripting language of choice for professional Web developers depends upon their particular preferences and programming needs. But no matter which language they choose, they can thank JavaScript for getting the scripting movement started.

depending on the type of browser a particular user has. The JavaScript program you are about to create will determine if the Web surfer is using Netscape Navigator or not, and then it will react accordingly.

STEP-BY-STEP 5.3

1. Open Notepad, SimpleText, or your favorite text editor (if it is not already open).

2. Retrieve the **js-two.htm** or **js-two.html** file you created in Step-by-Step 5.2. Add the bolded HTML and JavaScript code exactly as shown in Figure 5-5.

FIGURE 5-5
HTML/JavaScript document with *if-else* conditional statement

```
<HTML>
<HEAD>
<TITLE>HTML and JavaScript</TITLE>
</HEAD>
<BODY>
<CENTER>
<H1>
<SCRIPT>
  document.write("Hello World Wide Web!");
</SCRIPT>
</H1>
<H3>
<SCRIPT>
  document.write("Welcome to the exciting world of JavaScript");
</SCRIPT>
</H3>
<SCRIPT>
  if (navigator.appName == "Netscape")
  {
    document.write("You are using Netscape Navigator");
  }
  else
  {
    document.write("You are not using Netscape Navigator.<BR>");
    document.write("I'll bet you are using Microsoft Internet Explorer.");
  }
</SCRIPT>
</CENTER>
</BODY>
</HTML>
```

3. Save your newly created file as **js-three.html** or **js-three.htm**.

STEP-BY-STEP 5.3 Continued

4. Open your Web browser and view the **js-three.html** document you just created. You should see something that looks like either Figure 5-6A or Figure 5-6B. Continue to the next section, or shut down your computer if you are finished for the day.

FIGURE 5-6A
Resulting Web page when
viewed with Netscape Navigator

Hello World Wide Web!

Welcome to the exciting world of JavaScript

You are using Netscape Navigator.

FIGURE 5-6B
Resulting Web page when
viewed with Internet Explorer

Hello World Wide Web!

Welcome to the exciting world of JavaScript

You are not using Netscape Navigator.
I'll bet you are using Microsoft Internet Explorer.

Analyzing the Code You Have Just Entered

Even though we didn't add a lot of code to our JavaScript program, we did introduce several important concepts. Let's take a minute to review those concepts to make sure you have a solid understanding of what is happening here.

First of all, the condition that is being evaluated in this JavaScript code segment is:

```
(navigator.appName == "Netscape")
```

We mentioned earlier in this chapter that JavaScript objects contain special functions, called methods, that perform various tasks. Well, it just so happens that JavaScript objects also contain *properties* that programmers can access to obtain information about the object. In this case, we are utilizing the appName property of the navigator object in order to determine the application name of the current Web browser. (Please note that in this context, the word *navigator* can be used interchangeably with the word *browser*.) If this name is Netscape, then we know the user is running Netscape Navigator. Otherwise, we know the user is not running Netscape Navigator, so he or she is probably running Microsoft's Internet Explorer (although there is a small chance it could be some other browser).

The second important concept to learn here is that once the condition has been evaluated, either the *if* statement block will be executed or the *else* block will be executed—never both. If the result of the condition is true, the *if* block will run. If the condition is false, the *else* block will run. It's as simple as that.

There is a final point in this example you need to recognize. Until now, we have repeatedly mentioned the concept of embedding JavaScript source code in HTML documents. Well, it turns out that it is also possible, not to mention useful, to embed HTML tags in JavaScript text strings! Look carefully at the first call to document.write() inside the else statement block. Notice that the HTML <BR> tag is embedded within the output text string. The reason this tag is present is because we want the second string of text to appear on a separate line, rather than on the same line as the first string. In order to accomplish this, we have to put a <BR> tag in the output text stream so that the browser will recognize the BREAK command. Are you following?

Using the JavaScript Alert() Method

In the previous three activities, we have made use of the document.write() method, which is probably the most common way for JavaScript programs to communicate with the user. However, there are other ways in which scripts can get the user's attention. One such way is by means of the JavaScript alert() method.

The purpose of the alert() method is to allow the program to display a special dialog box that will alert the user that an expected event has occurred or that some kind of user input is required. Like the write() method and the appName property, the alert() method is part of an object called the window object. The window object is considered by the JavaScript interpreter to be the default object. Any method or property that appears in a script without an explicit reference to an object is automatically assumed to be part of the window object. For this reason, it is not necessary to include an object name and a period (.) character when it is invoked. Let's give the alert() method a try, shall we?

STEP-BY-STEP 5.4

1. Open Notepad, SimpleText, or your favorite text editor (if it is not already open).

2. Retrieve the **js-three.html** or **js-three.htm** file you created in Step-by-Step 5.3.

STEP-BY-STEP 5.4 Continued

3. Modify the HTML/JavaScript document by adding the text in bold shown in Figure 5-7.

FIGURE 5-7
HTML/JavaScript source code containing calls to the alert() method

```
<HTML>
<HEAD>
<TITLE>HTML and JavaScript</TITLE>
</HEAD>
<BODY>
<CENTER>
<H1>
<SCRIPT>
   document.write("Hello World Wide Web!");
</SCRIPT>
</H1>
<H3>
<SCRIPT>
   document.write("Welcome to the exciting world of JavaScript");
</SCRIPT>
</H3>
<SCRIPT>
   if (navigator.appName == "Netscape")
   {
       document.write("You are using Netscape Navigator");
       alert("Netscape Navigator detected.");
   }
   else
   {
       document.write("You are not using Netscape Navigator.<BR>");
       document.write("I'll bet you are using Microsoft Internet Explorer.");
       alert("Netscape Navigator required.");
   }
</SCRIPT>
</CENTER>
</BODY>
</HTML>
```

4. Save your newly created file as **js-four.html** or **js-four.htm**.

STEP-BY-STEP 5.4 Continued

5. Open your Web browser and view the **js-four.html** or **js-four.htm** document you just saved. You should see something that looks like either Figure 5-8A or Figure 5-8B. Continue to the next section, or shut down your computer if you are finished for the day.

FIGURE 5-8A
Resulting Web page when
viewed with Netscape Navigator

FIGURE 5-8B
Resulting Web page when
viewed with Internet Explorer

Analyzing the Code You Have Just Entered

Hopefully this activity has helped you to see how the alert() method could be useful in some situations. It normally is used in JavaScript programs when the user needs to be made aware that some unexpected error condition has occurred. It can also be used when the program needs some kind of user acknowledgment before proceeding. In either case, the alert() method is an alternative way for JavaScript software to generate output.

Accessing the Browser Status Line

You have probably noticed that when your Web browser is loading an HTML document that contains many objects, it displays various messages at the bottom of the window. This area of the screen is known as the *status line*, and it can be accessed from within a JavaScript program. In addition to the document.write() method and the alert() method, this is another way in which a JavaScript Web page can communicate information to the user.

The question you should be asking yourself now is, "How do I access the browser status line?" Once again, the answer to this question is very simple. The message displayed in the status line is nothing more than a string value that is stored in the status property of the window object. This means you can change the message at any time within a JavaScript program by including a statement like this:

```
window.status = "A string of text";
```

Now that you understand how easy it can be, let's add two new lines of code to the JavaScript program you wrote in the previous activity. This code will simply reinforce the messages that are displayed by the alert() method.

STEP-BY-STEP 5.5

1. Open Notepad, SimpleText, or your favorite text editor (if it is not already open).

2. Retrieve the **js-four.html** or **js-four.htm** file you created in Step-by-Step 5.4.

 Internet Milestone

Which Came First—Java or JavaScript?

Many people who have only a casual knowledge of Internet technologies tend to think that the Java programming language and the JavaScript scripting language are the same thing. Even those who know that they are *not* the same thing may not know how they relate to each other, or which one was created first. The answer is that Java was created first by Sun Microsystems, Inc. Sun released its cross-platform programming language to the general public in 1995, and it has continued to grow in popularity at an unprecedented rate ever since.

But Sun was not the only company looking for a way to enhance the capabilities of standard HTML. Netscape Communications Corporation was also busy working on finding a way to embed user-programmable scripts into static HTML Web pages, and they needed to incorporate a well-defined syntax into their design. When Netscape developers saw how popular the Java language was becoming, they decided to license the Java name from Sun, and use the Java syntax in their own scripting language. The result of Netscape's efforts became known as JavaScript, and it also has enjoyed a great deal of success in the Internet development sector.

STEP-BY-STEP 5.5 Continued

3. Modify the HTML/JavaScript document by adding the text in bold shown in Figure 5-9.

FIGURE 5-9
HTML/JavaScript source code that sets the browser status line

```
<HTML>
<HEAD>
<TITLE>HTML and JavaScript</TITLE>
</HEAD>
<BODY>
<CENTER>
<H1>
<SCRIPT>
   document.write("Hello World Wide Web!");
</SCRIPT>
</H1>
<H3>
<SCRIPT>
   document.write("Welcome to the exciting world of JavaScript");
</SCRIPT>
</H3>
<SCRIPT>
   if (navigator.appName == "Netscape")
   {
      document.write("You are using Netscape Navigator");
      window.status = "Netscape Navigator detected.";
      alert("Netscape Navigator detected");
   }
   else
   {
      document.write("You are not using Netscape Navigator.<BR>");
      document.write("I'll bet you are using Microsoft Internet Explorer.");
      window.status = "Netscape Navigator required.";
      alert("Netscape Navigator required");
   }
</SCRIPT>
</CENTER>
</BODY>
</HTML>
```

4. Save your newly created file as **js-five.html** or **js-five.htm**.

STEP-BY-STEP 5.5 Continued

5. Open your Web browser and view the **js-five.html** or **js-five.htm** document you just saved. You should see something that looks like either Figure 5-10A or Figure 5-10B. (Warning: Some versions of Internet Explorer may display the alert box before the status bar message.) Shut down your computer.

FIGURE 5-10A
Resulting Web page when viewed with Netscape Navigator

FIGURE 5-10B
Resulting Web page when viewed with Internet Explorer

Analyzing the Code You Have Just Entered

As we mentioned earlier in this lesson, the most common way for JavaScript to interact with a Web surfer is by means of the document.write() method. But the browser status line also can be an effective way of communicating information to the user. In this case, we simply used the status line to echo the message displayed in the alert dialog box. However, it is much more common to see JavaScript programs use the status line to let the user know what it is doing. Whenever your script is about to initiate a potentially lengthy process, such as downloading a large graphic image, for example, it is a good idea to display an appropriate message in the status line. This can go a long way toward making sure that the user knows her computer system hasn't crashed.

SUMMARY

In this lesson, you learned:

- You can explain the purpose of JavaScript.

- How to use the <SCRIPT> and </SCRIPT> tags.

- You can use JavaScript objects.

- You can use JavaScript methods.

- You can understand and apply JavaScript syntax.

 Internet Milestone

Hello, World!

The next time you are in your local bookstore, take a few minutes to skim through the first few chapters of several different programming books. In many cases, you will see that the first programming example introduced in these books demonstrates how to display the phrase *Hello, World!* in that particular language. Why do you suppose it is so common for authors to begin their books in this way? Well, the answer is simple.

In 1978, two employees of Bell Laboratories, Brian Kernighan and Dennis Ritchie, published a book entitled *The C Programming Language*. This book has proven itself to be one of the most enduring programming tutorials in the history of computer software. Over the past twenty years, this book has undergone only one revision, and the second edition is still in print! The very first programming exercise in this book explains how to use the C function called printf() to display the phrase *Hello, World*. Though it is unlikely Kernighan and Ritchie intended to start an informal tradition among authors of programming books, that is exactly what they did! And although we took the liberty of modifying the phrase somewhat (to *Hello World Wide Web!*), it is still based on this simple example from over twenty-five years ago.

VOCABULARY *Review*

Define the following terms:

<SCRIPT> and
   </SCRIPT> tags
Binary code
Compiler
Condition
Interpretation

Keywords
Methods
Objects
Operators
Parameter list
Programming language

Properties
Scripting language
Status line
Syntax
Token

REVIEW *Questions*

TRUE/FALSE

Circle T if the statement is true or F if the statement is false.

T   F   **1.** JavaScript is a programming language.

T   F   **2.** JavaScript requires a compiler.

T   F   **3.** You insert JavaScript in an HTML document between the <SCRIPT> and </SCRIPT> tags.

T   F   **4.** Method names are always followed by a parameter list.

T   F   **5.** Semicolons (;) are not always necessary in JavaScript statements.

FILL IN THE BLANK

Complete the following sentences by writing the correct word or words in the blanks provided.

1. The symbols { and } are called _____ braces.

2. The JavaScript *if* statement supports an optional _____ clause, which defines an action to take if the specified condition is not true.

3. A JavaScript condition will always consists of two _____ separated by a relational operator.

4. _____ Communications Corporation introduced JavaScript to the world in 1995.

5. The _____( ) method allows the program to display a special dialog box that will warn the user that an unexpected event has occurred, or that some kind of user input is required.

WRITTEN QUESTIONS

Write a brief answer to the following questions.

1. How does JavaScript enhance the capabilities of HTML?

2. What is a JavaScript object? What are object methods and object properties?

3. What JavaScript method is most commonly used to generate output?

4. What is the syntax of a conditional statement in JavaScript?

5. In what ways does the alert() method differ from the write() method?

PROJECTS

 PROJECT 5-1

GreatApplications, Inc., is looking for skilled Internet programmers who have a good understanding of HTML programming with JavaScript. In order to test the knowledge of potential employees, GreatApplications is giving a series of HTML/JavaScript tests. Here is the first question on the test:

As you know, there is nothing special about the phrase *Hello World Wide Web!* used in Step-by-Step 5.1 (**js-one.htm** or **js-one.html**). Replace this phrase with **Welcome to GreatApplications**. Change the message in the write() method. Just remember that the string you want to display must be enclosed within the double quote characters ("). Save your changed file as **js-test1.html**.

TEAMWORK PROJECT

Teamwork is one of the attributes that GreatApplications, Inc., is always looking for in its employees. Candidates for jobs at GreatApplications, Inc. are divided into teams of two to three members. Each team is asked to solve the following problems together. Prospective employees are judged not just on the correct answers, but on how team members communicate and work together in a cordial and creative manner to solve the problems. During a group interview, you are on a team that is given the following two projects.

Problem 1: Obviously <BR> is not the only HTML formatting tag that can be embedded in a JavaScript output string. You can use any formatting tags you wish in a document.write() statement. Try being creative for a moment, and see how many other tags you can put in the JavaScript code for this exercise. What effect, if any, do they have on the resulting Web page? Is it better to place HTML tags outside of the <SCRIPT></SCRIPT> tags, or embed them in JavaScript text strings? Are there times when you might want to do both? Think about it! Save this file as **js-test2.htm** or **js-test2.html**.

Problem 2: It should be clear to you that you can use any HTML tags with JavaScript, not just the heading and center tags. Try inserting some of the other HTML tags described in the first four lessons into this Lesson 5 Teamwork project to see what effect they will have. Specifically, try using the tags that affect the foreground and background colors of the Web page. See if you can get your JavaScript Web page to appear as yellow text on a blue background, for example. Or try to make the <H1> text appear in a different color than the <H3> text. Save this file as **js-test3.htm** or **js-test3.html**.

 WEB PROJECT

In Step-by-Step 5.3, you created a JavaScript program that identified whether your browser was Netscape Navigator or not. GreatApplications, Inc., has just assigned you the task of rewording this program so that it is oriented toward Microsoft Internet Explorer (IE) rather than toward Netscape's Navigator. This means that you'll have to change the JavaScript conditional statement, as well as the wording of the text strings inside the *if* and the *else* statement blocks in your **js-four.htm** or **js-four.html** file.

When you have completed your changes, view the new file with both Netscape Navigator and with Microsoft Internet Explorer if you have both of them available, just to make sure it operates correctly. Each browser can be downloaded on the Internet for free from their respective manufacturers and installed on your computer. Save your file as **js-test4.htm** or **js-test4.html**.

CRITICAL *Thinking*

 ACTIVITY 5-1

In the introduction of Step-by-Step 5.3, we mentioned that the conditional statement is one of JavaScript's most powerful features. This claim is merely an echo of the statement made more than 20 years ago by the great computer scientist Joseph Weizenbaum. In 1976, Mr. Weizenbaum wrote a book entitled *Computer Power and Human Reason,* in which he presented the idea that the real power of computer systems was their ability to make decisions. Think about this idea for a while, and then answer the following questions:

1. How useful would computers be if they could not make decisions?

2. Describe the general structure of the JavaScript decision-making statement.

3. What does it mean to "evaluate a condition"?

4. Why do you suppose the *else* clause of the *if-else* statement is optional?

 ACTIVITY 5-2

Try solving one or both of the following thinking activities:

Thinking Activity 5-2A: One way in which some JavaScript programmers utilize the browser status line is to display instructions to the user. In this case, it might make sense to display a message that tells the user what to do when the alert dialog box appears. That is, the status line could include a message that tells the user to click on the OK button to continue processing the script. Why don't you go ahead and make this change? Try to make the message as informative as possible without using a lot of words. Save your file as **js-test5.htm** or **js-test5.html**. (If you are using a version of Internet Explorer that does not display the status line until after the alert box is cleared, you may need to use a different approach.)

Thinking Activity 5-2B: In this activity, we have demonstrated how to define a conditional statement that evaluates the contents of the navigator.appName property to determine if it contains the value "Netscape." But if the appName property does not contain the value Netscape, what value does it contain? How can you find out? Well, think about the document.write() method for a minute. Can it be used to display more than just a literal string (in double quotes)? Of course it can. It can also be used to display the contents of a JavaScript variable or an object property. Now can you write a JavaScript statement that displays the value of appName? Sure you can. Save your file as **js-test6.htm** or **js-test6.html**.

 # SUMMARY *Project*

Put your newly acquired knowledge of JavaScript to work by revisiting a previous activity. Retrieve the HTML file you created in Step-by-Step 1.2, and saved as file **one.html** in Step-by-Step 1.3 (in Lesson 1). Replace all sentences in this file with JavaScript code. To be more specific, use the document.write() method to output the five sentences to your Web page. Your completed Web page should look like the one in Figure 5-11.

FIGURE 5-11
A simple Web page generated with JavaScript

PROJECT REQUIREMENTS

- Use the HTML code you created in Step-by-Step 1.2 in Lesson 1.

- Replace the text (sentences) with JavaScript document.write() statements.

- Save your new file as **project5.html** or **project5.htm**.

- View your new file in a Web browser to ensure that it looks right.

- Use your browser's View Source command to view the page source. Compare what you see to the page source you created in file **one.html**.

USING IMAGES WITH JAVASCRIPT

OBJECTIVES

Upon completion of this lesson, you should be able to:

- Understand the names and usage of JavaScript events.
- Create an image rollover.
- Make a hyperlink rollover.
- Build a cycling banner.
- Display random images.
- Create a JavaScript slide show.

Estimated Time: 1.5 hours

VOCABULARY

Array

Cycling banner (ad banner)

Decrement

Event

Function

Hyperlink rollover

Image rollover

Increment

Index

Instantiate

Real number (floating-point number)

Slide show

Variable

Making Graphic Images Come Alive

In Lesson 3, we mentioned how important the effective use of graphic images can be to the overall success of a Web page. Well, that principle holds true whether the Web page is based on HTML or JavaScript technology. Standard HTML gives you the ability to do several interesting things with images, but JavaScript gives you some additional capabilities.

In this lesson, we will focus on the JavaScript features that are commonly used to make graphic images come alive on Web pages. Once you have learned these new techniques, you will quickly recognize their usage all over the World Wide Web. Then you will no longer need to wonder how the designers of these interesting pages are able to create such eye-catching effects.

Before you can accomplish anything spectacular with images, you'll need to acquire an understanding of JavaScript events. For the purpose of this book you can think of an *event* as a system-level response to the occurrence of some specific condition. Some of these conditions are generated by the Web browser software itself, but most of them are caused by the user performing some action. Such actions might include moving the mouse, clicking on a button, or even selecting a block of text on the screen. But regardless of how a particular event is generated, JavaScript gives you the ability to create Web pages that react to it. And when these reactions are implemented skillfully, the user will definitely be impressed by your Web page.

Another important concept you'll need to master when working with images is the notion of JavaScript functions. A *function* is nothing more than a segment of JavaScript code that can be invoked or called just like the document.write() and alert() methods used in Lesson 5. In fact, there is really no difference between a method and a function, except that methods have already been defined as part of the JavaScript programming environment. Functions, on the other hand, are written by the programmer and may contain any number of JavaScript statements, including calls to JavaScript methods or other functions.

It may not be obvious to you at this point how JavaScript events and functions relate to the usage of graphic images in Web pages. But just be patient, and you'll see the connection very soon. In fact, that is the very purpose of the activities in this lesson. We will be using events and functions with images to create some interesting effects that will improve the quality of your Web pages immensely. So if you are ready to get started, let's get to work!

Teaching an Image to Roll Over

In Lesson 3, you learned how to include a graphic image in your Web page, and you also learned how to turn an image into a hyperlink. Now we are going to show you how to use the power of JavaScript to make a graphical hyperlink respond to mouse movements.

To be more specific, we are going to show you how you can change the appearance of an image whenever the user moves the mouse pointer over it. This JavaScript programming technique is called an *image rollover*.

The first thing you need to know in order to implement a rollover is how to make use of the JavaScript events called *onMouseOver* and *onMouseOut*. The *onMouseOver* event is generated whenever the user moves the mouse over a particular object. Likewise, the *onMouseOut* event is generated when the user moves the mouse pointer off of the object. All you need to learn is how to use JavaScript to detect when these events occur, and then take some appropriate action. In Step-by-Step 6.1, we are going to display a blue arrow on the screen and then change the arrow to red when the mouse pointer rolls over it. We will then change the arrow color back to blue when the mouse pointer rolls off of the image. Sound simple enough?

S TEP-BY-STEP 6.1

1. Enter the URL **www.course.com** in your Web browser.

2. Click in the search box and enter the title of this book (*HTML and JavaScript BASICS*).

3. Click **Search** and wait for the search results to appear. Then find the correct book title from the results list and click on it.

4. Choose the link called **Student Online Companion**.

5. Click the **Lesson 6** link and choose the **Data Files & Graphics** link from the list that appears.

6. Download the **bluearrow.gif** and **redarrow.gif** files (seen in Figures 6-2A and 6-2B) to the exact same folder where you have been saving your Web pages. If you need to review how to download these files, return to Step-by-Step 3.2 for assistance.

STEP-BY-STEP 6.1 Continued

7. Open your text editor or word processor and enter the HTML/JavaScript code exactly as it appears in Figure 6-1.

FIGURE 6-1
JavaScript code to create an image rollover

```
<HTML>
<HEAD>
<TITLE>HTML and JavaScript</TITLE>
<SCRIPT>
 var blueArrow = new Image;
 blueArrow.src = "bluearrow.gif";
 var redArrow = new Image;
 redArrow.src = "redarrow.gif";

 function turnBlue()
 {
     document.arrow.src = blueArrow.src;
     return;
 }

 function turnRed()
 {
     document.arrow.src = redArrow.src;
     return;
 }
</SCRIPT>
</HEAD>
<BODY>
<CENTER>
<A HREF="webpage.html" onMouseOut="turnBlue()" onMouseOver="turnRed()">
<IMG NAME="arrow" SRC="bluearrow.gif">
</A>
</CENTER>
</BODY>
</HTML>
```

8. Save this file in the appropriate folder as **js-six.html**.

9. Open your Web browser if it is not already open.

STEP-BY-STEP 6.1 Continued

10. View your **js-six.html** page. Your Web page should look initially like Figure 6-2A, but when you move the mouse pointer over the arrow image, its appearance should change to look like Figure 6-2B.

11. Move on to the next section, or shut down your computer if you are finished for the day.

Important

If you are a Windows XP user with Service Pack 2 installed, your browser may display a warning message about blocking active content. If this occurs, click on the warning and follow the subsequent prompts to enable JavaScript.

FIGURE 6-2A
Your Web page as it appears initially

FIGURE 6-2B
Your Web page when the mouse pointer rolls over the image

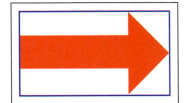

Analyzing the Code You Have Just Entered

Even though the HTML/JavaScript source code in Figure 6-1 is not very long, it does introduce several new features that you have not seen before. Let's take a moment to make sure you understand all of these concepts, because you will be seeing them throughout this lesson.

First of all, you should be aware that the <SCRIPT> and </SCRIPT> tags appear in the header section of the HTML document rather than in the body section. This means that the Web browser will process the JavaScript code before it begins to display the contents of the document on the screen. This is an important point for this particular document because we want the browser to load both the blue and the red arrow images into memory before it displays the body of the Web page. If we fail to do this, the browser would not know what images it is to load when the *onMouseOver* and *onMouseOut* events occur, and the result would be a JavaScript error message.

Next, it is important for you to understand what the JavaScript code (lines 5 through 8 of Figure 6-1) actually does. This statement in line 5 (var blueArrow = new Image;) tells the JavaScript interpreter to create a new Image object, and then to save a reference to that object in a variable that we have called *blueArrow*. Remember that a JavaScript *variable* is nothing more than a name that is assigned to a literal value or to an object. Once this assignment has been made, the name can be used throughout the HTML document to refer to that particular value or object.

The statement in line 6 (blueArrow.src = "bluearrow.gif";) tells JavaScript that the source (src) property of the *blueArrow* object will contain the graphic image stored in the file *bluearrow.gif*. This is the statement that actually causes the browser to load the blue arrow image into memory. Once this task is complete, the next two JavaScript statements perform essentially the same function as the first two statements.

The statement in line 7 (var redArrow = new Image;) causes the interpreter to create a new Image object and assigns it the name *redArrow*. The statement in line 8 (redArrow.src = "redarrow.gif";) sets the src property of the object to the image contained in the file *redarrow.gif*, so the browser will load this image into memory also. Do you follow?

Event Handling Logic

The next concept we need to discuss is the JavaScript event handling logic. This is an important feature of JavaScript because it demonstrates another way in which JavaScript code can interact with standard HTML tags.

Until now, all of the JavaScript statements you have used were located between the <SCRIPT> and </SCRIPT> tags, right? The JavaScript event handling statements are actually placed within a standard HTML tag. In this case, the statements that handle the *onMouseOver* and *onMouseOut* events are located within the opening anchor (<A>) tag. When the *onMouseOver* event occurs, the JavaScript function called turnRed() is invoked, and this function sets the source (src) property of the arrow object contained within the document object to the src property of the *redArrow* object.

Likewise, when the *onMouseOut* event occurs the turnBlue() function is called; this function sets the src property of the document's arrow object to the value of the *blueArrow.src* property.

Therefore, when the mouse pointer rolls over the arrow image, the *onMouseOver* event fires (occurs), and the image source is assigned the contents of the *redarrow.gif* file.

In a similar fashion, moving the mouse pointer off of the arrow image causes the *onMouseOut* event to fire, and the image source is assigned the contents of the *bluearrow.gif* file. Is this making sense?

The final point we would like to address concerns the origin of the *document.arrow* object. How does the browser know what object we are referring to when we use the name *arrow*? The answer, fortunately, is very simple. If you look closely at the <IMG> tag we used to define the original image, you will see that we included a new attribute that you have not used before.

Technology Careers

Client/Server Application Engineers

Wherever you may go throughout corporate America, you will find a high demand for software developers who can create fast, reliable client/server applications. The main idea behind a client/server application is that one process (or program) will run in a central location, and then multiple client processes, running in many different locations, will make requests of the server process and wait for responses.

Twenty years ago, this type of distributed system would be found only in large corporations, banks, or airline reservation agencies because it was difficult to install and expensive to maintain. Today, client/server architecture is well within the reach of small businesses, government agencies, or even school districts. Unfortunately, though, having the means to create a client/server software system does not mean it is easy to find someone who can actually create and write the programs necessary for such systems to work properly. That is why acquiring a solid knowledge of JavaScript today could prove to be very important for you someday. JavaScript is frequently used on the client side of client/server applications, so you can be sure that there are a lot of companies out there just waiting to hire you. Don't miss this great opportunity!

This attribute is called NAME, and its purpose is to allow you to assign a variable name to the Image object. In this example we gave the Image object the name *arrow*, and since this image is part of our HTML document it can be referenced in JavaScript code as *document.arrow*. This is getting fun now, isn't it?

Teaching a Hyperlink to Roll Over

Now that you know how to make an image rollover, let's learn how to create a hyperlink rollover. As you might expect, a hyperlink rollover is very similar to an image rollover. The only difference is that a *hyperlink rollover* is triggered when the user moves the mouse over a hyperlink, rather than when the mouse rolls over an image. Makes sense, doesn't it?

If you are expecting the JavaScript code required to make a hyperlink rollover to be similar to the code for an image rollover, you won't be disappointed. In fact, if we didn't tell you what changes to make, you would probably have to look at the new source code twice to determine what the differences are. Are you ready to give it a try? Let's do it.

S TEP-BY-STEP 6.2

1. Open your text editor or word processor and retrieve the **js-six.html** file you created in the previous Step-by-Step.

 Programming Skills

Using JavaScript Events

All of the activities in this lesson make use of one or more JavaScript events. However, several JavaScript events are available that are not discussed in this lesson. But that doesn't mean you can't do a little independent study and learn how to use them on your own. Here is an alphabetical list of possible JavaScript events that are available, along with a brief description of the condition that will trigger the event.

Event Name	Event Trigger
onAbort	The user aborted the loading of a Web page.
onBlur	The user deactivated an object (the object lost focus).
onChange	The user changed the object in some way.
onClick	The user clicked the mouse on an object.
onError	The JavaScript interpreter encountered a script error.
onFocus	The user activated an object (the object received focus).
onLoad	The Web browser finished loading a page.
onMouseOver	The mouse pointer passed over an object.
onMouseOut	The mouse pointer moved off an object.
onSelect	The user selected (highlighted) the contents of an object.
onSubmit	The user submitted an HTML form.
onUnload	The Web browser unloaded a page from memory.

STEP-BY-STEP 6.2 Continued

2. Next, key the changes in the HTML and JavaScript source code as shown in bold in Figure 6-3. You will need to delete some JavaScript code and a few HTML tags so your new file looks exactly like Figure 6-3.

FIGURE 6-3
JavaScript code to create a hyperlink rollover

```
<HTML>
<HEAD>
<TITLE>HTML and JavaScript</TITLE>
<SCRIPT>
var blueArrow = new Image;
blueArrow.src = "bluearrow.gif";
var redArrow = new Image;
redArrow.src = "redarrow.gif";

function turnBlue()
{
    document.arrow.src = blueArrow.src;
    return;
}

function turnRed()
{
    document.arrow.src = redArrow.src;
    return;
}
</SCRIPT>
</HEAD>
<BODY>
<CENTER>
<A HREF="webpage.html" onMouseOut="turnBlue()" onMouseOver="turnRed()">
Next Page
</A>
<P>
<IMG NAME="arrow" SRC="bluearrow.gif">
</CENTER>
</BODY>
</HTML>
```

3. Save this file in the appropriate folder as **js-seven.html**.

4. Open your Web browser if it is not already open.

STEP-BY-STEP 6.2 Continued

5. View your **js-seven.html** page. Your Web page should look initially like Figure 6-4A, but when you move the mouse pointer over the Next Page hyperlink its appearance should change to look like Figure 6-4B. Move on to the next section, or shut down your computer if you are finished for the day.

FIGURE 6-4A
Your Web page as it appears initially

FIGURE 6-4B
Your Web page when the mouse pointer rolls over the hyperlink

Analyzing the Code You Have Just Entered

If you are an astute observer, you will notice that the JavaScript statements in this HTML document (*js-seven.html*) are exactly the same as in the previous document (*js-six.html*). So let's make sure that you have a solid understanding of what changes were made in the HTML tags, and how these changes relate to the JavaScript code.

First of all, the <A> and the </A> anchor tags no longer enclose the <IMG> tag, so the arrow image is no longer part of the hyperlink reference. Instead, the anchor tags now enclose the Next Page text you just added. This means that the *onMouseOver* and *onMouseOut* events will be fired when the mouse rolls over the new hyperlink instead of when it rolls over the arrow image. However, the action performed by JavaScript code is the same as before, so the image changes color just like it did before.

You may be wondering why we inserted the paragraph tag between the hypertext and the arrow image. We did this because the paragraph tag forces the image down below the Next Page hyperlink. Otherwise, the image would appear to the right of the hypertext. (Feel free to remove the <P> tag and view the file again if you want to see what we mean.)

You may also be wondering why the arrow image was surrounded by a blue rectangle in the previous Step-by-Step, but not in this one. The answer to this question is that in Step-by-Step 6.1, the image was defined as a hyperlink, and the hyperlink images are normally displayed with a blue border by a Web browser. This is why the blue border is still visible when the arrow image is changed from blue to red. But in Step-by-Step 6.2, the image is not defined as a hyperlink, so the blue border is gone. Instead, the Next Page text is defined as the hyperlink, so it is displayed as blue and underlined, regardless of the color of the arrow image. Got it? (If you would like to know how to eliminate the blue rectangle in Step-by-Step 6.1, complete the Web project at the end of this lesson.)

> **Net Tip**
>
> When you can spare the time, spend an hour searching the Web for sites that include interesting images or hypertext rollover effects. Make a list of the sites you like best and try implementing the same types of rollovers yourself.

Creating a Cycling Banner

When you are surfing the Web, it is probably quite common for you to encounter commercial Web sites containing advertisements that are constantly changing. As it turns out, these cycling banners (also known as ad banners) can be created in various ways using different Internet technologies. However, one of the easiest and most efficient ways to create these types of advertisements is by using JavaScript events and functions.

A *cycling banner* is really nothing more than a sequence of graphic images that are displayed one after another with a small pause between each image change. After all of the images in the sequence have been displayed, the browser will cycle back to the first image and start the sequence all over again. This is the reason why this particular Web page enhancement is called a cycling banner.

You may think that creating a cycling banner takes a lot of time and effort, but this is not the case with JavaScript! In this next section, we will show you that it takes only a few minutes to integrate an effective ad display into your Web page. By utilizing a single JavaScript event, and by defining one simple JavaScript function, you will be well on your way to fame and fortune in the world of cycling banner design. Are you ready for this?

S TEP-BY-STEP 6.3

1. You will need four graphics in this activity, which you can download from the Student Guide. Enter the URL **www.course.com** in your Web browser.

2. Click in the search box and enter the title of this book (*HTML and JavaScript BASICS*).

3. Click **Search** and wait for the search results to appear. Then find the correct book title from the results list and click on it.

4. Choose the link called **Student Online Companion**.

5. Click the **Lesson 6** link and choose the **Data Files & Graphics** link from the list that appears.

6. Download the *lions.gif, tigers.gif, bears.gif*, and *ohmy.gif* (seen in Figures 6-6A, 6-6B, 6-6C, and 6-6D) images to the exact same folder where you have been saving your Web pages. If you accidentally download the files to a different folder, your Web page will not function correctly. (If you need to review how to download these files, return to Step-by-Step 3.2 in Lesson 3 for assistance.)

STEP-BY-STEP 6.3 Continued

7. Open your text editor or word processor and enter the HTML/JavaScript code exactly as it appears in Figure 6-5.

FIGURE 6-5
JavaScript code to create a cycling banner

```
<HTML>
<HEAD>
<TITLE>HTML and JavaScript</TITLE>
<SCRIPT>
var imgArray = new Array(4);
imgArray[0] = new Image;
imgArray[0].src = "lions.gif";
imgArray[1] = new Image;
imgArray[1].src = "tigers.gif";
imgArray[2] = new Image;
imgArray[2].src = "bears.gif";
imgArray[3] = new Image;
imgArray[3].src = "ohmy.gif";
var index = 0;

function cycle()
{
    document.banner.src = imgArray[index].src;
    index++;
    if (index == 4)
    {
        index = 0;
    }
    setTimeout("cycle()", 2000);
    return;
}
</SCRIPT>
</HEAD>
<BODY onLoad="cycle()">
<CENTER>
<IMG NAME="banner" SRC="lions.gif">
</CENTER>
</BODY>
</HTML>
```

8. Save this file in the appropriate folder as **js-eight.html**.

STEP-BY-STEP 6.3 Continued

9. Open your Web browser and view your **js-eight.html** page. Your Web page should look initially like Figure 6-6A, but after a two-second delay, it should change to look like Figure 6-6B. After an additional two-second delay, it should change to look like Figure 6-6C, and then finally to Figure 6-6D. Move on to the next section, or shut down your computer if you are finished for the day.

FIGURE 6-6A
The first image in your cycling banner

FIGURE 6-6B
The second image in your cycling banner

FIGURE 6-6C
The third image in your cycling banner

FIGURE 6-6D
The fourth image in your cycling banner

Analyzing the Code You Have Just Entered

Once again, we introduced several important JavaScript concepts within a relatively small amount of source code. Let's go through the source code listing in Figure 6-5 carefully to make sure you understand exactly what's happening here.

First, take a look at line 5 (var imgArray = new Array(4);). Here we are creating a new JavaScript object, which you have not used before, called an array. An *array* is simply a collection of similar objects that can be accessed by means of a variable name and an index. An *index* is simply an integer variable that identifies which element of an array is being referenced.

> **Net Tip**
>
> When a graphic is defined as a hyperlink, the browser will display the image with a rectangular border around it. If this border detracts from the appearance of the page, adjust the size of a hyperlink border with the BORDER attribute. The statement BORDER = 0 in the <IMG> tag will remove the border.

Arrays are available in virtually every modern computer language, so it's important for you to become familiar with them. In this case, our array is defined to contain a maximum of four elements, and its variable name is called *imgArray*. In this case, the array will contain four Image objects, but arrays can contain any other type of JavaScript object as well.

Second, consider the JavaScript statements in lines 6 through 13. These statements should look somewhat familiar to you, since they are essentially the same as those in lines 5 through 8 of Step-by-Step 6.2. Line 6 creates a new Image object and assigns it the name *imgArray* with an index of 0. Line 7 then sets the source (src) property of this new object to contain the contents of the file called *lions.gif*. Similarly, the JavaScript statements in lines 8, 10, and 12 also create new objects of the type Image, and these new objects are assigned the name *imgArray*, with index values of 1, 2, and 3, respectively.

The statements in lines 9, 11, and 13 set the src property of these three new objects to the contents of files *tigers.gif, bears.gif,* and *ohmy.gif,* respectively. Now these four graphic images can be displayed very quickly by other JavaScript statements, which we will describe shortly.

Third, the statement in line 14 (var index = 0;) simply creates a JavaScript variable named index and assigns the value 0 to it. This variable will be used to access the various elements in the *imgArray* array.

Fourth, the JavaScript statements in lines 16 through 26 define a function called *cycle(),* and this function will cause the images in the cycling banner to appear one after the other. This is accomplished by setting the src property of the *document.banner* object to the src property of the current element of the *imgArray* array. Then we increment the value stored in the index variable (using the ++ operator) in order to access the next element of our image array. The term *increment* means to add 1 to a value. Since the only valid indices for this array are 0 to 3, we must test the value of index to see if it has exceeded the acceptable range. In other words, if index contains the value 4, we must set it back to 0 in order to make the banner images cycle back to the beginning of the sequence. Then our final task is to set a timer that will call the *cycle()* function again after 2000 milliseconds have elapsed (2000 milliseconds is equal to 2 seconds). Are you still with us so far?

Finally, the last thing we need to explain is how the whole cycling banner process gets started. If you take a close look at the <BODY> tag of our HTML document (in line 29 of the source code listing), you will see that we have inserted a new JavaScript event. This event is called *onLoad,* and it is triggered when the Web browser has finished loading the body of the HTML Web page. In this example, the browser loads the image called *lions.gif* (which is assigned the

---

Internet Milestone

Improving Programming Languages with Zero-Based Arrays

Arrays were invented to solve complex problems in defining elements in a program. Nearly every programming language supports the concept of arrays, but they don't all implement array indexing in the same way. If you define a 10-element array in other programming languages such as Basic, Fortran, or Pascal, for example, you would use index values of 1, 2, 3,... 10 to access those 10 elements. But some other languages (including C++, Java, and JavaScript) do not use this one-based indexing technique. Instead, they implement a zero-based technique that makes the valid array indices for a 10-element array 0, 1, 2,... 9. At first you might think that the one-based approach makes more sense because it is easier for novice programmers to understand. However, if you were to look at the low-level machine code generated by different language compilers, you would see that the one-based approach is less efficient for the computer hardware to process. This is one reason why professional programmers tend to use zero-based languages for their software development projects.

variable name *banner* by the NAME attribute), and then fires the *onLoad* event, which in turn causes the *cycle()* function to be invoked. The *cycle()* function will then be called continuously every 2 seconds in response to the JavaScript *setTimeout()* method, which is called inside the same function. Have you got it all straight now? You've learned a lot in this activity!

Displaying Random Images

In the previous activity, you learned how to display a sequence of graphic images in a specific order. There are also times when Web page designers want their images to appear in a random order. This approach is normally used when a particular Web site contains a large collection of graphic images, and the site owner would like the system to randomly select an image for display.

At first, you might assume that displaying images in a fixed sequence is much easier than displaying them in a random order. But this is not the case when you're programming in JavaScript. In fact, it actually requires fewer lines of code to display random images than it does to create a cycling banner. This is primarily due to JavaScript's built-in ability to support random number generation.

Since much of the source code for this activity is the same as for the previous activity, you'll be able to use your previous file and make just a few changes. In fact, all you will need to do is replace the cycle() function with a similar function called select(). You don't even need to worry about downloading graphics files to the correct folder because we will use the same images as in the previous activity. Are you ready for this?

STEP-BY-STEP 6.4

1. Open your text editor or word processor and retrieve the **js-eight.html** file you created in the previous Step-by-Step.

STEP-BY-STEP 6.4 Continued

2. Next, modify the HTML and JavaScript source code. Replace the **cycle()** function with the **select()** function, and modify the onLoad event in the <BODY> tag as shown in bold in Figure 6-7.

FIGURE 6-7
JavaScript code to display random images

```
<HTML>
<HEAD>
<TITLE>HTML and JavaScript</TITLE>
<SCRIPT>
var imgArray = new Array(4);
imgArray[0] = new Image;
imgArray[0].src = "lions.gif";
imgArray[1] = new Image;
imgArray[1].src = "tigers.gif";
imgArray[2] = new Image;
imgArray[2].src = "bears.gif";
imgArray[3] = new Image;
imgArray[3].src = "ohmy.gif";
var index = 0;

function select()
{
    index = Math.floor(Math.random() * 4);
    document.banner.src = imgArray[index].src;
    setTimeout("select()", 2000);
    return;
}
</SCRIPT>
</HEAD>
<BODY onLoad="select()">
<CENTER>
<IMG NAME="banner" SRC="lions.gif">
</CENTER>
</BODY>
</HTML>
```

3. Save this file in the appropriate folder as **js-nine.html**.

4. Open your Web browser if it is not already open.

5. View your **js-nine.html** page. Your Web page should look initially like Figure 6-6A, 6-6B, 6-6C, or 6-6D, and then the image should change every two seconds. Unlike the previous Step-by-Step, the images will not appear in a predictable order. Move on to the next section, or shut down your computer if you are finished for the day.

Analyzing the Code You Have Just Entered

Let's quickly review the JavaScript concepts that are introduced in Step-by-Step 6.4.

First, we changed the function name from cycle() to select() because it more accurately reflects the purpose and behavior of the function. As a result of this name change, we also need to modify the *onLoad* event statement in the HTML <BODY> tag so that it will invoke the proper function name. If we had failed to make this change, the Web browser would have responded with an unpleasant error message.

Second, we needed to include the appropriate JavaScript code to generate a random number, and then convert that number into a valid array index in the range 0 to 3. The JavaScript method random(), which is part of the Math object, is guaranteed to return a real number that is greater than or equal to 0.0 and less than 1.0. A *real number*, also called a floating-point number, is a numerical value that includes a decimal portion. Since the numbers in this restricted range are not usable as array indices, we need to scale them to the proper range. In this case, we have four elements in our array, so we multiply (with the * operator) the random value by 4. Now we have a real number that is guaranteed to be greater than or equal to 0.0 and less than 4.0. The final step is to invoke the Math.floor() method, which will eliminate the decimal part of the resulting number. This means that the only possible values remaining are 0, 1, 2, and 3, and these are exactly the values we need to use as array indices.

Just to be sure you feel comfortable with this process, let's walk through an example. Let's suppose that the first three times the select() function is called, the Math.random() method generates random values of 0.137, 0.8312, and 0.54. When we multiply these numbers by 4, the resulting values are 0.548, 3.3248, and 2.16, respectively. Then when we run these new real numbers through the Math.floor() method, the final numbers stored in the index variable will be 0, 3, and 2.

Obviously, these are all valid array index values, so the images displayed will be the contents of the files *lions.gif*, followed by *ohmy.gif*, and finally *bears.gif*. Or in other words, you would see Figure 6-6A, followed by Figure 6-6D, and finally Figure 6-6C on your screen. Do you understand?

Net Tip

HTML is not case sensitive. The browser will interpret <IMG>, <Img>, or <img> in the same way. However, this is not true of programming languages like JavaScript. When naming JavaScript objects, variables, or functions, you must make certain to use the same case each time, because the JavaScript interpreter will treat INDEX, index, and Index as three different variables. This will cause the variable name to be interpreted differently each time the script runs.

Creating a JavaScript Slide Show

In the previous two Step-by-Steps, we showed you how to create JavaScript programs that will automatically change the image on the screen every two seconds. But sometimes it is more desirable to let users decide for themselves when they want the image to change. When you allow the user to change the image by clicking on some object with the mouse, the end result is something akin to an electronic *slide show*.

In the next Step-by-Step, you will create a JavaScript program that will provide the user with two hyperlinks labeled <u>Back</u> and <u>Next</u>. When the user clicks on one of these links, the image displayed will change appropriately.

In order to accomplish this task, you will need to modify the *js-nine.html* file you created in the previous Step-by-Step. You will remove the select() function and insert two new functions named doBack() and doNext(). Then you will add some additional HTML tags to make the screen look good and to provide the user with the appropriate hyperlinks that will cause the slide show image to change. You are probably excited to get started on this exercise, so let's do it! For the sake of simplicity, we will be using the same graphic images that we used in the previous two exercises.

S TEP-BY-STEP 6.5

1. Open your text editor or word processor and retrieve the **js-nine.html** file you created in the previous activity.

2. Delete the **select()** function and replace it with two new functions called **doBack()** and **doNext()**.

3. Change the <BODY> tag by deleting the **onLoad** event and the call to the **select()** function.

4. Between the center tags, you'll need to add additional HTML tags and text shown in Figure 6-8 to make your slide show look good on the screen.

STEP-BY-STEP 6.5 Continued

5. When you are finished making your edits, the resulting file should look just like the source code listing shown in Figure 6-8.

FIGURE 6-8
JavaScript code needed to create a slide show

```
<HTML>
<HEAD>
<TITLE>HTML and JavaScript</TITLE>
<SCRIPT>
var imgArray = new Array(4);
imgArray[0] = new Image;
imgArray[0].src = "lions.gif";
imgArray[1] = new Image;
imgArray[1].src = "tigers.gif";
imgArray[2] = new Image;
imgArray[2].src = "bears.gif";
imgArray[3] = new Image;
imgArray[3].src = "ohmy.gif";
var index = 0;

function doBack()
{
    if   (index > 0)
    {
        index--;
        document.slideshow.src = imgArray[index].src;
    }
    return;
}

function doNext()
{
    if (index < 3)
    {
        index++;
        document.slideshow.src = imgArray[index].src;
    }
    return;
}
</SCRIPT>
</HEAD>
<BODY>
<CENTER>
<H2>My JavaScript Slide Show</H2>
<P>
```

STEP-BY-STEP 6.5 Continued

FIGURE 6-8 Continued
JavaScript code needed to create a slide show

```
<IMG NAME="slideshow" SRC="lions.gif">
<P>
<A HREF="javascript:doBack()">Back</A>
   
<A HREF="javascript:doNext()">Next</A>
</CENTER>
</BODY>
</HTML>
```

6. Save your new file as **js-ten.html**.

7. Open your Web browser and view your **js-ten.html** file. Your screen should initially look like Figure 6-9A. However, as you continually click the Next hyperlink, the image will change and look like Figures 6-9B, 6-9C, and 6-9D. Move on to the next section, or shut down your computer if you are finished for the day.

FIGURE 6-9A
The first image of your slide show

FIGURE 6-9B
The second image of your slide show

FIGURE 6-9C
The third image of your slide show

FIGURE 6-9D
The fourth image of your slide show

Analyzing the Code You Have Just Entered

Once again, we introduced new JavaScript concepts in the previous Step-by-Step, so let's run through them to make sure nothing gets by you. The first several lines of JavaScript code (lines 5 through 14) are the same as in the previous two Step-by-Steps, so you should feel comfortable with them by now. But you may not be completely familiar with everything in the doBack() and doNext() functions. Let's walk through them.

The first thing we do in the doBack() function is to test the value of the index variable. If it is greater than 0, then we know we are not displaying the first image in a slide show, so we need to back up to the previous image in the sequence. This is done by decrementing the value stored in index (with the -- operator) and then loading a new image source into the slideshow object of our HTML document. As you might expect, the term *decrement* means to subtract 1 from the current value of a variable. But you should know that if the current value of index is 0, then the doBack() function performs no action.

The content of the doNext() function is, of course, very similar to that of the doBack() function. We first check the value of index to see that its current value is less than 3. If it is, then we know we are not displaying the last image in our slide show sequence, so we need to change the image on the screen. This is done by incrementing the index variable, and then setting the src property of the slideshow object to the next image in the list. But if the value of index is 3, then the doNext() function performs no action.

If you have a firm understanding of the material in Lesson 1 through 4, then you should feel perfectly comfortable with most of the HTML code contained within the body tags of this Web page. However, there are a couple of things that you have not seen before, so let's explain them also.

You may have noticed that the HREF attribute of the Back hyperlink does not include our reference to another HTML document. Instead, it contains a reference to a JavaScript function named doBack(). This means that when the user clicks on this hyperlink, the Web browser will perform the specified function rather than loading a new HTML page! Neat stuff, isn't it?

The final item we would like to address in this lesson concerns the three cryptic symbols * * that occur on line 44 of the source code listing in Figure 6-8. Suffice it to say that the symbols are HTML commands that tell the Web browser to put a little extra space between the Back hyperlink and the Next hyperlink. They are not required for this JavaScript program to function correctly, but they improve the appearance of the page somewhat. Feel free to remove this line from your file if you wish.

 Net Ethics

Copyright Code Infringement

We mentioned in Lesson 3 that it is very unethical for Web page developers to download copyrighted images from commercial Web sites and then use those images for their own purposes. This obviously holds true whether the images are used in standard HTML pages or in JavaScript pages. But when you start developing JavaScript enhanced Web pages, you should also be aware that script piracy is just as unethical as picture piracy. In fact, it is not just unethical, it is also illegal! Although downloading and studying script that has been created by other people is sometimes a great way to learn JavaScript, you must keep in mind that the copyright laws still apply. You should feel free to use publicly accessible JavaScript code for educational purposes, but you should not simply copy scripts from someone else's Web site to use on your own unless you receive the owner's permission to do so.

SUMMARY

In this lesson you learned:

- You can understand the names and uses of JavaScript events.
- To create an image rollover.
- To make a hyperlink rollover.
- To build a cycling banner.
- To display random images.
- To create a JavaScript slide show.

VOCABULARY *Review*

Define the following terms:

Array	Image rollover	Real number (floating-point
Cycling banner (ad banner)	Increment	number)
Decrement	Index	Slide show
Event	Instantiate (see Web Project	Variable
Function	on page 165)	
Hyperlink rollover		

REVIEW *Questions*

TRUE/FALSE

Circle T if the statement is true or F if the statement is false.

T   F   **1.** Conditions that fire or trigger events are always caused by the user.

T   F   **2.** <SCRIPT></SCRIPT> tags can appear in the header section of an HTML document.

T   F   **3.** After a variable has been named, it can be used throughout an HTML document to refer to that particular value or object.

T   F   **4.** All rollovers are hyperlink images.

T   F   **5.** The JavaScript method random() will return a real or floating-point number.

FILL IN THE BLANK

Complete the following sentences by writing the correct word or words in the blanks provided.

1. A(n) _____ is a system-level response to the occurrence of some specific condition.

2. A(n) _____ is nothing more than a segment of JavaScript code that can be called, just like the document.write() method.

3. An image _____ is created with the help of the *onMouseOver* and *onMouseOut* events.

4. A JavaScript _____ is nothing more than a name that is assigned to a literal value or to an object.

5. _____ banners are also known as ad banners.

WRITTEN QUESTIONS

Write a brief answer to the following questions.

1. What is a JavaScript event? How are events generated?

2. What is a JavaScript function? How does a function differ from a method?

3. How does an image rollover differ from a hyperlink rollover?

4. What is a cycling banner? Why is it called "cycling"?

5. What is the purpose of the Math object methods random() and floor()?

6. What is a JavaScript electronic slide show?

PROJECTS

 PROJECT 6-1

In this project, GreatApplications, Inc., has just hired you to replace a JavaScript programmer who recently left the company for a higher paying job. Unfortunately, your predecessor left an important project unfinished. You must fix the script created in Step-by-Step 6.1. You may have noticed that if you click the mouse button when your mouse pointer is over the arrow image, your Web browser displays an error message. Why do you suppose this happens? Well, if you think about it for a minute, the arrow image was defined as a hyperlink in this document, and the purpose of a hyperlink is to tell the browser to load a new HTML document when the user clicks on it.

Look carefully at the HREF attribute in your <A HREF=> tag and attribute. What Web page file will the browser try to load if you click on this particular hyperlink? Obviously, the answer is the webpage.html file. But does this file really exist? Of course not; someone will need to create it, right? We think that someone should be you!

Go ahead and create an exciting HTML page and save it with the name **webpage.html**. Then, view your js-six.html page again and verify that your browser will really display your new page by clicking on the arrow image as it changes color. Don't forget that your new file must be saved in the same folder as your js-six.html file.

  TEAMWORK PROJECT

The management team of GreatApplications, Inc., has decided that they want to create an Electronic Zoo, and they want to make it available to the public on their corporate Web site. Consequently, they have given your team the assignment of creating a JavaScript slide show that contains the images of many different types of animals. Form and organize teams of three or four members. Each member should spend some time searching the Web for suitable animal images, and then you must create a JavaScript slide show program to display them. Start with the source code listed in Figure 6-8, and then make the necessary modifications to get the program to display the animal images that you have collected. Some things you might want to change include:

■ The Web page title

■ The image file names

■ The size (dimensions) of your slide show window

Save your team's work as **js-test7.html**.

WEB PROJECT

In the Teamwork project you found out how easy it is to replace graphics and to change the look and feel of your slide show. Let's suppose for a moment that instead of just four graphic images, your collection has increased to eight. What changes would you need to make in your JavaScript program to make it work properly with eight images? To start with, you would need to change your array size from four to eight. Then, you will need to learn a new word, *instantiate*, which is the process of creating a new object and assigning it a value. You will need to instantiate the four new array elements just like you did for the first four in Step-by-Step 6.5. What do you suppose would be the valid index values for the four new array elements? If you guessed 4, 5, 6 and 7 you're absolutely right! After you have completed this step, though, you still need to modify the code further. Can you recognize what needs to change? What about changing the last index value in the doNext() function?

Save your work as **js-test8.html**.

CRITICAL *Thinking*

 ACTIVITY 6-1

In Step-by-Step 6.3, we showed you how to create a cycling banner, or ad banner, as it is sometimes called. We also mentioned that numerous commercial Web sites include ad banners, usually at the top of their Web pages. But one thing we haven't explained is the reason there are so many sites like this online. It basically boils down to a monetary issue. The owner of the site will charge companies a certain amount to include their advertisements on the host Web pages. In this way, many Web sites can provide services to their users, but still cover their own operating costs. Analyze some of these Web sites by considering the following questions:

1. What types of businesses might choose to pay other companies to host their ad banners?

2. What types of products and services are most likely to be advertised in this manner?

3. Why do you suppose most ad banners are defined as hyperlinks?

4. What types of Web sites are most likely to host ad banners?

 ACTIVITY 6-2

In Step-by-Step 6.1, we showed you how to create a rollover that reacts when the mouse passes over an image. In Step-by-Step 6.2, we showed you how to create a rollover that changes the color of the arrow when the mouse pointer passes over a hyperlink. But now we want to know if you can create a rollover that would react to either condition.

Can you make a small modification in your js-seven.html file that will cause the arrow image to change color when the mouse passes over either the hyperlink or the arrow? Of course you can! All you need to do is move one HTML tag from its current position to a new position. But which one? By examining and thinking about the code, can you figure out what tag needs to be moved and where it needs to go? Try it!

Save your work as **js-test9.html**.

SCANS **ACTIVITY 6-3**

In Step-by-Step 6.3 (**js-eight.html**) you used a timeout value of 2000 milliseconds. But sometimes different values can be more effective. Try changing the delay value in the setTimeout() method called to see what effect different numbers will have.

Save your work as **js-test10.html**.

If you are extremely clever, take this exercise a little further. You may recognize the fact that there may be occasions when providing a different delay value for each image in the banner sequence could be desirable. If you are feeling up to the challenge, try creating a second four-element array in the header section of your HTML document called delay. Then assign different values to each element in the new array (such as 1000, 4000, 3000, and 2000), and use these values in the setTimeout() method call. That is, replace the constant value 2000 with the variable name delay[index]. If you can complete this task correctly, then you are well on your way to understanding the fundamentals of JavaScript arrays. You should be proud of yourself!

Save your more advanced work as **js-test10advanced.html**.

SCANS **ACTIVITY 6-4**

Sometimes Web designers like to create slide shows that function in a circular fashion rather than in a linear way. This means that whenever the user reaches either end of the image sequence, the program will jump to the opposite end and continue displaying the images. In other words, if the user is currently viewing the first page in the slide show sequence and she clicks on the back hyperlink, the next image display will be the last image in the set. Similarly, when the user is viewing the last image in the sequence and then clicks on the next hyperlink, she will immediately see the first slide show image. Do you think that you can modify your js-ten.html file to operate in this way? We're sure you can do it! If the answer isn't immediately obvious to you, go back to study the JavaScript cycle() function in Step-by-Step 6.3. It should tell you all you need to know!

Save your work as **js-test11.html**.

SCANS **SUMMARY** *Project*

In this lesson you learned many valuable JavaScript skills that allow you to create cycling banners, random image displays, and electronic "slide shows." You should recognize, however, that these techniques are not mutually exclusive. In other words, you do not necessarily have to choose only one of these techniques for a given Web page. If you wish, you can use all three techniques together. Demonstrate that you have mastered all of the concepts presented in this lesson by creating a Web page that uses all three of these JavaScript image techniques. When you are finished, your Web page should look something like Figure 6-10.

FIGURE 6-10
A Web page containing three JavaScript image techniques

PROJECT REQUIREMENTS

■ Use the same image files you downloaded for Step-by-Step 6.3.

■ Create a cycling banner in the upper third of your Web page.

■ Create a random image display in the middle third of your Web page.

■ Create a slide show in the lower third of your Web page.

■ Devise a way to get both the cycling banner and the random image display started when your Web page loads.

CREATING FORMS WITH JAVASCRIPT

OBJECTIVES

Upon completion of this lesson, you should be able to:

- Understand the purpose and usage of JavaScript input controls.

- Understand the benefits of data validation.

- Create an HTML form.

- Enhance the functionality of HTML forms with JavaScript.

Estimated Time: 2 hours

VOCABULARY

Check box

Controls/components

Data validation

Radio button

Text field

Making HTML Forms More Functional

In Lesson 3, you received a brief introduction to HTML forms. In this lesson we will begin by reviewing the information presented in Lesson 3 and then show you how JavaScript can enhance the capabilities of HTML forms.

We begin the process of creating a fully functional, robust form by defining the general layout of the form on a Web page. This step is accomplished by using the appropriate HTML tags as described in Lesson 3. The next step is to identify the various objects in the HTML form with which the user will interact. Each of these interactive objects (also called *controls* or *components*) must be given a name so that it can be referenced within JavaScript code. Then the final step is to write the JavaScript functions that will be invoked when the user triggers a specific JavaScript event.

One of the most important concepts you will learn in this lesson is the idea of data validation. *Data validation* is simply the process of checking user input data to make sure that it is complete and accurate. Although it is not always possible to catch every error a user might make when filling out a form, there are many kinds of mistakes that can be detected. For example, if the user forgets to fill out a portion of a form, it is an easy task for JavaScript to detect the absence of required data and alert the user accordingly.

In order for you to learn these JavaScript form-processing concepts effectively, we would like you to pretend that you work for a newly established pizza company called The JavaScript Pizza Parlor. As an employee of this new company, your job will be to create a Web page that will allow customers to place their pizza orders over the Internet. As you work through the following Step-by-Steps, you will learn how to make your electronic order form better and better.

We're sure you can't wait to get started, so here we go!

Creating a Pizza Order Form

The first step in creating an effective order form for The JavaScript Pizza Parlor is to define its appearance on the Web page with the appropriate HTML tags. In the following Step-by-Step, you'll use several tags and attributes that were introduced in Lesson 3 to make your form look appealing and well organized. The completed form will consist of nothing more than headings, labels, and user input controls, but it takes time and practice to make them all look good on the screen. Take note of the ways in which the heading, font, and break tags are used to control the final appearance of the pizza order form.

You should also pay close attention to the NAME attribute that appears in several of the HTML tags used in Step-by-Step 7.1. Although these names do not affect the appearance of the form at all, they are critical elements of the document. They will be used extensively by the JavaScript functions you will create in subsequent Step-by-Steps.

STEP-BY-STEP 7.1

1. Open your text editor or word processor and enter the HTML code exactly as it appears in Figure 7-1.

FIGURE 7-1
HTML code to create a pizza order form

```
<HTML>
<HEAD>
<TITLE>HTML and JavaScript</TITLE>
</HEAD>
<BODY>
<FORM NAME="PizzaForm">
<H1>The JavaScript Pizza Parlor</H1>
<BR>
<H4>Step 1: Enter your name, address, and phone number:</H4>
<FONT FACE="Courier">
Name:    <INPUT NAME="customer" TYPE="TEXT" SIZE=50><BR>
Address: <INPUT NAME="address" TYPE="TEXT" SIZE=50><BR>
City:    <INPUT NAME="city" TYPE="TEXT" SIZE=16>
State: <INPUT NAME="state" TYPE="TEXT" SIZE=4>
Zip: <INPUT NAME="zip" TYPE="TEXT" SIZE=8><BR>
Phone:   <INPUT NAME="phone" TYPE="TEXT" SIZE=50><BR>
</FONT>
<BR><BR>
<H4>Step 2: Select the size of pizza you want:</H4>
<FONT FACE="Courier">
<INPUT NAME="size" TYPE="RADIO">Small
<INPUT NAME="size" TYPE="RADIO">Medium
<INPUT NAME="size" TYPE="RADIO">Large<BR>
</FONT>
<BR><BR>
<H4>Step 3: Select the pizza toppings you want:</H4>
<FONT FACE="Courier">
<INPUT NAME="toppings" TYPE="CHECKBOX">Pepperoni
<INPUT NAME="toppings" TYPE="CHECKBOX">Canadian Bacon
<INPUT NAME="toppings" TYPE="CHECKBOX">Sausage<BR>
<INPUT NAME="toppings" TYPE="CHECKBOX">Mushrooms
<INPUT NAME="toppings" TYPE="CHECKBOX">Pineapple
<INPUT NAME="toppings" TYPE="CHECKBOX">Black Olives<BR>
</FONT>
<BR><BR>
<INPUT TYPE="BUTTON" VALUE="Submit Order">
<INPUT TYPE="BUTTON" VALUE="Clear Entries">
</FORM>
</BODY>
</HTML>
```

2. Save this file in the appropriate folder as **js-eleven.html**.

3. Open your Web browser if it isn't already open.

STEP-BY-STEP 7.1 Continued

4. View your **js-eleven.html** file. Your Web page should look like Figure 7-2.

FIGURE 7-2
An HTML pizza order form

5. Continue to the next section or close your software and shut down your computer if you're finished for the day.

Analyzing the Code You Have Just Entered

As we indicated before, all of the HTML tags used in Step-by-Step 7.1 were previously introduced in Lesson 3. But, to make sure you understand everything completely, let's review some of these concepts before continuing to the JavaScript portion of this lesson. Since the form itself is divided into three sections (or steps), let's take a closer look at each section to see exactly how it works.

The section we call Step 1 consists of a heading and six labeled text fields. A *text field* is an input control that allows the user to key a string value into a specific location on the Web page. Each text field is assigned a name and a size. The * * symbols are used to align the left edges of the Name, Address, City, and Phone fields.

The Step 2 section is composed of a heading and three labeled radio buttons. A *radio button* is an input control that allows the user to select just one option from a set of options. In this case, the radio buttons are labeled Small, Medium, and Large to correspond to the available pizza sizes. The Web browser will treat these three options as a set because they all have been given the same name (*size*).

The final section, called Step 3, consists of the heading and six labeled check boxes. A *check box* is an input control that allows the user to select any number of options from a set of options. As is the case with Step 2, these check boxes were given labels that correspond to the six kinds of pizza toppings available. The Web browser will also treat these six options as a set because they all have been assigned the name *toppings*.

The final part of this pizza order form contains two buttons that are located at the bottom of the page, labeled Submit Order and Clear Entries. These input controls are defined with the <INPUT> tag just like the other controls, but the TYPE attribute is set to BUTTON rather than TEXT, RADIO, or CHECKBOX. If you try to click either of these controls, you will find that they currently do not perform any action. Making these buttons functional is the object of the next two Step-by-Steps.

Making the Submit Order Button Functional

Now that we have a solid HTML foundation for our pizza order form, let's start adding some extra functionality with JavaScript. The first thing we will do is to add a JavaScript function that will be invoked (called) when the user clicks the Submit Order button. In this case, we will simply display an alert box to let the user know that his or her pizza order has been submitted to The JavaScript Pizza Parlor. This is an important part of our form because it is usually a good idea to let the user know what the program is doing.

In order to get the Submit Order button to call a JavaScript function when it is clicked, you'll need to make use of a new JavaScript event. As you might expect, this event is called *onClick*, and it is triggered whenever an input control of type BUTTON is clicked.

Now that you know what needs to be done, go ahead and do it!

STEP-BY-STEP 7.2

1. Open your text editor or word processor and retrieve the **js-eleven.html** file you created in the previous activity.

2. Add the **doSubmit()** JavaScript function definition, as shown in bold in Figure 7-3.

STEP-BY-STEP 7.2 Continued

3. Add the **onClick** event statement to the <INPUT> tag that defines the Submit Order button. This change is also shown in bold in Figure 7-3.

FIGURE 7-3
A pizza order form with a functional Submit Order button

```
<HTML>
<HEAD>
<TITLE>HTML and JavaScript</TITLE>
<SCRIPT>
function doSubmit()
{
 alert("Your pizza order has been submitted.");
 return;
}
</SCRIPT>
</HEAD>
<BODY>
<FORM NAME="PizzaForm">
<H1>The JavaScript Pizza Parlor</H1>
<BR>
<H4>Step 1: Enter your name, address, and phone number:</H4>
<FONT FACE="Courier">
Name:    <INPUT NAME="customer" TYPE="TEXT" SIZE=50><BR>
Address: <INPUT NAME="address" TYPE="TEXT" SIZE=50><BR>
City:    <INPUT NAME="city" TYPE="TEXT" SIZE=16>
State: <INPUT NAME="state" TYPE="TEXT" SIZE=4>
Zip: <INPUT NAME="zip" TYPE="TEXT" SIZE=8><BR>
Phone:   <INPUT NAME="phone" TYPE="TEXT" SIZE=50><BR>
</FONT>
<BR><BR>
<H4>Step 2: Select the size of pizza you want:</H4>
<FONT FACE="Courier">
<INPUT NAME="size" TYPE="RADIO">Small
<INPUT NAME="size" TYPE="RADIO">Medium
<INPUT NAME="size" TYPE="RADIO">Large<BR>
</FONT>
<BR><BR>
<H4>Step 3: Select the pizza toppings you want:</H4>
<FONT FACE="Courier">
<INPUT NAME="toppings" TYPE="CHECKBOX">Pepperoni
<INPUT NAME="toppings" TYPE="CHECKBOX">Canadian Bacon
<INPUT NAME="toppings" TYPE="CHECKBOX">Sausage<BR>
<INPUT NAME="toppings" TYPE="CHECKBOX">Mushrooms
<INPUT NAME="toppings" TYPE="CHECKBOX">Pineapple
<INPUT NAME="toppings" TYPE="CHECKBOX">Black Olives<BR>
</FONT>
<BR><BR>
<INPUT TYPE="BUTTON" VALUE="Submit Order" onClick="doSubmit()">
```

STEP-BY-STEP 7.2 Continued

FIGURE 7-3 (continued)

```
<INPUT TYPE="BUTTON" VALUE="Clear Entries">
</FORM>
</BODY>
</HTML>
```

4. Save your new file as **js-twelve.html**.

5. Open your Web browser and view your **js-twelve.html** file. Your screen should look initially like Figure 7-2, but when you click the Submit Order button, an alert box should be displayed, as shown in Figure 7-4.

> **Important**
>
> Users of Windows XP with Service Pack 2 installed may see a warning about active content. Simply click OK to acknowledge the warning, then follow the prompts to enable JavaScript.

FIGURE 7-4
The pizza order form after the Submit Order button is clicked

6. Continue to the next section or close your software and shut down your computer if you're finished for the day.

Analyzing the Code You Have Just Entered

If you think about the code you just keyed for a moment, you should recognize the fact that there is not much new. The doSubmit() function you just added does nothing more than call the JavaScript alert() method, which was described in Lesson 5. And the concept of defining a JavaScript function was covered in some detail in Lesson 6. Consequently, you should feel very comfortable with this part of your program.

As for the *onClick* event you added to the submit button <INPUT> tag, it also looks and acts just like the *onMouseOver, onMouseOut*, and *onLoad* events you used in Lesson 6. In other words, you should have had no trouble at all understanding the concepts presented in Step-by-Step 7.2. At least we hope you had no trouble!

Making the Clear Entries Button Functional

You probably know from personal experience that it is very common for people to make mistakes while filling out paper forms. Unfortunately, this is also true of electronic forms, especially when they require a large amount of information to be entered. For this reason, it is customary for Web page designers to include some type of clear button that allows the user to erase form entries with a single click.

In the case of our pizza order form, it would be nice to give the customer the ability to clear the form after an order has been submitted. Then, a second order could be placed without having to change all of the existing data one field at a time.

In order to accomplish this task, you will need to add another function to your HTML/JavaScript document called *doClear()*. Next, you should add an *onClick* event to the <INPUT> tag of the Clear Entries button, just as you did for the Submit Order button in the previous Step-by-Step. This event will call the *doClear()* function to erase any existing form data. Got it?

S TEP-BY-STEP 7.3

1. Open your text editor or word processor and retrieve the **js-twelve.html** file you created in the previous Step-by-Step.

 Netiquette

Over the past two decades, many software developers have learned the importance of giving users adequate feedback. In other words, it is essential for programmers to give the user some kind of visual (or sometimes audio) clue as to what the program is doing or when it has completed its operation. Think about it for a minute. What do you suppose an average computer user would do if he or she clicked the Submit Order button on an electronic form and nothing happened?

Unless a message appears to confirm that the order has actually been submitted, a user would probably click the button again. Maybe the customer might click it several more times in hopes of receiving some response. Some other users might even erroneously conclude that their computer has stopped responding and needs to be rebooted!

This is an especially significant issue when a program has to perform an operation that takes a long time to complete. When your Web browser is downloading large graphic images over a slow Internet connection, for example, it is essential for the JavaScript program to give some kind of visual feedback to let you know it is actually doing something. Otherwise you would see a lot of impatient users rebooting their computers for no reason. So, please be considerate of users and design your JavaScript programs to give lots of appropriate feedback.

STEP-BY-STEP 7.3 Continued

2. Just above the closing script tag, add the JavaScript code for the **doClear()** function, as shown in bold in Figure 7-5.

3. Next, add the **onClick** event to the <INPUT> tag of the Clear Entries button, also shown in bold in Figure 7-5.

FIGURE 7-5
A pizza order form with a functional Clear Entries button

```
<HTML>
<HEAD>
<TITLE>HTML and JavaScript</TITLE>
<SCRIPT>
function doSubmit()
{
 alert("Your pizza order has been submitted.");
 return;
}

function doClear()
{
 document.PizzaForm.customer.value = "";
 document.PizzaForm.address.value = "";
 document.PizzaForm.city.value = "";
 document.PizzaForm.state.value = "";
 document.PizzaForm.zip.value = "";
 document.PizzaForm.phone.value = "";
 document.PizzaForm.size[0].checked = false;
 document.PizzaForm.size[1].checked = false;
 document.PizzaForm.size[2].checked = false;
 document.PizzaForm.toppings[0].checked = false;
 document.PizzaForm.toppings[1].checked = false;
 document.PizzaForm.toppings[2].checked = false;
 document.PizzaForm.toppings[3].checked = false;
 document.PizzaForm.toppings[4].checked = false;
 document.PizzaForm.toppings[5].checked = false;
 return;
}
</SCRIPT>
</HEAD>
<BODY>
<FORM NAME="PizzaForm">
<H1>The JavaScript Pizza Parlor</H1>
<BR>
<H4>Step 1: Enter your name, address, and phone number:</H4>
<FONT FACE="Courier">
Name:    <INPUT NAME="customer" TYPE="TEXT" SIZE=50><BR>
Address: <INPUT NAME="address" TYPE="TEXT" SIZE=50><BR>
City:    <INPUT NAME="city" TYPE="TEXT" SIZE=16>
State: <INPUT NAME="state" TYPE="TEXT" SIZE=4>
```

STEP-BY-STEP 7.3 Continued

FIGURE 7-5 (continued)

```
Zip: <INPUT NAME="zip" TYPE="TEXT" SIZE=8><BR>
Phone:   <INPUT NAME="phone" TYPE="TEXT" SIZE=50><BR>
</FONT>
<BR><BR>
<H4>Step 2: Select the size of pizza you want:</H4>
<FONT FACE="Courier">
<INPUT NAME="size" TYPE="RADIO">Small
<INPUT NAME="size" TYPE="RADIO">Medium
<INPUT NAME="size" TYPE="RADIO">Large<BR>
</FONT>
<BR><BR>
<H4>Step 3: Select the pizza toppings you want:</H4>
<FONT FACE="Courier">
<INPUT NAME="toppings" TYPE="CHECKBOX">Pepperoni
<INPUT NAME="toppings" TYPE="CHECKBOX">Canadian Bacon
<INPUT NAME="toppings" TYPE="CHECKBOX">Sausage<BR>
<INPUT NAME="toppings" TYPE="CHECKBOX">Mushrooms
<INPUT NAME="toppings" TYPE="CHECKBOX">Pineapple
<INPUT NAME="toppings" TYPE="CHECKBOX">Black Olives<BR>
</FONT>
<BR><BR>
<INPUT TYPE="BUTTON" VALUE="Submit Order" onClick="doSubmit()">
<INPUT TYPE="BUTTON" VALUE="Clear Entries" onClick="doClear()">
</FORM>
</BODY>
</HTML>
```

4. Save this file in the appropriate folder as **js-thirteen.html**.

5. Open your Web browser if it is not already open.

6. View your **js-thirteen.html** page. Your Web page should initially look like Figure 7-2.

7. Next, key your information into the text fields of Step 1.

8. Choose a pizza size in Step 2 of your online form.

9. Select several toppings in Step 3 of your online form.

10. Now click the **Clear Entries** button at the bottom of your form. The entire form should instantly become blank, and then look like Figure 7-2 again.

11. Continue to the next section or close your software and shut down your computer if you're finished for the day.

Analyzing the Code You Have Just Entered

As you can see, the steps required to make the Clear Entries button functional are very similar to those we used to make the Submit Order button active. However, some new concepts are introduced in the doClear() function that are important for you to understand. So let's take a closer look at what these JavaScript statements are doing.

The first statement of the doClear() function makes use of the *value* property of the TEXT input control object. In this particular case, the text control is assigned the name *customer*, and it is an element within the FORM object that we named *PizzaForm*. The form object, in turn, is contained with the document object that we first introduced in Lesson 5. Therefore, we can easily clear the value stored in that text field by assigning an empty string ("") to the *document.PizzaForm.customer.value* property.

The next five statements of the doClear() function perform essentially the same action, except that they reference the text control objects named *address*, *city*, *state*, *zip*, and *phone*. Since these five controls also belong to the FORM object within the HTML document, they are referenced with a *document.PizzaForm* prefix. In addition, we clear these five controls by assigning an empty string to their value property, just like we did with the *customer* field.

Clearing the pizza size value in Step 2 is performed in a similar fashion, but there's a new concept at work here. Since we gave all three RADIO input controls the same name (*size*), the JavaScript interpreter will treat them as an array of objects. This means that we must use an index value to indicate which radio button we wish to access. The index values assigned to the array elements will always start at 0, and they will increase sequentially for each new element encountered. In this case, the radio buttons labeled *Small*, *Medium*, and *Large* will be assigned index values of 0, 1, and 2 respectively. Each of these objects contains a property called *checked* that indicates whether the option is selected or not. We can clear all of these options simply by setting their checked property to the logical value *false*.

Technology Careers

As you work through the various activities in this lesson, you may wonder how an actual pizza business would receive orders by means of a Web page. After all, the JavaScript code in these programs does nothing more than display various items of information on the screen. There are no programmed instructions included in these examples that would actually cause the data entered into the form to be sent to another location, right? Well, you can rest assured that JavaScript is capable of sending information to another location. This data transfer normally travels through a Common Gateway Interface (CGI) that resides on a Web server somewhere. When the server receives the form data, it is processed by another program that is typically written in CGI script.

CGI script looks a lot like JavaScript code, and it is processed in an interpretive fashion, just like JavaScript. CGI script programs are capable of many different functions, but they are most frequently used to update a database system. This means that the pizza company, or any other type of business for that matter, can use any number of software packages to collect information from electronic forms that are distributed over the Web. But the main point we want to make here is that CGI script programs do not appear out of thin air. Someone has to write them, and that someone could be you! Individuals who can add knowledge of CGI scripting to their JavaScript coding skills should have a relatively easy time finding a job in the software field. Think about it!

The pizza topping options of Step 3 work just like the pizza size options of Step 2. Since we have defined six of these CHECKBOX objects with the same name (*toppings*), they are treated as a six-element array. Their index values are, of course, assigned as 0 through 5, and they are cleared when their checked property is set to false. Got it?

Validating Text Fields

Practically every business that provides its customers with electronic forms has the need to validate the data those customers enter in some way. Consider The JavaScript Pizza Parlor for example. What good will it do a pizza business to receive an order form with the address field left blank? How could they possibly deliver a pizza to an unknown address? Or even worse, what if an inconsiderate prankster decided to submit dozens of pizza orders that were left completely blank? Scenarios like these would cause the business more harm than good.

For the sake of the next Step-by-Step, let's assume that the owner of the JavaScript Pizza Parlor would like your JavaScript program to accept only orders that have valid data in the customer, address, city, and phone fields. If a customer attempts to submit an order with any one of these fields left blank, the program will display an appropriate error message.

This is one type of data validation we promised you would learn about in this lesson. So, let's get busy coding.

STEP-BY-STEP 7.4

1. Open your text editor or word processor and retrieve the **js-thirteen.html** file you created in the previous Step-by-Step.

2. Add an **if** statement to the *doSubmit()* function, as shown in bold in Figure 7-6.

3. Next, just before the closing script tag, add the **validateText()** JavaScript function, as shown in bold in Figure 7-6.

FIGURE 7-6
A JavaScript form that validates text fields

```
<HTML>
<HEAD>
<TITLE>HTML and JavaScript</TITLE>
<SCRIPT>
function doSubmit()
{
   if (validateText() == false)
   {
      alert("Required data missing in Step 1");
      return;
   }
   alert("Your pizza order has been submitted.");
   return;
}
```

STEP-BY-STEP 7.4 Continued

FIGURE 7-6 (continued)

```
function doClear()
{
 document.PizzaForm.customer.value = "";
 document.PizzaForm.address.value = "";
 document.PizzaForm.city.value = "";
 document.PizzaForm.state.value = "";
 document.PizzaForm.zip.value = "";
 document.PizzaForm.phone.value = "";
 document.PizzaForm.size[0].checked = false;
 document.PizzaForm.size[1].checked = false;
 document.PizzaForm.size[2].checked = false;
 document.PizzaForm.toppings[0].checked = false;
 document.PizzaForm.toppings[1].checked = false;
 document.PizzaForm.toppings[2].checked = false;
 document.PizzaForm.toppings[3].checked = false;
 document.PizzaForm.toppings[4].checked = false;
 document.PizzaForm.toppings[5].checked = false;
 return;
}

function validateText()
{
 if (document.PizzaForm.customer.value == "") return false;
 if (document.PizzaForm.address.value == "") return false;
 if (document.PizzaForm.city.value == "") return false;
 if (document.PizzaForm.phone.value == "") return false;
 return true;
}
</SCRIPT>
</HEAD>
<BODY>
<FORM NAME="PizzaForm">
<H1>The JavaScript Pizza Parlor</H1>
<BR>
<H4>Step 1: Enter your name, address, and phone number:</H4>
<FONT FACE="Courier">
Name:    <INPUT NAME="customer" TYPE="TEXT" SIZE=50><BR>
Address: <INPUT NAME="address" TYPE="TEXT" SIZE=50><BR>
City:    <INPUT NAME="city" TYPE="TEXT" SIZE=16>
State: <INPUT NAME="state" TYPE="TEXT" SIZE=4>
Zip: <INPUT NAME="zip" TYPE="TEXT" SIZE=8><BR>
Phone:   <INPUT NAME="phone" TYPE="TEXT" SIZE=50><BR>
</FONT>
<BR><BR>
<H4>Step 2: Select the size of pizza you want:</H4>
<FONT FACE="Courier">
<INPUT NAME="size" TYPE="RADIO">Small
<INPUT NAME="size" TYPE="RADIO">Medium
```

STEP-BY-STEP 7.4 Continued

FIGURE 7-6 (continued)

```
<INPUT NAME="size" TYPE="RADIO">Large<BR>
</FONT>
<BR><BR>
<H4>Step 3: Select the pizza toppings you want:</H4>
<FONT FACE="Courier">
<INPUT NAME="toppings" TYPE="CHECKBOX">Pepperoni
<INPUT NAME="toppings" TYPE="CHECKBOX">Canadian Bacon
<INPUT NAME="toppings" TYPE="CHECKBOX">Sausage<BR>
<INPUT NAME="toppings" TYPE="CHECKBOX">Mushrooms
<INPUT NAME="toppings" TYPE="CHECKBOX">Pineapple
<INPUT NAME="toppings" TYPE="CHECKBOX">Black Olives<BR>
</FONT>
<BR><BR>
<INPUT TYPE="BUTTON" VALUE="Submit Order" onClick="doSubmit()">
<INPUT TYPE="BUTTON" VALUE="Clear Entries" onClick="doClear()">
</FORM>
</BODY>
</HTML>
```

4. Save this modified file as **js-fourteen.html**.

5. Open your Web browser and view your **js-fourteen.html** file. If you enter a value for all of the required fields and click the Submit Order button, you should see a confirmation message, as shown in Figure 7-4. However, if any one of the required text fields is left blank, you will see an error message, as shown in Figure 7-7.

FIGURE 7-7
A text field validation error message

STEP-BY-STEP 7.4 Continued

6. Continue to the next section or close your software and shut down your computer if you're finished for the day.

Analyzing the Code You Have Just Entered

As is often the case, we have added a relatively small amount of JavaScript code to our Web page, but this code illustrates a couple of important concepts.

First, the *validateText()* function is a little different from any other function you have written up to now because it returns a value. Returning a value means that whenever any other function is called (in the doSubmit() function in this case), its name is essentially replaced by the value it returns. The validateText() function can only return one of two possible values: *false* or *true*. The *false* value is returned if the value property of the *customer* object, the *address* object, the *city* object, or the *phone* object is an empty string. That is, the *false* value is returned if any one of these fields is left blank. If none of the required text fields are blank, then the function returns the *true* value.

Second, the return value of the validateText() function is compared to the value *false* by the new *if* statement in the doSubmit() function. If the return value is false, then the doSubmit() function displays an alert box to let the user know that he or she has left a required text field blank. Otherwise, the user will see a different alert box confirming that the pizza order has been submitted. Is this concept clear to you now?

Internet Milestone

Assignment vs. Comparison

You may have noticed that many of the JavaScript statements in this lesson use a single equal sign (=), while others use two equal signs (= =). The reason for this is that all programming languages must make a distinction between assigning a value to a variable and comparing the content of a variable to some other value. In the case of C, C++, Java, and JavaScript, the assignment operation is accomplished with the "=" character, while the comparison operation is performed by two "= =" characters.

So what happens if you confuse these two operators? Well, the answer depends on the language you're using. For many years, the C and C++ languages have been criticized because they allow the programmer to easily confuse the assignment operator with the comparison operator. This type of mistake is usually difficult to find because the program will compile and run just fine, but it will yield unexpected results.

The Java language designers, however, took this common pitfall into account when they defined its syntax rules. As a result, you'll see a compilation error if you attempt to use the wrong operator. Unfortunately, the architects of JavaScript did not follow the Java experts in this regard. Like C and C++, JavaScript will use the wrong operator without a single complaint. Unexpected or erratic program behavior is the only clue you will get when you make this kind of mistake, so please use extreme caution in this regard!

Validating Radio Buttons

Now that you know how to check for blank text fields, let's consider another type of data validation. In Step 2 of our pizza order form, we ask the customer to select the size of pizza he or she wants. But what will happen if the customer fails to do this? As of now, the order will be submitted whether this information is available or not. This means that the person who receives the order at The JavaScript Pizza Parlor will have no idea what size of pizza the customer wants.

Fortunately, we will be adding some new JavaScript code in the next Step-by-Step that will prevent this situation from occurring. All we have to do is add another data validation function to the program and a new *if* statement to the existing doSubmit() function.

Are you ready to complete the final activity in this lesson? Then let's go for it!

S TEP-BY-STEP 7.5

1. Open your text editor or word processor and retrieve the **js-fourteen.html** file you created in the previous Step-by-Step.

2. Add a new **if** statement to the doSubmit() function, as shown in bold in Figure 7-8.

3. Next, insert a new function called **validateRadio()** just before the </SCRIPT> tag in your file, as shown in bold in Figure 7-8.

FIGURE 7-8
A JavaScript form that validates radio button selections

```
<HTML>
<HEAD>
<TITLE>HTML and JavaScript</TITLE>
<SCRIPT>
function doSubmit()
{
    if (validateText() == false)
    {
        alert("Required data missing in Step 1");
        return;
    }
    if (validateRadio() == false)
    {
        alert("Required data missing in Step 2");
        return;
    }
    alert("Your pizza order has been submitted.");
    return;
}

function doClear()
{
```

STEP-BY-STEP 7.5 Continued

FIGURE 7-8 (continued)

```
    document.PizzaForm.customer.value = "";
    document.PizzaForm.address.value = "";
    document.PizzaForm.city.value = "";
    document.PizzaForm.state.value = "";
    document.PizzaForm.zip.value = "";
    document.PizzaForm.phone.value = "";
    document.PizzaForm.size[0].checked = false;
    document.PizzaForm.size[1].checked = false;
    document.PizzaForm.size[2].checked = false;
    document.PizzaForm.toppings[0].checked = false;
    document.PizzaForm.toppings[1].checked = false;
    document.PizzaForm.toppings[2].checked = false;
    document.PizzaForm.toppings[3].checked = false;
    document.PizzaForm.toppings[4].checked = false;
    document.PizzaForm.toppings[5].checked = false;
    return;
}

function validateText()
{
 if (document.PizzaForm.customer.value == "") return false;
 if (document.PizzaForm.address.value == "") return false;
 if (document.PizzaForm.city.value == "") return false;
 if (document.PizzaForm.phone.value == "") return false;
 return true;
}

function validateRadio()
{
 if (document.PizzaForm.size[0].checked) return true;
 if (document.PizzaForm.size[1].checked) return true;
 if (document.PizzaForm.size[2].checked) return true;
 return false;
}
</SCRIPT>
</HEAD>
<BODY>
<FORM NAME="PizzaForm">
<H1>The JavaScript Pizza Parlor</H1>
<BR>
<H4>Step 1: Enter your name, address, and phone number:</H4>
```

STEP-BY-STEP 7.5 Continued

FIGURE 7-8 (continued)

```
<FONT FACE="Courier">
Name:    <INPUT NAME="customer" TYPE="TEXT" SIZE=50><BR>
Address: <INPUT NAME="address" TYPE="TEXT" SIZE=50><BR>
City:    <INPUT NAME="city" TYPE="TEXT" SIZE=16>
State: <INPUT NAME="state" TYPE="TEXT" SIZE=4>
Zip: <INPUT NAME="zip" TYPE="TEXT" SIZE=8><BR>
Phone:   <INPUT NAME="phone" TYPE="TEXT" SIZE=50><BR>
</FONT>
<BR><BR>
<H4>Step 2: Select the size of pizza you want:</H4>
<FONT FACE="Courier">
<INPUT NAME="size" TYPE="RADIO">Small
<INPUT NAME="size" TYPE="RADIO">Medium
<INPUT NAME="size" TYPE="RADIO">Large<BR>
</FONT>
<BR><BR>
<H4>Step 3: Select the pizza toppings you want:</H4>
<FONT FACE="Courier">
<INPUT NAME="toppings" TYPE="CHECKBOX">Pepperoni
<INPUT NAME="toppings" TYPE="CHECKBOX">Canadian Bacon
<INPUT NAME="toppings" TYPE="CHECKBOX">Sausage<BR>
<INPUT NAME="toppings" TYPE="CHECKBOX">Mushrooms
<INPUT NAME="toppings" TYPE="CHECKBOX">Pineapple
<INPUT NAME="toppings" TYPE="CHECKBOX">Black Olives<BR>
</FONT>
<BR><BR>
<INPUT TYPE="BUTTON" VALUE="Submit Order" onClick="doSubmit()">
<INPUT TYPE="BUTTON" VALUE="Clear Entries" onClick="doClear()">
</FORM>
</BODY>
</HTML>
```

4. Save this file as **js-fifteen.html**.

STEP-BY-STEP 7.5 Continued

5. Open your Web browser and view your **js-fifteen.html** file. Your Web page should initially look like Figure 7-2. However, if you click the Submit Order button before the pizza size has been selected, you will see the alert box shown in Figure 7-9.

FIGURE 7-9
A radio button validation error message

The JavaScript Pizza Parlor

Step 1: Enter your name, address, and phone number:

Name : E. Shane Turner
Address : 305 Lincoln St.
City : Afton   State :   Zip :
Phone : 307-555-1234

Step 2: Select the s [dialog box overlapping]

> **Microsoft Internet Explorer** ⊠
> ⚠ Required data missing in Step 2
> [OK]

○ Small   ○ Medi [obscured]

Step 3: Select the pizza toppings you want:

☐ Pepperoni ☐ Canadian Bacon ☐ Sausage
☐ Mushrooms ☐ Pineapple ☐ Black Olives

[Submit Order]   [Clear Entries]

6. Continue to the next section or close your software and shut down your computer if you're finished for the day.

Internet Milestone

The Logical NOT Operator

Like C, C++, and Java, JavaScript gives you the ability to invert the value of a logical variable with the NOT operator (!). In other words, you can invert a true value to false or a false value to true by placing a single ! in front of the variable. This operator is most commonly used when the programmer wants to test for a false condition. This means that whenever a variable (or function return value) is being compared to the false value (= = false), the comparison can be shortened by using the ! operator instead. Here's a specific example:

If (validateText() = = false) is equivalent to If (!validateText())

The preferred way of testing for a false value is a matter of personal taste. However, it is very common to see novice programmers use the former approach, while professional coders tend to use the latter technique. Either way will work just fine.

Analyzing the Code You Have Just Entered

The main idea behind the section you just completed is similar to the previous Step-by-Steps, but let's make sure you understand the subtle differences.

In order to validate the contents of a text field, we check the contents of the object's *value* property to see if it contains an empty string. To validate a set of radio buttons, we need to test the value of each object's *checked* property to see if it is set to *true* or *false*. Consequently, the validateRadio() function subsequently tests the value of each checked property in the object set, and returns a *true* value if it encounters a selected radio button. However, if none of the radio buttons in the set is selected, the function returns a *false* value.

The true/false value returned by the validateRadio() function is evaluated by the doSubmit() function, just as it was for the validateText() function. If the return value is false, then the user will see an appropriate alert box to let him or her know that Step 2 was not completed correctly. The end result of this activity is that customers will not be able to submit an order to The JavaScript Pizza Parlor without selecting a pizza size first.

SUMMARY

In this lesson you learned:

- You can understand the purpose of JavaScript input controls.

- To use JavaScript input controls.

- You can understand the benefits of data validation.

- To create an HTML form that will accept JavaScript code.

- To enhance HTML forms with JavaScript.

 Internet Milestone

The Origin of the Term *Radio Button*

The term *radio button* has been around the software industry ever since Microsoft introduced its Windows operating system in the late 1980s. But very few people know where the term originated or exactly what it means. The Microsoft programmers who designed the Windows interface recognized that it is often necessary to treat a set of options as mutually exclusive. In other words, only one option can be selected at any given time. They also wanted to give this type of action a special name that would help the user understand this behavior. The term they chose to use was *radio button* because the behavior of these options is similar to the function selection buttons found on old-style stereo systems. These old stereos typically contained several buttons labeled AM, FM, FM STEREO, PHONO, TAPE, and AUX that allowed the user to select the music source. And since it was possible to listen to only one music source at a time, pushing any one of these buttons caused any other selected button to pop out. These mechanical radio buttons were usually round, so the Windows programmers gave the round shape to their radio buttons, too.

VOCABULARY *Review*

Define the following terms:

Check box	Data validation	Text field
Controls/components	Radio button	

REVIEW *Questions*

TRUE/FALSE

Circle T if the statement is true or F if the statement is false.

T   F   **1.** Data validation is the process of checking user input data to make sure it is complete and accurate.

T   F   **2.** The NAME attribute helps to define selection options in HTML forms.

T   F   **3.** The term *radio button* is derived from the word *radial*, which means *round*.

T   F   **4.** To get a button to call a JavaScript function when it is clicked, you'll need to make use of the *onClick* event.

T   F   **5.** Because users now have so much experience on the Internet, it is considered annoying for programmers to provide visual or audio feedback on the progress of Web form events.

FILL IN THE BLANK

Complete the following sentences by writing the correct word or words in the blanks provided.

1. The text field is a(n) _____ control that allows the user to key a string value into a specific location on a Web page.

2. The _____ button is an input control that allows the user to select just one option from a set of options.

3. A(n) _____ is an input control that allows the user to select any number of options from a set of options.

4. JavaScript statements use a single equal sign (=) for the _____ operation.

5. JavaScript statements use a double equal sign (= =) for the _____ operation.

WRITTEN QUESTIONS

Write a brief answer to the following questions.

1. What is an input control or component?

2. How are text fields, radio buttons, check boxes, and buttons defined in HTML?

3. What is data validation? Why is it important?

4. How do you validate the contents of a text field?

5. How do you validate a set of radio buttons?

PROJECTS

 PROJECT 7-1

GreatApplications, Inc., has just won a major business contract with a pizza company called The Four Corners Pizza Palace. This company wants GreatApplications to create a Web-based pizza order form like the one you created for The JavaScript Pizza Parlor in the Step-by-Steps in this lesson.

The Four Corners Pizza Palace does business in the famous "Four Corners" area of the United States. The Four Corners is a geographical area located on the corners of the states of Arizona (AZ), Colorado (CO), New Mexico (NM), and Utah (UT). Therefore, The Four Corners Pizza Palace will need a drop-down list that contains two-letter abbreviations for each of the states. This information will help the company tabulate the sales tax for each state. You are to create a pizza order form and add the state code drop-down list selection box. If you don't remember how to create a drop-down list control, refer to Step-by-Step 3.5 in lesson 3. Once you create the form, clear the contents of this new element with the Clear button and check for input when the Submit button is selected.

Save your work as **js-test12.html**.

 ## WEB PROJECT

The pizza order form you have been working with in this lesson is obviously designed for educational, rather than business, purposes. Nevertheless, do you think there might be some pizza companies out there that really do sell pizza on the Net? Conduct an Internet search for pizza businesses that maintain their own Web pages. Listed as a percentage, how many of your local pizza parlor establishments give you the ability to order pizza over the Web? List some of the things they do to make the ordering experience easy for their customers.

Save your work as **js-research1.txt**.

 ## TEAMWORK PROJECT

Your supervisor at GreatApplications, Inc. is fairly happy with the electronic order form you have been working on for The JavaScript Pizza Parlor in this lesson. However, she is asking for some changes! Make these changes as a team. First, add a new text field labeled *E-mail:* that will be located directly below the *Phone:* field of Step 1. Next, add a new pizza size radio button, labeled *Jumbo*, to the right of the Large radio button under Step 2. And finally, add two new pizza topping options to the Step 3 section of the form area, label your two new toppings *Anchovies* and *Extra Cheese*, and position them to the right of the existing toppings (one per row). Can you do it?

Save your work as **js-test13.html**.

CRITICAL *Thinking*

 ## ACTIVITY 7-1

In this lesson, we have discussed the concept of data validation at length. In Step-by-Steps 7.4 and 7.5, you learned to implement simple validation techniques. But what if you were asked to explain the concept to a fellow student, including reasons why it is important to use these techniques? Could you do it? Data validation is a fundamental part of virtually every professional computer program, no matter what type of program it is or in what programming language it is written. So, it is essential that you attain a solid understanding of the concept. To help make sure you do, answer the following questions.

1. What types of data must be validated for a typical form?

2. Is checking for blank fields always sufficient for text validation? Explain.

3. What characteristics of the zip code field could be tested for validity?

4. Is it always possible for a computer program to validate every field on the form? Why or why not?

SCANS ACTIVITY 7-2

You can never provide too much feedback. Return to and review the information presented in Step-by-Step 5.5 about the browser status line. Then add a statement to the doSubmit() function in The JavaScript Pizza Parlor program (saved as **js-fifteen.html**) that will cause an appropriate message to appear in the status line in addition to the alert box. This should be a relatively easy task to accomplish, don't you think?

Save your work as **js-test14.html**.

SCANS ACTIVITY 7-3

Your supervisor still is not completely satisfied with The JavaScript Pizza Parlor form because one or more of the data validation functions can fail. If a required text field in Step 1 is left blank, for example, she would like an error message to appear that specifies which field is empty. In addition, she would like the cursor to appear in that particular text field when the user dismisses the alert box. She would also like the Step 2 error message to be reworded so that it includes the words *pizza size* in some way.

In order to accomplish this assignment, you will need to remove the generic error message from the doSubmit() function and insert specific error messages into the validateText() function. You will also need to make use of the focus() method to get the cursor into the appropriate text field. Can you get the job done?

Save your work as **js-test15.html**.

> **Hot Tip**
>
> To get the text cursor into the name field, use the following JavaScript statement:
> **document.PizzaForm.customer. focus();**

SUMMARY *Project*

If you have gained a firm understanding of the material presented in this lesson, you should be able to create a professional-looking order form for almost any situation. Demonstrate that you have mastered the concepts of Lesson 7 by creating an order form for the fictitious JavaScript Computer Company. This company wants you to build a JavaScript-enabled Web page that allows customers to order a custom computer system containing the exact components they want. Some of the characteristics of a computer system that affect both its capabilities and its price include CPU speed, RAM, and hard disk capacity. Create a computer order form that looks something like the one shown in Figure 7-10.

FIGURE 7-10

An example computer system order form

PROJECT REQUIREMENTS

■ Give your order form an appropriate heading.

■ Include a section for customer information that contains text fields for customer name, company name, address line 1, address line 2, city, state, and zip code. All of these fields should be required except company name and address line 2.

■ Include a section for computer information that contains radio button options for CPU speed, RAM size, hard drive capacity, and at least three other categories of your choice. The first three options should be required, but the last three can be optional.

■ Add two buttons to your order form. One button should validate the form and submit the order if it passes validation. The other button should clear the form completely.

USING JAVASCRIPT WITH FRAMES

OBJECTIVES

Upon completion of this lesson, you should be able to:

■ Create a JavaScript function with a parameter list.

■ Create JavaScript-enabled hyperlinks that affect frames.

■ Create JavaScript-enabled buttons that affect frames.

■ Create top-level JavaScript functions.

Estimated Time: 1.5 hours

VOCABULARY

Child document

Function parameter

Parameter list

Parent document

Parent object

Top object

Advanced JavaScript Programming

All of the JavaScript code you have written in Lessons 5, 6, and 7 has been limited in scope to a single HTML document. But if you recall the material that was presented in Lesson 4, you should realize that not all Web pages consist of just one file. In fact, any Web page that contains a frame set is always composed of multiple files. There must be one file that defines the frame set, and two or more additional files that define the frames within that frame set. The frame set file is known as the *parent document*, and the frame files contained within the frame set are known as *child documents*.

So the question becomes, is it possible for a Web user to perform an action in one frame that affects the appearance of a different frame? The answer is yes. All of the frames that make up a Web page can communicate with each other by means of JavaScript functions, because the Web browser provides a common environment in which frames can interact. The JavaScript code that accomplishes such cross-frame cooperation is a little more complicated than single document code, but it is still well within your reach. You are probably anxious to get started, so let's get to it.

Creating a JavaScript-Ready Frame Set

Before you can write JavaScript code that allows different frames to interact, you must create HTML documents that define a frame set. In the following Step-by-Step, we will show you how to create a frame set that contains an image in one frame and a standard HTML table in another frame. The table will initially contain nonfunctional file names, which you will later convert into hyperlinks. But for now, the goal is simply to create an appropriate frame-based Web page.

S TEP-BY-STEP 8.1

1. Open your text editor or word processor, and enter the HTML code exactly as it appears in Figure 8-1.

FIGURE 8-1
HTML code to create a frame set

```
<HTML>
<HEAD>
<TITLE>HTML and JavaScript</TITLE>
</HEAD>
<FRAMESET ROWS="140,*">
<FRAME NAME="upperFrame" SRC="upper1.html">
<FRAME NAME="lowerFrame" SRC="lower1.html">
</FRAMESET>
</HTML>
```

2. Save this file in the appropriate folder as **js-sixteen.html**.

3. Clear the contents of your editor or word processor, and enter HTML code exactly as it appears in Figure 8-2.

> **Note**
>
> The Step-by-Step activities in Lesson 8 will reference the same image files that were used in Step-by-Step 6.3, 6.4, and 6.5 in Lesson 6. If you no longer have access to the lions.gif, tigers.gif, bears.gif, and ohmy.gif image files, you will need to download them again. Refer to Step-by-Step 6.3 if you need to review the process for downloading these files.

FIGURE 8-2
HTML code to create an upper frame

```
<HTML>
<HEAD>
<TITLE>HTML and JavaScript</TITLE>
</HEAD>
<BODY>
<CENTER>
<IMG NAME="upperImage" SRC="lions.gif">
</CENTER>
</BODY>
</HTML>
```

4. Save this file in the appropriate folder as **upper1.html**.

STEP-BY-STEP 8.1 Continued

5. Clear the contents of your editor or word processor, and enter HTML code exactly as it appears in Figure 8-3.

FIGURE 8-3
HTML code to create a lower frame

```
<HTML>
<HEAD>
<TITLE>HTML and JavaScript</TITLE>
</HEAD>
<BODY>
<CENTER>
<H2>IMAGE LIST</H2>
<TABLE>
<TR><TD>1: LIONS.GIF</TD></TR>
<TR><TD>2: TIGERS.GIF</TD></TR>
<TR><TD>3: BEARS.GIF</TD></TR>
<TR><TD>4: OHMY.GIF</TD></TR>
</TABLE>
</CENTER>
</BODY>
</HTML>
```

6. Save this file in the appropriate folder as **lower1.html**.

7. Open your Web browser and view your **js-sixteen.html** file. Your screen should look like Figure 8-4.

FIGURE 8-4
A frame-based Web page

IMAGE LIST

1: LIONS.GIF

2: TIGERS.GIF

3: BEARS.GIF

4: OHMY.GIF

8. Continue to the next section or close your software and shut down your computer if you're finished for the day.

Analyzing the Code You Have Just Entered

You should feel very comfortable with all of the HTML code in the previous Step-by-Step. But just to make sure that nothing gets by you, let's review the most important concepts presented in the preceding three HTML files.

The first file defines a frame set as it was initially presented in Lesson 4. This particular frame set contains two horizontal frames named *upperFrame* and *lowerFrame*. The second file you created, *upper1.html*, will be loaded and displayed in the upper frame, and the third file, *lower1.html*, will be presented to the user in the lower frame.

The second file is also very simple, as it does nothing more than display an image that is horizontally centered on the screen. Note that the NAME attribute of this image is *upperImage*.

The third file defines a simple table that is also horizontally centered on the screen. The table contains four rows, and each row contains the name of an image file. For now, these filenames are nothing more than plain text, but they can be easily converted into hyperlinks. In fact, this is one of the tasks you will perform in the next Step-by-Step.

Adding JavaScript Code to Your Frame Set

Now that you have created a frame-based Web page to work with, we can show you how to make your frame set functional with JavaScript. The first thing you will do is to add a JavaScript function to the HTML document that is displayed in the lower frame. The purpose of this function is to change the image that is displayed in the upper frame document.

Once you have defined this function you will convert the plain text file names listed in the HTML table to hyperlinks. These links will then invoke the JavaScript function when the user clicks on them. Are you ready for this?

STEP-BY-STEP 8.2

1. Open your text editor or word processor and retrieve the **js-sixteen.html** file you created in the previous Step-by-Step.

2. Modify the name of the file that will be loaded into the lower frame as shown in bold in Figure 8-5.

FIGURE 8-5
HTML code to define a frame set

```
<HTML>
<HEAD>
<TITLE>HTML and JavaScript</TITLE>
</HEAD>
<FRAMESET ROWS="140,*">
<FRAME NAME="upperFrame" SRC="upper1.html">
<FRAME NAME="lowerFrame" SRC="lower2.html">
</FRAMESET>
</HTML>
```

STEP-BY-STEP 8.2 Continued

3. Save this modified file as **js-seventeen.html**.

4. Using your text editor or word processor retrieve the **lower1.html** file you created in the previous Step-by-Step.

5. Add the JavaScript function and hyperlink anchor (<A>) tags as shown in bold in Figure 8-6.

FIGURE 8-6
HTML/JavaScript code to add functionality to your frame set

```
<HTML>
<HEAD>
<TITLE>HTML and JavaScript</TITLE>
<SCRIPT>
function setImage(number)
{
  if (number == 1)
  {
    parent.upperFrame.document.upperImage.src = "lions.gif";
  }
  if (number == 2)
  {
    parent.upperFrame.document.upperImage.src = "tigers.gif";
  }
  if (number == 3)
  {
    parent.upperFrame.document.upperImage.src = "bears.gif";
  }
  if (number == 4)
  {
    parent.upperFrame.document.upperImage.src = "ohmy.gif";
  }
  return;
}
</SCRIPT>
</HEAD>
<BODY>
<CENTER>
<H2>IMAGE LIST</H2>
<TABLE>
<TR><TD><A HREF="javascript:setImage(1)">1: LIONS.GIF</A></TD></TR>
<TR><TD><A HREF="javascript:setImage(2)">2: TIGERS.GIF</A></TD></TR>
<TR><TD><A HREF="javascript:setImage(3)">3: BEARS.GIF</A></TD></TR>
<TR><TD><A HREF="javascript:setImage(4)">4: OHMY.GIF</A></TD></TR>
</TABLE>
</CENTER>
</BODY>
</HTML>
```

STEP-BY-STEP 8.2 Continued

6. Save the file as **lower2.html**.

7. Open your Web browser and view your **js-seventeen.html** file. Your screen should initially look like Figure 8-7A. But when you click one of the available hyperlinks, the image in the upper frame should change to look like Figure 8-7B, 8-7C, or 8-7D in accordance with the filename you clicked.

> **Important**
>
> Users of Windows XP with Service pack 2 installed may see a warning regarding active content. If this occurs, click OK to acknowledge the warning, then follow the prompts to enable JavaScript.

FIGURE 8-7A
Frame-based Web page after clicking the LIONS.GIF hyperlink

LIONS

IMAGE LIST

1: LIONS.GIF
2: TIGERS.GIF
3: BEARS.GIF
4: OHMY.GIF

FIGURE 8-7B
Frame-based Web page after clicking the TIGERS.GIF hyperlink

and TIGERS

IMAGE LIST

1: LIONS.GIF
2: TIGERS.GIF
3: BEARS.GIF
4: OHMY.GIF

STEP-BY-STEP 8.2 Continued

FIGURE 8-7C
Frame-based Web page after clicking the BEARS.GIF hyperlink

and BEARS

IMAGE LIST

1: LIONS.GIF
2: TIGERS.GIF
3: BEARS.GIF
4: OHMY.GIF

FIGURE 8-7D
Frame-based Web page after clicking the OHMY.GIF hyperlink

Oh My!

IMAGE LIST

1: LIONS.GIF
2: TIGERS.GIF
3: BEARS.GIF
4: OHMY.GIF

8. Continue to the next section or close your software and shut down your computer if you're finished for the day.

Analyzing the Code You Have Just Entered

Although this frame-based Web page does not look or behave much differently from the ones you created in Lesson 6, some important new concepts are at work here. We'll explain them in detail to make sure you understand them.

First, take a good look at the JavaScript function called *setImage*. All JavaScript function definitions include a *parameter list*, which is simply a list of data items that the function needs to perform its intended action. All of the JavaScript functions you have written up to now have had empty parameter lists, but this newest function contains one parameter called *number*. This parameter is used by the *setImage* function to determine which graphic file to use as the source for the upper frame image.

Another important concept you should understand is that the *number* parameter in the *setImage* function gets its value from one of the four hyperlinks defined in the lower frame. Notice that all four HREF attributes within the anchor tags contain calls to the same JavaScript function, but the parameter passed to that function is different for each graphic file name. If we did not make use of the JavaScript *function parameter* to distinguish one hyperlink from another, it would be necessary to define four different functions. The parameter approach is more efficient, especially when there are ten, twenty, or a hundred different hyperlinks, rather than just four.

One final note of significance is the use of the JavaScript *parent object* in the setImage function. To learn more, read the *Internet Milestone* called *The Parent and Child Relationship*.

Creating a Frame-Based Slide Show

In Lesson 6 you created an electronic slide show that would allow the user to change the image displayed on the screen by clicking hyperlinks or buttons. In this lesson we will show you how to create a frame-based Web page that performs essentially the same function. Later, we will teach you how to write JavaScript code that will make this Web page functional. But for now we will do as we did in Step-by-Step 8.1. That is, we will begin by helping you create the basic frame set, and the frames that it contains.

The HTML document that you will use in the upper frame of the next Step-by-Step will be the same one you used in the two previous Step-by-Steps (*upper1.html*), but the lower frame will contain a new document with two control buttons. Initially these buttons will not be functional, but we will address this issue later. Shall we begin?

 Internet Milestone

The Parent and Child Relationship

If you refer back to the JavaScript functions you wrote in Lesson 6 to manipulate images, you should realize that the functions are defined in the same file as the images they access. However, in Step-by-Step 8.2 the setImage function is defined in the lower2.html file, and the image it accesses is defined in the upper1.html file.

In order for a JavaScript function to access an object in a different file, the two files must be linked in some fashion. In this particular example, the upper1.html and the lower2.html files are both contained within a common parent frame set, and this frame set can be referenced via the JavaScript object called parent. Keep in mind also that the frame set file defines two child frames, and these frames were given the names upperFrame and lowerFrame. The upper frame contains an HTML document, and this document contains an image object called upperImage (as defined in the upper1.html file in Figure 8-2). Putting all this information together should help you understand exactly how the src property of the image object is set with the following JavaScript code:

```
parent.upperFrame.document.upperImage.src = "<filename>";
```

Bear in mind also that image objects are not the only type of object that can be referenced across frames by JavaScript functions. The same technique may be used to access text field objects, drop-down list objects, button objects, etc.

S TEP-BY-STEP 8.3

1. Open your text editor or word processor and retrieve the **js-seventeen.html** file you created in the previous Step-by-Step.

2. Modify the name of the file that will be loaded into the lower frame as shown in bold in Figure 8-8.

FIGURE 8-8
HTML code to define a frame set

```
<HTML>
<HEAD>
<TITLE>HTML and JavaScript</TITLE>
</HEAD>
<FRAMESET ROWS="140,*">
<FRAME NAME="upperFrame" SRC="upper1.html">
<FRAME NAME="lowerFrame" SRC="lower3.html">
</FRAMESET>
</HTML>
```

3. Save this modified file as **js-eighteen.html**.

4. Clear the contents of your text editor or word processor and then enter the following HTML code exactly as shown in Figure 8-9.

FIGURE 8-9
HTML code for an electronic slide show

```
<HTML>
<HEAD>
<TITLE>HTML and JavaScript</TITLE>
</HEAD>
<BODY>
<CENTER>
<H2>WELCOME</H2>
<H3>to my</H3>
<H3>Electronic Slide Show</H3>
<BR>
<INPUT TYPE="BUTTON" VALUE="Prev Image">
<INPUT TYPE="BUTTON" VALUE="Next Image">
</CENTER>
</BODY>
</HTML>
```

5. Save this file as **lower3.html**.

STEP-BY-STEP 8.3 Continued

6. Open your Web browser and view your **js-eighteen.html** file. Your screen should look like Figure 8-10.

FIGURE 8-10
A frame-based Web page for an electronic slide show

7. Continue to the next section or close your software and shut down your computer if you're finished for the day.

Analyzing the Code You Have Just Entered

As was the case in Step-by-Step 8.1, the HTML code you just created contains nothing that was not already presented in previous lessons. The primary purpose of Step-by-Step 8.3 is to make sure you feel comfortable working with frame sets and frames. The next Step-by-Step will show you how to make the *Prev Image* and *Next Image* buttons functional by using JavaScript events and functions.

Making Your Slide Show Buttons Functional

The primary purpose of the next Step-by-Step is to show you how to make the slide show buttons functional. Note that there is more than one way to accomplish this objective. In fact, when you are working with frame sets, there will always be multiple ways in which a particular problem may be solved.

 Internet Milestone

The Progress of Programming Languages

Now that you have had an introduction into JavaScript, you may be interested in pursuing a career in programming. This is a good time to become a programmer, because many advances have been made in programming languages. There is a long history of programming languages, each developed to make the task of programming progressively easier.

Machine language was one of the first ways programmers communicated with computers. Machine language commands look like binary numbers. For example:

```
01010101
100001011 11101100
01001100
01001100
```

Machine language is a system computers can relate to. However, it's difficult for programmers to learn. Assembly language followed, which uses words as assembly commands that are then turned into machine-specific commands. Here is an example of assembly language:

```
PUSH BP
MOV BP,SP
DEC SP
DEC SP
```

Assembly language is also very difficult, so an entire group of new languages emerged to make programming easier, including Basic, Fortran, Pascal and Cobol. A sample of Pascal code looks like this:

```
program AddIt;
var
i, j, k : integer;
begin
i := 3;
j ;= 2;
k := i + j;
```

Pascal begins to look a bit more like what you have been learning in JavaScript. However, JavaScript is more like other, more highly developed languages including C++, Visual Basic, and Java. Much of what you have learned while discovering JavaScript can be applied to these other languages. In fact, many concepts found in these higher-level languages will be very familiar to you.

Think back for a moment to the overall design of the frame-based Web page you created in Step-by-Step 8.2. In that instance, we chose to create a JavaScript function in the lower frame document that is invoked by hyperlinks in that same document, but that accesses an image object in the upper frame document. In the next Step-by-Step we will take a slightly different approach. To be specific, we will create two JavaScript functions in the upper frame document that will access the image object in that same document, but that will be invoked by buttons contained in the lower frame document.

There are not necessarily any advantages or disadvantages in following the former approach, or by implementing JavaScript code using the latter technique. We simply want you to understand that you have various options available to you, and you may produce JavaScript solutions in different ways. The method you choose is up to you.

STEP-BY-STEP 8.4

1. Open your text editor or word processor and retrieve the **js-eighteen.html** file you created in the previous Step-by-Step.

2. Modify the names of the files that will be loaded into the upper frame and the lower frame as shown in bold in Figure 8-11.

FIGURE 8-11
HTML code to define a frame set

```
<HTML>
<HEAD>
<TITLE>HTML and JavaScript</TITLE>
</HEAD>
<FRAMESET ROWS="140,*">
<FRAME NAME="upperFrame" SRC="upper2.html">
<FRAME NAME="lowerFrame" SRC="lower4.html">
</FRAMESET>
</HTML>
```

3. Save this modified file as **js-nineteen.html**.

4. Using your text editor or word processor retrieve the **upper1.html** file you created in Step-by-Step 8.1.

STEP-BY-STEP 8.4 Continued

5. Add the JavaScript image array and functions code as shown in bold in Figure 8-12.

FIGURE 8-12
HTML/JavaScript code to implement a slide show

```
<HTML>
<HEAD>
<TITLE>HTML and JavaScript</TITLE>
<SCRIPT>
var images = new Array(4);
images[0] = new Image;
images[0].src = "lions.gif";
images[1] = new Image;
images[1].src = "tigers.gif";
images[2] = new Image;
images[2].src = "bears.gif";
images[3] = new Image;
images[3].src = "ohmy.gif";
var index = 0;

function prevImage()
{
  if (index > 0)
  {
    index--;
    document.upperImage.src = images[index].src;
  }
  return;
}

function nextImage()
{
  if (index < 3)
  {
    index++;
    document.upperImage.src = images[index].src;
  }
  return;
}
</SCRIPT>
</HEAD>
<BODY>
<CENTER>
<IMG NAME="upperImage" SRC="lions.gif">
</CENTER>
</BODY>
</HTML>
```

STEP-BY-STEP 8.4 Continued

6. Save the file as **upper2.html**.

7. Using your text editor or word processor retrieve the **lower3.html** file you created in the previous Step-by-Step.

8. Add the JavaScript events as shown in bold in Figure 8-13.

FIGURE 8-13
HTML/JavaScript code to make two buttons functional

```
<HTML>
<HEAD>
<TITLE>HTML and JavaScript</TITLE>
</HEAD>
<BODY>
<CENTER>
<H2>WELCOME</H2>
<H3>to my</H3>
<H3>Electronic Slide Show</H3>
<BR>
<INPUT TYPE="BUTTON" VALUE="Prev Image"
  onClick="parent.upperFrame.prevImage()">
<INPUT TYPE="BUTTON" VALUE="Next Image"
  onClick="parent.upperFrame.nextImage()">
</CENTER>
</BODY>
</HTML>
```

9. Save the file as **lower4.html**.

STEP-BY-STEP 8.4 Continued

10. Open your Web browser and view your **js-nineteen.html** file. Your screen should initially look like Figure 8-14A. But when you click the Next Image button, you should see your screen change to look like Figures 8-14B, 8-14C, and 8-14D.

FIGURE 8-14A
First image in the slide show

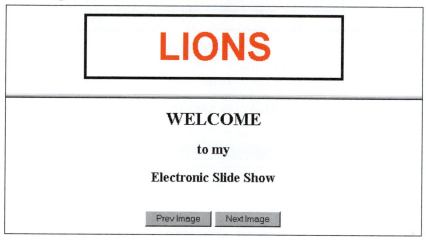

FIGURE 8-14B
Second image in the slide show

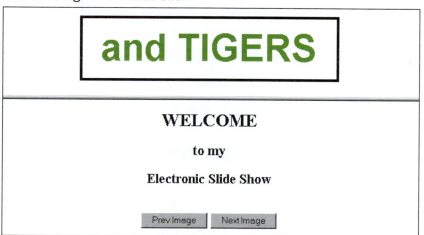

STEP-BY-STEP 8.4 Continued

FIGURE 8-14C
Third image in the slide show

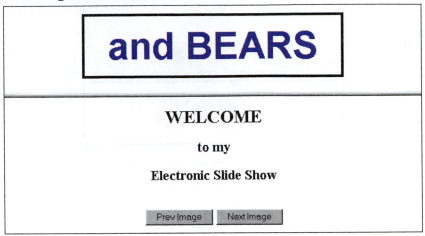

FIGURE 8-14D
Fourth image in the slide show

11. Continue to the next section or close your software and shut down your computer if you're finished for the day.

Analyzing the Code You Have Just Entered

Let's begin our analysis of the previous Step-by-Step activity by taking a closer look at the new JavaScript code we added to the upper frame document.

First, we created a four-element image array to contain the four graphics that make up our slide show. We also added two new JavaScript functions called *prevImage()* and *nextImage()* that change the image that is currently displayed on the screen. This code is almost identical to the JavaScript code you created in Lesson 6. (Please refer to that lesson if you have forgotten the details of JavaScript arrays and array indices.)

Next, we added an *onClick* event to each of the two buttons that were defined in the lower frame document. You should note that these *onClick* events will cause the Web browser to invoke the appropriate function in the upper frame document when its corresponding button is clicked. Once again, these JavaScript functions make use of the JavaScript parent object to access the parent frame set, and the *upperFrame* frame name to access the HTML document in the upper frame.

Creating a Top-Level JavaScript Function

As you saw in the previous Step-by-Steps, it is not terribly difficult for one HTML document to access an object in another document, if the two documents are contained within a common frame set. However, you should recognize that this process can get a little more complex if you are working within a Web page that contains nested frame sets. (If you don't remember what nested frame sets are, refer back to Lesson 4.)

If you have a frame set nested within a second frame set that is nested within a third frame set and so on, you may access any frame you wish by utilizing the proper sequence of JavaScript parent objects. In other words, if an HTML document wants to access its parent frame set, it may do so by using the parent object. If that page needs to access the parent frame set of its own parent, it can use two instances of the JavaScript parent object. To access the frame set three levels up would require the use of three parent objects, and so forth. For example:

```
onClick="parent.parent.parent.someFrame.someFunction()"
```

The problem with this approach is that your JavaScript code is long, confusing, and difficult to maintain if you make numerous references to the parent object. In many cases you may find it much more convenient to place many JavaScript function definitions in the top-level frame set file, and then every HTML document—no matter how deeply it is nested within the Web page framework—can easily access these functions by using the JavaScript *top object*.

In this final Step-by-Step we will show you how to create a top-level JavaScript function, and how to access that function from within lower-level documents. In one case, you will convert the image object in the upper frame into a hyperlink that invokes the function. In addition, you will add a new button to the lower frame document that will also call the top-level function. We're sure you are anxious to learn these new concepts, so let's get it done!

Netiquette

I think you'll have to admit that JavaScript is a valuable tool. However, like any tool in the wrong hands, it can become a destructive thing. Unfortunately, many hackers have used JavaScript to create viruses that infect computers and cause considerable damage to computer data. Not only is this activity extremely illegal, it's also unethical and harmful to the important work people do on their computers. Think about it. What would you do if you knew that a friend of yours was writing viruses using JavaScript and distributing them online?

STEP-BY-STEP 8.5

1. Open your text editor or word processor and retrieve the **js-nineteen.html** file you created in the previous Step-by-Step.

2. Add the JavaScript function, and modify the names of the files that will be loaded into the upper frame and the lower frame as shown in bold in Figure 8-15.

FIGURE 8-15
HTML code to define a frame set

```
<HTML>
<HEAD>
<TITLE>HTML and JavaScript</TITLE>
<SCRIPT>
function message()
{
  alert("We're off to see the wizard!");
  return;
}
</SCRIPT>
</HEAD>
<FRAMESET ROWS="140,*">
<FRAME NAME="upperFrame" SRC="upper3.html">
<FRAME NAME="lowerFrame" SRC="lower5.html">
</FRAMESET>
</HTML>
```

3. Save this modified file as **js-twenty.html**.

4. Using your text editor or word processor retrieve the **upper2.html** file you created in the previous Step-by-Step.

5. Convert the image into a hyperlink by adding the anchor tags shown in bold in Figure 8-16.

FIGURE 8-16
HTML/JavaScript code to invoke a top-level function from an image hyperlink

```
<HTML>
<HEAD>
<TITLE>HTML and JavaScript</TITLE>
<SCRIPT>
var images = new Array(4);
images[0] = new Image;
images[0].src = "lions.gif";
images[1] = new Image;
images[1].src = "tigers.gif";
```

STEP-BY-STEP 8.5 Continued

FIGURE 8-16 (continued)

```
images[2] = new Image;
images[2].src = "bears.gif";
images[3] = new Image;
images[3].src = "ohmy.gif";
var index = 0;

function prevImage()
{
  if (index > 0)
  {
    index--;
    document.upperImage.src = images[index].src;
  }
  return;
}

function nextImage()
{
  if (index < 3)
  {
    index++;
    document.upperImage.src = images[index].src;
  }
  return;
}
</SCRIPT>
</HEAD>
<BODY>
<CENTER>
<A HREF="javascript:top.message()"><IMG NAME="upperImage"
  SRC="lions.gif"></A>
</CENTER>
</BODY>
</HTML>
```

6. Save the file as **upper3.html**.

7. Using your text editor or word processor retrieve the **lower4.html** file you created in the previous Step-by-Step.

STEP-BY-STEP 8.5 Continued

8. Add the new button as shown in bold in Figure 8-17.

FIGURE 8-17
HTML/JavaScript code to invoke a top-level function from a button

```
<HTML>
<HEAD>
<TITLE>HTML and JavaScript</TITLE>
</HEAD>
<BODY>
<CENTER>
<H2>WELCOME</H2>
<H3>to my</H3>
<H3>Electronic Slide Show</H3>
<BR>
<INPUT TYPE="BUTTON" VALUE="Prev Image"
  onClick="parent.upperFrame.prevImage()">
<INPUT TYPE="BUTTON" VALUE="Next Image"
  onClick="parent.upperFrame.nextImage()">
<BR><BR>
<INPUT TYPE="BUTTON" VALUE="Show Message"
  onClick="top.message()">
</CENTER>
</BODY>
</HTML>
```

9. Save the resulting file as **lower5.html**.

STEP-BY-STEP 8.5 Continued

10. Open your Web browser and view your **js-twenty.html** file. Your screen should initially look like Figure 8-18A. If you click on the image in the upper frame, or click the Show Message button in the lower frame, you should see an alert box displayed as shown in Figure 8-18B.

FIGURE 8-18A
Web page as it initially appears

FIGURE 8-18B
Web page after top-level JavaScript function is invoked

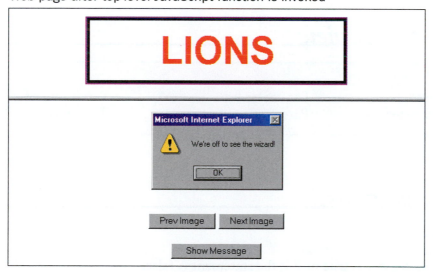

Analyzing the Code You Have Just Entered

First, let's take a look at the JavaScript function called *message()* that we added to the *js-twenty.html* file. There is nothing special about the function itself. In fact, it does nothing more than invoke the JavaScript *alert()* method to display its message. What is unusual about this function, however, is that it is contained in a frame set file rather than a standard

HTML document. And since this particular frame set file happens to define the top-level frame set, this function becomes accessible to any lower-level document by using the JavaScript top object.

Second, we convert the image in the upper frame document to a hyperlink in order to show you that our top-level function can be accessed from an image hyperlink. We also added a new button to the lower frame document to illustrate that the same top-level function can be invoked by clicking a button, and that this button can reside in a different HTML document from the image hyperlink.

The final concept we would like to present is that this top-level function, and any other JavaScript function for that matter, can be called from any HTML hyperlink (text or image), or by any JavaScript event. (Please refer to Lesson 6 if you need to review the names and usage of JavaScript events.)

SUMMARY

In this lesson you learned:

- You can create a JavaScript function with a parameter list.
- You can create JavaScript-enabled hyperlinks that affect other frames.
- You can create JavaScript-enabled buttons that affect other frames.
- You can create top-level JavaScript functions.

VOCABULARY *Review*

Define the following terms:

Child document	Parameter list	Parent object
Function parameter	Parent document	Top object

REVIEW *Questions*

TRUE/FALSE

Circle T if the statement is true or F if the statement is false.

T   F   **1.** Any Web page that contains a frame set is always composed of multiple files.

T   F   **2.** There must be one file that defines the frame set, and one additional file that defines the frames within the frame set.

T   F   **3.** The frame set file is known as the child file or document.

T   F   **4.** The JavaScript function definitions include a parameter list, which is a list of data items that the function needs in order to perform its intended action.

T   F   **5.** A JavaScript function can be called from any HTML hyperlink, even if that hyperlink is text or an image.

FILL IN THE BLANK

Complete the following sentences by writing the correct word or words in the blanks provided.

1.   The frame set file is also known as the _____ document.

2.   The frame files contained within the frame set are known as _____ documents.

3.   A(n) _____ list is a list of data items that a function needs to perform its intended action.

4.   If a page needs to access the parent frame set of its own parent, it can use two instances of the JavaScript parent _____.

5.   A four-element image _____ was used in Step-by-Step 8.2 to contain four graphics that made up the slide show.

WRITTEN QUESTIONS

Write a brief answer to the following questions.

1.   What does the parent document in a frame set file do or accomplish?

2.   How can you identity or define a child document in a frame set file?

3.   Write a short sample of HTML code that will create four rows with each row containing the name of an image.

4.   What does the *onClick* event do?

5. What does the *alert()* method do when it is invoked?

PROJECTS

 ### PROJECT 8-1

GreatApplications, Inc., is finishing its important contract with The Four Corners Pizza Palace. At the last minute, it has decided to reexamine the project. Can you enhance the project by making a frame set and using additional JavaScript code to handle some information?

Reexamine the project you completed in Step-by-Step 7.5 and improve it in this project. Determine what it would take to convert the content to a frames-style Web site integrating additional JavaScript. In particular, think about how the Four-Corners area information listing the states of Arizona (AZ), Colorado (CO), New Mexico (NM), and Utah (UT) can be redesigned using JavaScript. You don't actually need to create the Web site, simply plan and sketch your ideas out on paper. Then, take your design to a team meeting found in the following Teamwork Project.

  ### TEAMWORK PROJECT

You, and other members of your team, planned on paper a redesign of the Web site for The Four Corners Pizza Palace integrating new JavaScript elements learned in this lesson. Pull your ideas together as a team and re-create the project after analyzing all the various options that your team has come up with. See if you can redesign the site as a team, assigning various parts of the project to different team members. The project must have at least two frames and data must be accessed by one frame and appear in the other using JavaScript.

Save your parent page as **js-test16.html** and name the other files as you see fit.

  ### WEB PROJECT

Conduct a search of five JavaScript-enabled Web pages. Use the View Source command and see what new ideas you can learn from these Web page resources. What new pieces of code can you find? What new methods can you observe? What types of things does the JavaScript accomplish in these Web pages? Are there any ideas that you could use in the future when creating your own JavaScript pages?

Save your research as **js-test17.html**.

CRITICAL*Thinking*

SCANS **ACTIVITY 8-1**

In this lesson, you learned many new techniques. You've become an expert in coding! One of the new employees at GreatApplications, Inc., is having trouble understanding what some of the code does. Explain the following segment of code to this new employee. Explain what this segment of code does in your own words. Save your description as **js-test18.html**.

```
<TABLE>
<TR><TD>1: LIONS.GIF</TD></TR>
<TR><TD>2: TIGERS.GIF</TD></TR>
<TR><TD>3: BEARS.GIF</TD></TR>
<TR><TD>4: OHMY.GIF</TD></TR>
</TABLE>
```

SCANS **ACTIVITY 8-2**

Another segment of code needs analyzing for the GreatApplications, Inc. team. Evaluate this next segment of code and explain, in your own words, what it accomplishes. Save your explanation as **js-test19.html**.

```
<INPUT TYPE="BUTTON" VALUE="Prev Image"
 onClick="parent.upperFrame.prevImage()">
<INPUT TYPE="BUTTON" VALUE="Next Image"
 onClick="parent.upperFrame.nextImage()">
<BR><BR>
<INPUT TYPE="BUTTON" VALUE="Show Message"
 onClick="top.message()">
```

SCANS **ACTIVITY 8-3**

Here is a final segment of code that needs explaining. Evaluate this next segment of code and explain what the code is, what it does, and what it accomplishes. Save your explanation as js-test20.html.

```
var images = new Array(4);
images[0] = new Image;
images[0].src = "lions.gif";
images[1] = new Image;
images[1].src = "tigers.gif";
images[2] = new Image;
images[2].src = "bears.gif";
images[3] = new Image;
images[3].src = "ohmy.gif";
var index = 0;
```

SCANS **SUMMARY** *Project*

Think back to the electronic zoo that was described in the Teamwork Project of Lesson 6. GreatApplications, Inc. would now like you to create an electronic zoo that makes use of HTML frames and JavaScript. Your new Web page should display a navigation bar on the left containing a list of the animals in your e-Zoo. The right frame will display an appropriate title, and a picture of whatever animal the user selects from your list. When the user clicks an animal hyperlink on the left, a JavaScript function will be invoked to change the image displayed on the right. Your completed Web page should look something like the one shown in Figure 8-19.

FIGURE 8-19
An electronic zoo with frames and JavaScript

PROJECT REQUIREMENTS

■ Your navigation bar (left side) should occupy about 25% of the screen width.

■ Your navigation bar should contain an appropriate title and at least five animal hyperlinks.

■ Your main page (right side) should display a Web page title and a picture of the currently selected animal.

■ Neither your navigation bar, nor your main Web page should contain a JavaScript function definition. Your JS function should be defined in the parent (frameset) page.

■ Use the JavaScript **top** object to access your JavaScript function.

THE EXCITING WORLD OF JAVASCRIPT

JAVASCRIPT TAG, METHODS AND FUNCTIONS SUMMARY

TAGS OR ATTRIBUTES	RESULT	LESSON
!=	Symbol that means *is not equal to*.	5
<	Symbol that means *is less than*.	5
<=	Symbol that means *is less than or equal to*.	5

`<FRAMESET ROWS="140,*">`
`<FRAME NAME="upperFrame" SRC="upper1.html">`
`<FRAME NAME="lowerFrame" SRC="lower1.html">`
`</FRAMESET>`
	Sample HTML code used to establish a frame set.	8

`<INPUT NAME=" " TYPE="TEXT" SIZE=number>`	Sample HTML tag used to create a text box for data entry.	7
`<INPUT NAME="size" TYPE="RADIO">`	Sample HTML tag used to create radio buttons.	7
`<INPUT NAME="toppings" TYPE="CHECKBOX">`	Sample HTML tag used to create a check box.	7
`<INPUT TYPE="BUTTON" VALUE="The string of text">`	Sample HTML tag used to create a button.	7
`<SCRIPT> </SCRIPT >`	HTML tags that indicate the beginning and the end of JavaScript code imbedded in a Web page.	5
= =	Symbol that means *is equal to*.	5
>	Symbol that means *is greater than*.	5
>=	Symbol that means *is greater than or equal to*.	5
`alert("A string of text");`	Method that allows a program to display a special dialog box that will alert the user when an expected event has occurred or some kind of user input is required.	5
`document.write("A string of text.");`	The write method of the JavaScript object called document.	5

`else`
`{`
`    statement e1;`
`    statement e2;`
`    statement e3;`
`    statement eN;`
`}`
	A sample JavaScript *else* clause, which defines the action if the specified condition is not true.	5

TAGS OR ATTRIBUTES	RESULT	LESSON
| ```
function cycle()
{
  document.banner.src = imgArray[index].src;
  index++;
  if (index == 4)
  {
    index = 0;
  }
  setTimeout("cycle()", 2000);
  return;
}
``` | Sample of JavaScript code used to define a function called *cycle()* which sets a timer that will trigger an action after 2000 milliseconds have elapsed. | 6 |
| ```
function doBack()
{
  if (index > 0)
  {
    index--;
    document.slideshow.src = imgArray[index].src;
  }
  return;
}
``` | Sample of JavaScript code used to create a function called *doBack()*, which tests the value of the index variable. If the index variable is greater than 0, the function will decrement or subtract 1 from the current value. | 6 |
| ```
function doClear()
{
  document.PizzaForm.customer.value = "";
  return;
}
``` | Sample of code used to create a function called *doClear()*, which clears the contents of input boxes. | 7 |
| ```
function doNext()
{
  if (index < 3)
  {
    index++;
    document.slideshow.src = imgArray[index].src;
  }
  return;
}
``` | Sample of JavaScript code used to create a function called *doNext()*, which tests the value of the index variable. If the index variable is less than 3, the function will increment or add 1 to the current value. | 6 |
| ```
function nextImage()
{
  if (index < 3)
  {
    index++;
    document.upperImage.src = images[index].src;
  }
  return;
}
``` | Sample of JavaScript code used to create a function called *nextImage()*, which changes an image to the next image defined in an array. | 8 |
```

TAGS OR ATTRIBUTES	RESULT	LESSON
| ```
function prevImage()
{
  if (index > 0)
  {
    index--;
    document.upperImage.src = images[index].src;
  }
  return;
}
``` | Sample of JavaScript code used to create a function called *prevImage()*, which changes an image to the previous image defined in an array. | 8 |
| ```
function select()
{
  index = Math.floor(Math.random() * 4);
  document.banner.src = imgArray[index].src;
  setTimeout("select()", 2000);
  return;
}
``` | Sample of JavaScript code used to create a function called *select()*, which allows the random selection of images. | 6 |
| ```
function setImage(number)
{
  if (number == 1)
  {
    parent.upperFrame.document.upperImage.src =
"lions.gif";
  }
  if (number == 2)
  {
    parent.upperFrame.document.upperImage.src = "tigers.gif";
  }
  if (number == 3)
  {
    parent.upperFrame.document.upperImage.src = "bears.gif";
  }
  if (number == 4)
  {
    parent.upperFrame.document.upperImage.src = "ohmy.gif";
  }
  return;
}
``` | Sample of JavaScript code used to create a function called *setImage(number)* which sets the source (src) property of an image based on the value of an input parameter (number). | 8 |
| ```
function validateText()
{
  if (document.PizzaForm.customer.value == "")
return false;
  return true;
}
``` | Sample of JavaScript code used to create a function called *validateText()*, which alerts users if they have failed to input data. Can only return a true or false answer. | 7 |
| ```
if ( <condition> )
{
    statement 1;
    statement 2;
    statement 3;
    . . .
    statement N;
}
``` | A shell or sample of the JavaScript conditional *if* statement. | 5 |
```

TAGS OR ATTRIBUTES	RESULT	LESSON
| ```
if (validateRadio() == false)
{
  alert("Required data missing in Step 2");
  return;
}
────────
function validateRadio()
{
  if (document.PizzaForm.size[0].checked) return true;
  if (document.PizzaForm.size[1].checked) return true;
  if (document.PizzaForm.size[2].checked) return true;
  return false;
}
``` | Sample of JavaScript code used to create a function called *validateRadio()*, which alerts users if they have failed to select a radio button. | 7 |
math.random()	A method capable of generating random numbers.	6
onAbort	A JavaScript event where the user aborts the loading of a Web page.	6
onBlur	A JavaScript event where the user deactivates an object (the object loses focus).	6
onChange	A JavaScript event where the user changes the object in some way.	6
onClick	A JavaScript event where the user clicks the mouse on an object.	6
onError	A JavaScript event where the JavaScript interpreter encounters a script error.	6
onFocus	A JavaScript event where the user activates an object (the object receives focus).	6
onLoad	A JavaScript event where the Web browser finishes loading a page.	6
onMouseOut	A JavaScript event that is generated when a user moves the mouse pointer off of an object.	6
onMouseOver	A JavaScript event that is generated whenever the user moves the mouse over a particular object.	6
onSelect	A JavaScript event where the user selects (highlights) the contents of an object.	6
onSubmit	A JavaScript event where the user submits an HTML form.	6
onUnload	A JavaScript event where the Web browser unloads a page from memory.	6
var	Used to indicate a programmer-defined variable.	6
```

TAGS OR ATTRIBUTES	RESULT	LESSON

`var imgArray = new Array(4);`
`imgArray[0] = new Image;`
`imgArray[0].src = "lions.gif";`
`imgArray[1] = new Image;`
`imgArray[1].src = "tigers.gif";`
`imgArray[2] = new Image;`
`imgArray[2].src = "bears.gif";`
`imgArray[3] = new Image;`
`imgArray[3].src = "ohmy.gif";`
`var index = 0;`
	Sample of JavaScript code used to create an array. The variable names are assigned by a programmer.	6

`window.status = "A string of text";`	A JavaScript statement that changes the value stored in the status property of the window object.	5

REVIEW *Questions*

MATCHING

Match the correct term in the right column to its description in the left column.

_____ 1. Software that converts human-readable code into a machine-readable form.

_____ 2. The process where JavaScript code is converted by a browser into machine-readable form.

_____ 3. Well-defined set of capabilities or invisible entities that are called upon by one or more specialized functions known as methods.

_____ 4. A segment of JavaScript code that can be invoked or called.

_____ 5. A system-level response to the occurrence of some specific condition.

_____ 6. A collection of similar objects that can be accessed by means of a variable name in an index.

_____ 7. The process of checking user input data to make sure that it is complete and accurate.

_____ 8. An input control that allows the user to key a string value into a specific location on a Web page.

_____ 9. A file that defines the frame set and two or more additional files that define the frames within that frame set.

_____ 10. Frame files contained within the frame set.

A. Interpretation

B. Array

C. Objects

D. Data validation

E. Function

F. Compiler

G. Parent document

H. Child document

I. Event

J. Text field

WRITTEN QUESTIONS

Compose a brief answer to each of the following questions. Save the answers in a single file named **Unit 2 Summary**.

1. Explain the difference between compiled and interpreted programming and scripting languages.

2. Explain the concept of a parameter list.

3. What is an array? Give an example in JavaScript.

4. What is a function? Give an example in JavaScript.

5. Explain the relationship between a parent and a child document within a frame set and how JavaScript can be used to have these documents interact with each other.

CROSS-CURRICULAR *Projects*

In this exercise, you will use HTML and JavaScript to create an online Web page quiz for learners in language arts, science, social studies, math, and a subject of your choice. Here's the trick—you have to create only one test form, and then add different questions for each of the subjects later. In other words, create a master quiz, and then change the questions for each subject area. Save each quiz separately, so you will have five separate quizzes at the end of your effort.

Create an online quiz form that asks ten questions. Combine HTML and JavaScript to create your master question-and-answer HTML/JavaScript document. Use a variety of questioning types: text boxes, to allow short written answers; check boxes, to allow learners to choose from a number of possible answers; and radio buttons, to allow learners to select a single response from a list of alternatives. Use JavaScript to create a *clear* button that will clear all of the answers from each quiz at the end of the test.

Revisit the sites you listed in the Unit 1 Review Cross-Curricular projects. Imagine that you are to visit each of the sites you recommended in those projects. Your job is to create a quiz that will test to see if learners have truly visited the sites and learned something from the content found on those pages. Add questions to your master online quiz form for the following subject areas. Save each quiz separately.

LANGUAGE ARTS 2

Write ten questions and insert them into your HTML/JavaScript quiz. Name this file **la-quiz.html** or **la-quiz.htm**.

SCIENCE 2

Write ten questions and insert them into your HTML/JavaScript quiz. Name this file **sci-quiz.html** or **sci-quiz.htm**.

SOCIAL STUDIES 2

Write ten questions and insert them into your HTML/JavaScript quiz. Name this file **ss-quiz.html** or **ss-quiz.htm**.

MATH 2

Write ten questions and insert them into your HTML/JavaScript quiz. Name this file **m-quiz.html** or **m-quiz.htm**.

YOUR CHOICE OF SUBJECT 2

Write ten questions and insert them into your HTML/JavaScript quiz. Name this file **mychoice-quiz.html** or **mychoice-quiz.htm**.

REVIEW *Projects*

 ## PROJECT 2-1

This is your chance to create a JavaScript project combining HTML and JavaScript to make something happen! For example, consider the hyperlinks in the left-hand navigation frame. Can you use the JavaScript *onMouseOver* event to display a brief description of each Web page in the browser status bar when the mouse pointer passes over it? What else can you create? What type of open-ended project can you design that will enhance your use and understanding of JavaScript within a Web page? Save your work as **Project 2-1**.

> **Extra for Experts**
>
> You may choose to enhance the project you created in the Unit 1 Review, Project 1-1 by animating it with JavaScript.

PROJECT 2-2

It is time to show your handiwork to your peers who have also created some innovative functionality with JavaScript in Project 2-1. Form groups of three or four members. Demonstrate one of your HTML/JavaScript quizzes that you created for your Cross-Curricular projects.

If any team member is having problems making elements of their pages work, solve these problems as a group. Give suggestions to each other on how these JavaScript-enabled pages can be improved.

SIMULATION

 JOB 2-1

Search the Web for five sites that use JavaScript in some way to enhance the Web site. List the sites and include a short sample of the JavaScript code used on each site in a single word-processing file named **Job 2-1**.

 JOB 2-2

Do you want to learn more about JavaScript? Search the Web and see if there are any online tutorials that can help you learn more about implementing JavaScript into your Web pages. Learn at least one new technique and create a Web page with your newly learned JavaScript code. Save your work as **Job 2-2**.

SUMMARY *Project*

In this unit you learned how to manipulate images with JavaScript. In addition, you learned how to use JavaScript functions to validate the information that users enter in order forms. Now you can demonstrate that you have mastered all of these concepts by creating a Web page that implements image processing *and* form validation logic.

GreatApplications, Inc. would like to start selling computer systems over the Internet, and they need you to create an online order form for them. Your order form should allow customers to select different types of computer cases, monitors, and printers. And as customers are making their selections, the total system price should be updated. The order form should also allow customers to enter their name, shipping address, phone number and e-mail address, and the entire form should be validated before being submitted to GreatApplications. When your entire order form is complete, it should look something like the one in Figure U2-1.

FIGURE U2-1
A sample computer system order form

PROJECT REQUIREMENTS

■ Give your order form an appropriate title.

■ Give the customer at least three choices of case styles, monitors and printers.

■ Display a 125x125 pixel image of the customer's selections.

■ You may use the computer component images provided on your instructor's resource CD, or you may download your own images from the Internet.

■ The total system price should be updated automatically when the customer selects system components, but it should not be updatable by the user. (*Hint:* use the READONLY attribute in the <INPUT> tag for this text field.)

Hot Tip

Use the **onClick** event within the <INPUT> tag for each radio button to update the image.

■ When the customer clicks the "Submit Order" button, a JavaScript function should be invoked to validate the form. All fields should be required except the second line of the address field. (This field should be optional.)

■ If any part of the order form fails the validation checks, an appropriate error message should be displayed.

■ If the form passes all validation checks, a message should alert the customer that their order has been submitted successfully.

■ The "Clear Values" button should clear the entire order form when clicked.

Hot Tip

Use the **blank.gif** image provided to clear the computer component images.

PORTFOLIO *Checklist*

Include the following files from this unit in your student portfolio:

___ JavaScript Unit Summary Questions

___ Language Arts Quiz

___ Science Quiz

___ Social Studies Quiz

___ Math Quiz

___ Your Choice of Subject Quiz

___ Project 2-1

___ Job 2-1

___ Job 2-2

ADVANCED INTERNET TECHNOLOGIES

Unit 3

 Estimated Time for Unit: 7 hours

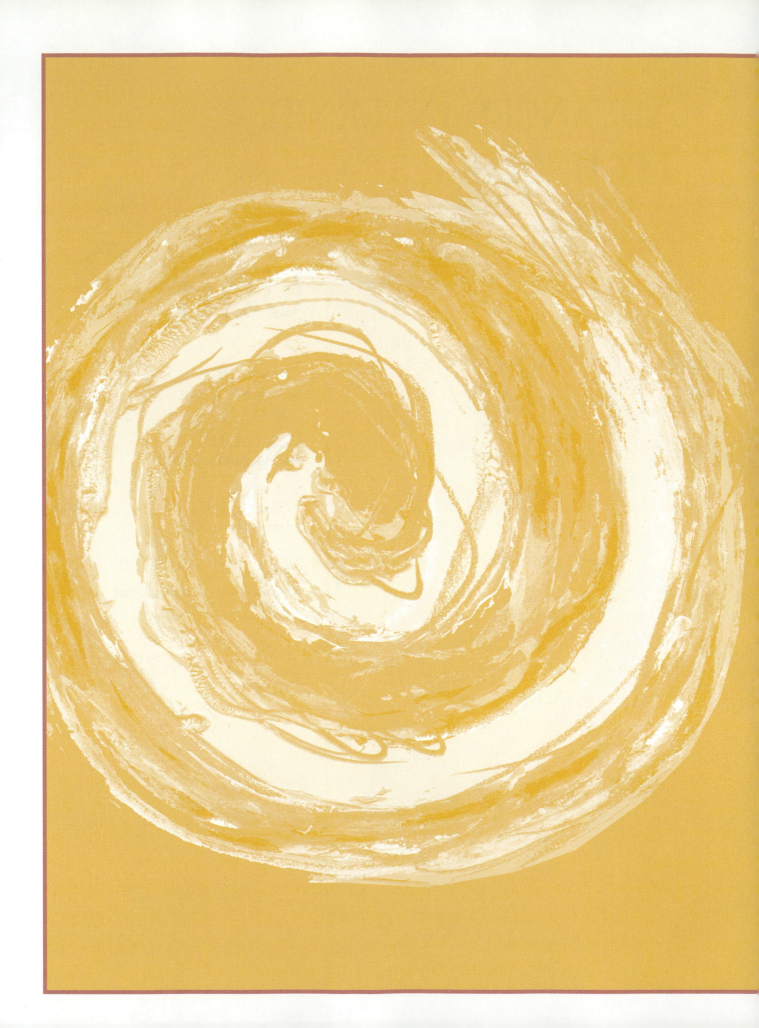

INTRODUCTION TO XML

OBJECTIVES

Upon completion of this lesson, you should be able to:

- Create simple XML documents.
- Define the syntax rules of XML tags.
- Create and use XML shortcut tags.
- Understand the usage of nested XML tags.
- Properly define XML tag attributes.

Estimated Time: 1.5 hours

VOCABULARY

Directive tag

Extensible

eXtensible Markup Language

Name-value pair

Platform neutral

Shortcut tags

Tag nesting

XML Basics

The HyperText Markup Language (HTML) has enjoyed a tremendous rate of growth over the past decade, and is currently the most widely used Internet technology. However, many other technologies are also designed to take advantage of the Internet's infrastructure. One such technology is XML, which is an acronym for *eXtensible Markup Language*. Since XML is also a markup language, it probably will not surprise you to learn that it has several things in common with HTML. However, it also has some fundamental differences that you will learn about in this lesson.

XML has become increasingly popular among professional software developers for various reasons. For one thing, XML is *platform neutral*, which means that it can be used on any number of different computer systems. Like HTML, XML can be read and processed by virtually any type of computer system including Macintosh workstations, Windows-based PCs, minicomputers running some form of UNIX, or even large-scale mainframe computers. XML is ideal for many software applications that need to function in a heterogeneous computing environment. Additionally, XML documents, like HTML documents, are composed of text that can be created very easily by anyone with a text editor.

XML vs. HTML

HTML is composed of nothing more than text with special tags embedded throughout the text. The tags serve as instructions to a Web browser that describe how the text in the HTML document should be displayed. For example, the tags <B> and </B> tell the browser that the text between these tags should be displayed in a bold font. Likewise, the <I> and </I> tags let the browser know that the intervening text should be displayed in an italic font. However, these example HTML tags do not convey any meaning to the browser, nor to the user. They do not tell what kind of data is being displayed in a bold or an italic font. The text could be a name, a sentence, or a meaningless string of gibberish. There is no way to know simply by looking at the HTML tags.

XML, on the other hand, takes the exact opposite approach. XML tags describe the meaning of the text located between the opening and closing tags. They do not, however, provide any instructions as to how the text should be displayed. These characteristics make XML a useful technology for certain situations, but it is not sufficient to construct Web pages. You will learn more about combining other technologies with XML to create Web pages in subsequent lessons. For now, the following exercise will help you gain experience with XML.

> **Hot Tip**
>
> Students who are using Internet Explorer on Windows XP with Service Pack 2 installed may see a warning message appear when they attempt to view their XML files for the first time. If this occurs, simply acknowledge the warning by clicking the **OK** button. Then select the IE option to allow blocked content, and click **Yes** to proceed.

S TEP-BY-STEP 9.1

1. Open your preferred text editor and enter the XML code exactly as it appears in Figure 9-1.

FIGURE 9-1
Example XML code to describe a student

```
<?xml version="1.0" ?>
<student>
    <name>John Q. Smith</name>
    <address>123 Oak St. Denver, CO 80717</address>
    <phone>303-555-1212</phone>
</student>
```

2. Save this file as **one.xml**.

3. Open your Web browser and view your *one.xml* file. Your screen should look like Figure 9-2.

STEP-BY-STEP 9.1 Continued

FIGURE 9-2

Example XML file when viewed in a Web browser

4. Close your Web browser but keep your *one.xml* file open in your text editor.

Analyzing the Results

As you can see, your Web browser does not treat XML documents the same as HTML documents. Since the XML tags do not convey any information to the browser as to how the data should be displayed, it simply displays the entire document—including the tags. If your *one.xml* file had been interpreted as a standard HTML document, the XML tags would have been processed as invalid HTML tags, and simply ignored.

The first tag displayed on the browser screen is known as an XML *directive tag* rather than a standard data tag. The purpose of a directive tag is simply to convey some piece of information to the XML parser (interpreter) rather than to describe a piece of data in the XML document. In this case, the directive tag tells the browser that it should process the XML document in accordance with the XML version 1.0 syntax rules. Directive tags are created by placing a question mark character (?) immediately after the opening angle bracket and immediately before the closing angle bracket.

You should also take note of the fact that the Web browser will automatically format XML documents when it displays them. Notice how the </student> tag lines up with the <student> tag, and the other tags are indented within them. Notice also that the XML directive tag is displayed in a blue font while the data tags are displayed in red. Data fields are displayed in a bold black font. The browser will always format XML documents this way, regardless of the way in which they were written. If you want to see the "raw" formatting of the XML document your browser is displaying, you can use the View Source option the same as you would for an HTML document. (Refer to Lesson 1 if you have forgotten how to view the source of a Web page.)

Note

The red dash seen next to the XML text will be explained later in this lesson.

Understanding XML Tags

As is apparent in the simple XML document you created for the previous Step-by-Step, XML tags are formed in the same way as HTML tags. That is, they are enclosed in angle brackets (< >). All HTML tags could be legitimate XML tags, but the reverse is not true. XML tags are *extensible*, which means that they are not limited to a predefined set. An XML document may contain any tag that appropriately describes the data it defines, and there is no limit to the number of tags that can be created. This means that tags such as <NAME>, <ADDRESS>, and <PHONE> could all be considered valid within a particular XML document. And, as you might expect, closing tags are also formed as they are in HTML. That is, the tag name is preceded by a slash character (/). The closing XML tags that would correspond to the opening tags in our example would be </NAME>, </ADDRESS>, and </PHONE>, respectively.

Even though XML tags can contain virtually anything, they still must conform to various rules of syntax. For example, every opening XML tag must have a corresponding closing tag. This rule is not enforced in HTML since there are a few HTML tags (such as </BR>, <IMG>, <INPUT>, and so forth) that do not require the presence of matching closing tags.

Another XML rule of syntax is that closing tags must always appear in the reverse order of their corresponding opening tags. This rule is also not enforced in HTML. Consider the following example:

<B><I>Welcome to the wonderful world of XML!</B></I>

This line of text would be deemed acceptable in HTML, and would cause a Web browser to display the sentence in a bold, italic font. However, this same line of text would not be considered valid according to the rules of XML. The </B> tag would be matched up with the most recently used opening tag, which in this case is the <I> tag. Since </B> is not a valid closing tag for <I>, this line of text would be rejected by an XML interpreter. To correct the error, the order of the closing tags must be reversed as shown here:

<B><I>Welcome to the wonderful world of XML!</I></B>

The following exercise will give you more experience working with XML tags.

S TEP-BY-STEP 9.2

1. If necessary, open your preferred text editor and retrieve the **one.xml** file you created in the previous Step-by-Step.

2. Add two new lines of XML code exactly as shown in Figure 9-3. These lines should be added before the closing </student> tag.

FIGURE 9-3
Example XML code containing syntax errors

```
<grade>10</gpa>
<gpa>3.34</grade>
```

STEP-BY-STEP 9.2 Continued

3. Save this file as **two-a.xml**.

4. Open your Web browser and view your *two-a.xml* file. You should see an error message similar to the one shown in Figure 9-4.

FIGURE 9-4

Example XML error message as seen in a Web browser

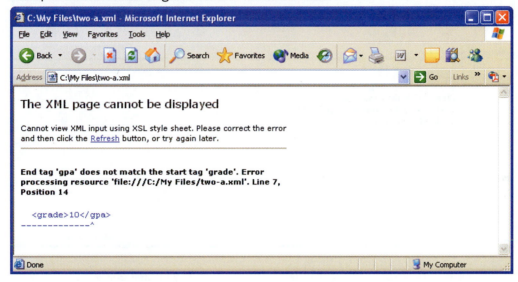

5. Return to your text editor and retrieve your **two-a.xml** file (if necessary).

6. Modify the "grade" and "gpa" data fields as shown in Figure 9-5.

FIGURE 9-5

Example XML code with syntax errors corrected

```
<grade>10</gpa>
<gpa>3.34</grade>
```

7. Save your modified file as **two-b.xml**.

STEP-BY-STEP 9.2 Continued

8. Open your Web browser (if necessary) and view your *two-b.xml* file. Your document should appear something like Figure 9-6.

FIGURE 9-6
XML document after syntax error correction

```
<?xml version="1.0" ?>
- <student>
    <name>John Q. Smith</name>
    <address>123 Oak St. Denver, CO 80717</address>
    <phone>303-555-1212</phone>
    <grade>10</grade>
    <gpa>3.34</gpa>
  </student>
```

9. Close your Web browser but keep your *two-b.xml* file open in your text editor.

Analyzing the Results

Figure 9-4 demonstrates how an XML interpreter reacts when it encounters an error in the structure of an XML document. In this case, the browser displays an error message to let the user know that the </GPA> closing tag does not match the <GRADE> opening tag. After this error is corrected, the browser displays the document correctly as in Figure 9-6. Notice that the browser still formats and colors the tags and data values as it did in Step-by-Step 9.1.

XML Shortcut Tags

Within HTML documents, it is possible to see a tag that is immediately followed by its matching closing tag. Consider the following examples:

```
<BR></BR>
<IMG SRC="bear.jpg"></IMG>
<INPUT TYPE=TEXT SIZE=20></INPUT>
```

Although these examples are considered acceptable to a Web browser, it is somewhat unusual to see an HTML document written this way. Most HTML developers would simply leave out the closing tags, and the resulting Web page would still be considered valid, and would be displayed just fine by a Web browser.

However, this is not the case for XML documents. As was stated earlier in this lesson, all XML tags must be accompanied by a matching closing tag. Simply leaving the closing tags out would result in an XML syntax error. Therefore, XML supports the concept of *shortcut tags*, which allows XML developers to combine an opening and a closing tag into a single tag whenever there is no intervening data. Shortcut tags are created by placing the slash character (/) inside the closing angle bracket. To illustrate this point, consider how the previous example tags could be rewritten using XML shortcut tags:

```
<BR/>
<IMG SRC="bear.jpg"/>
<INPUT TYPE=TEXT SIZE=20/>
```

The following exercise will give you some experience with shortcut tags.

S TEP-BY-STEP 9.3

1. If necessary, open your preferred text editor and retrieve the **two-b.xml** file you created in the previous Step-by-Step.

2. Add new XML tags exactly as shown in Figure 9-7. (Add the tags that are shown in bold.)

FIGURE 9-7
Example XML code containing an unmatched tag

```
<?xml version="1.0"?>
<student>
  <marker1>
  <name>John Q. Smith</name>
  <address>123 Oak St. Denver, CO 80717</address>
  <phone>303-555-1212</phone>
  <grade>10</grade>
  <gpa>3.34</gpa>
  <marker2>
</student>
```

3. Save this file as **three-a.xml**.

STEP-BY-STEP 9.3 Continued

4. Open your Web browser and view your *three-a.xml* file. You should see an error message similar to the one shown in Figure 9-8.

FIGURE 9-8
XML error message as seen in a Web browser

5. Return to your text editor and retrieve your **three-a.xml** file (if necessary).

6. Add a closing tag and a shortcut tag as shown in bold in Figure 9-9.

FIGURE 9-9
XML code with closing tag and shortcut tag included

```
<?xml version="1.0"?>
<student>
    <marker1></marker1>
    <name>John Q. Smith</name>
    <address>123 Oak St. Denver, CO 80717</address>
    <phone>303-555-1212</phone>
    <grade>10</grade>
    <gpa>3.34</gpa>
    <marker2>
</student>
```

7. Save your modified file as **three-b.xml**.

8. Open your Web browser (if necessary) and view your *three-b.xml* file. Your document should appear like Figure 9-10.

STEP-BY-STEP 9.3 Continued

FIGURE 9-10
XML document with shortcut tag

```
<?xml version="1.0" ?>
- <student>
    <marker1 />
    <name>John Q. Smith</name>
    <address>123 Oak St. Denver, CO 80717</address>
    <phone>303-555-1212</phone>
    <grade>10</grade>
    <gpa>3.34</gpa>
    <marker2 />
  </student>
```

9. Close your Web browser but keep your *three-b.xml* file open in your text editor.

Analyzing the Results

As you can see from the Web browser's error message in Figure 9-8, it is not acceptable to simply leave out the closing tags for <MARKER1> and <MARKER2>. When the browser's XML parser reaches the closing </STUDENT> tag, it tries to match it with the most recent opening tag, in this case <MARKER>. Since the tags don't match, an XML syntax error results.

There are two ways to correct the errors in the *three-a.xml* file. The first way is to add a closing tag to match the appropriate opening tags. This is the approach taken for the <MARKER1> tag. The second solution is to turn an unmatched opening tag into a shortcut tag by adding the slash character. This solution was used for the <MARKER2> tag. These two corrections allow the browser to display the XML document correctly.

You should also notice that your Web browser's XML interpreter displays both the <MARKER1> and the <MARKER2> fields as shortcut tags, even though <MARKER1> was not written this way. For this reason, it is important for you to be able to recognize and understand XML shortcut tags when you see them.

Nested XML Tags

Like HTML, XML supports the concept of *tag nesting*. Nesting is simply placing XML tags inside of other XML tags. The XML document in Figure 9-1 shows the tags <NAME>, <ADDRESS>, and <PHONE>, and their corresponding closing tags, nested within the <STUDENT> </STUDENT> tag pair. This example illustrates a single level of nesting, but XML allows tags to be nested to many levels. In fact, there is no predetermined limit to the number of levels that XML tags may be nested.

XML supports tag nesting because it allows XML developers to break down data into smaller, more useful components. For example, it is often useful to break down a name into its first name, middle name, and last name components. Likewise, it is very common to divide a complete address into street, city, state, and zip code parts. Even a phone number can be dissected into its area code, prefix, and suffix components, and it is sometimes useful to do so.

It is common for those who create XML documents to indent nested tags. This is not necessary, but it is helpful in giving a visual clue as to which tags are nested within other tags. Keep in mind that your Web browser will indent all XML documents as it sees fit, regardless of the way in which you write them.

STEP-BY-STEP 9.4

1. If necessary, open your preferred text editor and retrieve the *three-b.xml* file you created in the previous Step-by-Step.

2. Modify the XML code by adding nested tags as shown in bold in Figure 9-11.

FIGURE 9-11
Modified XML code containing nested tags

```xml
<?xml version="1.0"?>
<student>
  <marker1></marker1>
  <name>
        <first>John</first>
        <middle>Q.</middle>
        <last>Smith</last>
  </name>
  <address>
        <street>123 Oak St.</street>
        <city>Denver</city>
        <state>CO</state>
        <zip_code>80717</zip_code>
  </address><phone>
        <area_code>303</area_code>
        <prefix>555</prefix>
        <suffix>1212</suffix>
  </phone>
  <grade>10</grade>
  <gpa>3.34</gpa>
  <marker2/>
</student>
```

3. Save this file as **four.xml**.

4. Open your Web browser and view your *four.xml* file. You should see a screen similar to the one shown in Figure 9-12.

STEP-BY-STEP 9.4 Continued

FIGURE 9-12
XML document with nested XML tags

5. Close your Web browser but keep your *four.xml* file open in your text editor.

Analyzing the Results

As expected, the Web browser correctly displays your new XML document with two levels of nesting. The browser indents the appropriate data fields in order to provide a visual indication of which values are nested within higher level tags. You should also note that the browser displays a small red dash (–) next to each tag that has other data fields nested within it. This is just one more way in which the XML interpreter can help you verify that the overall structure of your XML document is correct.

XML Tag Attributes

Nearly every HTML tag supports one or more optional attributes. Most tag attributes consist of a name and a value separated by the equals (=) character. This sequence is commonly called a ***name-value pair***, and it is located inside the angle brackets that define a tag. XML supports tag attributes also, but the rules for attributes in XML are a little more stringent than in

HTML. For instance, all XML tag attributes require values, whereas some HTML tag attributes do not—the attribute name alone is sufficient. Consider these HTML examples:

```
<OPTION SELECTED>
<INPUT TYPE=RADIO CHECKED>
<INPUT TYPE=TEXT READONLY>
```

In these examples, the attributes SELECTED, CHECKED, and READONLY will cause a Web browser to perform the appropriate function despite the fact that they have no associated values. It is possible to add values to these attributes, but doing so will not change the behavior of the HTML processor.

One other difference between HTML tag attributes and XML tag attributes is that XML requires all attribute values to be enclosed in double quotes ("). In HTML, attribute values do not necessarily require double quotes. Here are some additional HTML examples:

```
<HR SIZE=5>
<TABLE WIDTH=640 HEIGHT=480>
<IMG SRC=MyIcon.gif WIDTH=32 HEIGHT=32>
```

As these example tags illustrate, HTML does not require double quotes around attribute values. If the HTML developer chooses to use double quotes, the document will be interpreted correctly, but it is not necessary to do so. The Web browser will display exactly the same results, with or without quotes.

If the previous six examples of HTML tags were rewritten to conform to the rules of XML syntax, they would be written as follows:

```
<OPTION SELECTED="TRUE">
<INPUT TYPE="RADIO" CHECKED="TRUE">
<INPUT TYPE="TEXT" READONLY="TRUE">
<HR SIZE="5">
<TABLE WIDTH="640" HEIGHT="480">
<IMG SRC="MyIcon.gif" WIDTH="32" HEIGHT="32">
```

Now you know how to create tag attributes correctly in XML, but you may be asking yourself why you might want to use attributes in an XML document. The answer is simply that tag attributes are an effective way of distinguishing between tags of the same name. This is true in HTML also. For example, the <INPUT> tag tells the Web browser to display an input control on a Web page, but it is the TYPE attribute that identifies what type of control to display (text field, radio button, check box, and so forth). There are times when XML developers want to accomplish the same thing. For example, it may be desirable to use an attribute to distinguish between a billing address and a shipping address. Or perhaps there may be a need to identify different types of phone numbers—home numbers versus work numbers, for instance.

The following exercise will help you gain experience with XML tag attributes.

S TEP-BY-STEP 9.5

1. If necessary, open your preferred text editor and retrieve the **four.xml** file you created in the previous Step-by-Step.

2. Modify the XML code by adding the tag attributes shown in bold in Figure 9-13.

STEP-BY-STEP 9.5 Continued

FIGURE 9-13
Modified XML code containing tag attributes

```
<?xml version="1.0"?>
<student type=high school>
  <marker1></marker1>
  <name>
      <first>John</first>
      <middle>Q.</middle>
      <last>Smith</last>
  </name>
  <address type=street>
      <street>123 Oak St.</street>
      <city>Denver</city>
      <state>CO</state>
      <zip_code>80717</zip_code>
  </address>
  <phone type=home>
      <area_code>303</area_code>
      <prefix>555</prefix>
      <suffix>1212</suffix>
  </phone>
  <grade>10</grade>
  <gpa>3.34</gpa>
  <marker2/>
</student>
```

3. Save this file as **five-a.xml**.

4. Open your Web browser and view your *five-a.xml* file. You should see an error message as shown in Figure 9-14.

FIGURE 9-14
Error message for XML document containing invalid tag attributes

STEP-BY-STEP 9.5 Continued

5. Return to your text editor and retrieve your *five-a.html* file (if necessary).

6. Enclose the attribute values in double quotes as shown in Figure 9-15.

FIGURE 9-15
Modified XML code with double quotes included

```xml
<?xml version="1.0"?>
<student type="high school">
  <marker1></marker1>
  <name>
        <first>John</first>
        <middle>Q.</middle>
        <last>Smith</last>
  </name>
  <address type="street">
        <street>123 Oak St.</street>
        <city>Denver</city>
        <state>CO</state>
        <zip_code>80717</zip_code>
  </address>
  <phone type="home">
        <area_code>303</area_code>
        <prefix>555</prefix>
        <suffix>1212</suffix>
  </phone>
  <grade>10</grade>
  <gpa>3.34</gpa>
  <marker2/>
</student>
```

7. Save your modified file as **five-b.xml**.

8. Open your Web browser (if necessary) and view your *five-b.xml* file. Your document should appear something like Figure 9-16.

STEP-BY-STEP 9.5 Continued

FIGURE 9-16
XML document with valid tag attributes

9. Close your Web browser but keep your *five-b.xml* file open in your text editor.

Analyzing the Results

As you can see from Figure 9-14, the XML parser will indicate if tag attribute values are not properly enclosed in double quotes. Once this problem is corrected, the XML document will be displayed without errors as it appears in Figure 9-16.

In this particular example, we added a TYPE attribute to the <STUDENT>, <ADDRESS>, and <PHONE> tags. Hypothetically, these attributes could be used to distinguish different types of students (for example, high school vs. college), addresses (for example, street vs. mailing), or phone numbers (for example, home vs. work).

SUMMARY

In this lesson you learned:

- How to create simple XML documents.

- How to define XML tags properly.

- How to create and use XML shortcut tags.

- How to nest tags within an XML document.

- How to properly define XML tag attributes.

VOCABULARY *Review*

Define the following terms:

Directive tag
Extensible
eXtensible Markup Language

Name-value pair
Platform neutral

Shortcut tags
Tag nesting

REVIEW *Questions*

TRUE/FALSE

Circle T if the statement is true or F if the statement is false.

T F **1.** XML tags tell a Web browser how their associated data should be displayed.

T F **2.** All opening XML tags require a corresponding closing tag.

T F **3.** XML shortcut tags are formed by adding a slash character inside the closing angle bracket.

T F **4.** Nested tags are not supported in XML, and will cause a syntax error if used.

T F **5.** All XML tags require the presence of a value, but the double quotes around the value are optional.

FILL IN THE BLANK

Complete the following sentences by writing the correct word or words in the blanks provided.

1. XML is an acronym that stands for _____.

2. XML tags are _____, which means there is no predetermined limit on the number of tags you can create.

3. Whenever an opening XML tag is immediately followed by its matching closing tag, the two tags can be replaced by a single _____.

4. Placing XML tags inside of other XML tags is known as _____.

5. All XML tag attributes consist of a(n) _____, which is an identifier followed by an equals character followed by a string enclosed in double quotes.

WRITTEN QUESTIONS

Write a brief answer to each of the following questions.

1. What is the fundamental difference in purpose between HTML tags and XML tags?

2. Why is it that all HTML tags could be considered valid XML tags, but not all XML tags are necessarily valid HTML tags?

3. What is the difference between a directive tag and a data tag in XML?

4. What are XML shortcut tags? When may they be used?

5. What are name-value pairs, and how are they used in XML?

PROJECTS

 PROJECT 9-1

GreatApplications, Inc. has decided to enter the business of selling products over the Web. They have also decided that they want to use XML technology in this new business venture. Your first assignment is to create a simple XML document that will adequately describe the various data fields that comprise a customer. Such fields should include a unique identifier (customer ID), a name, an address, and so forth.

Create an XML document that has a structure similar to that shown in Figure 9-9 (which describes a student). Include at least five data fields within your customer XML document. Save your completed XML document as **project9-1.xml**, and then view it in a Web browser to make sure your XML structure is correct. If your document contains any syntax errors your browser will display an error message. If not, your customer record should look similar to the student record displayed in Figure 9-6.

  TEAMWORK PROJECT

GreatApplications, Inc. management has reviewed your XML document design for customers, and they have decided they need more detailed information. In a team of three or four students, collectively analyze your customer XML documents and determine where nested tags can be used to provide more useful information about a customer. Identify which XML data fields can be broken down into two or more components. Compile your results in a table that looks something like the one in Table 9-1. Save your document as **teamwork.doc**.

TABLE 9-1
Table of nested XML tags

XML DATA FIELD	DATA COMPONENTS
data field 1	component 1
	component 2
	. . .
	component N
data field 2	component 1
	component 2
	. . .
	component N
data field 3	component 1
	component 2
	. . .
	component N
.	
.	
.	
.	
.	
data field N	component 1
	component 2
	. . .
	component N

WEB PROJECT

After you have completed your data analysis in the teamwork project, go ahead and implement your design. You should begin by retrieving your **project9-1.xml** file. Make the necessary changes to add nested XML tags that define the data components you identified in your teamwork project. After you have completed your changes, save the resulting file as **web-project.xml**, and then view your file in a Web browser. If the browser displays an error message, fix the XML syntax error (or errors) that caused it and try again. Continue this process until the browser displays your document correctly.

CRITICAL *Thinking*

 ACTIVITY 9-1

Create a table that identifies and explains the XML rules of syntax that are not necessarily enforced in HTML. Your table should include a brief description of the rule, and examples of XML and HTML code that further illustrate the differences. Your resulting work should look something like Table 9-2. Save your table as **activity9-1.doc**

TABLE 9-2
Table of XML syntax rules that differ from HTML

RULE DESCRIPTION	XML EXAMPLES	HTML EXAMPLES
XML syntax rule description 1	XML example 1	HTML example 1
XML syntax rule description 2	XML example 2	HTML example 2
XML syntax rule description 3	XML example 3	HTML example 3
. . .	. . .	. . .
XML syntax rule description *N*	XML example *N*	HTML example *N*

 ACTIVITY 9-2

Even though XML is not designed for Web page development, one of the most effective ways to validate the structure of an XML document is to view it in a Web browser. Write a short paragraph that identifies those aspects of the Web browser's display format that can help XML developers identify errors in their documents.

 ACTIVITY 9-3

Your supervisor at GreatApplications, Inc. has instructed you to include some additional information in your customer XML document. Management has decided that it is necessary to maintain both a billing and a shipping address for each customer. In addition, they want to support at least three phone numbers (home, work, other) to be used by the telemarketing department.

Retrieve your **web-project.xml** file and make the appropriate changes. Use XML tag attributes to distinguish one type of address from the other and one type of phone number from another. Save the modified version of your file under the name **activity9-3.xml,** and then view your new document in a Web browser. Make all necessary corrections if your document does not display properly.

SUMMARY*Project*

Hopefully you have learned a lot about XML in this lesson, and this is your chance to demonstrate how well you know the concepts that were presented.

You should recognize the fact that it does GreatApplications, Inc. little good to maintain customer information by itself. It is also necessary for them to store data about the products they wish to sell to those customers. Create an XML document that describes several data fields associated with a product. Use nested XML tags and tag attributes where necessary, and save your completed document as **summary-project.xml.** When viewed in a Web browser, your completed document should look something like Figure 9-17.

FIGURE 9-17
XML document to describe a product

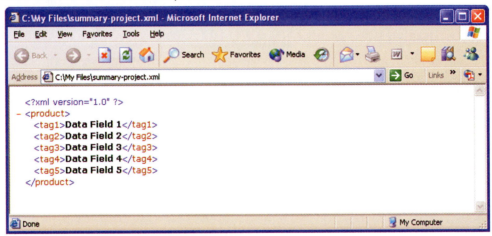

PROJECT REQUIREMENTS

- Your product XML document must contain at least five data fields.

- One of your data fields must be a unique product identifier (product ID).

- You must include at least one nested data field.

- Include at least one XML tag attribute.

INTRODUCTION TO XHTML

OBJECTIVES

Upon completion of this lesson, you should be able to:

- Create simple XHTML documents.
- Recognize common HTML tags that do not conform to XHTML syntax rules.
- Transition HTML tags and attributes to XHTML format.
- Convert HTML attributes that do not include values.
- Transition HTML frame sets to XHTML.

Estimated Time: 1.5 hours

VOCABULARY

Case sensitive

Document Type Definition (DTD)

Document type tag (<DOCTYPE>)

eXtensible HyperText Markup Language (XHTML)

HTML transitioning

Shortcut tags

XML namespace

XHTML Basics

In the previous lesson you learned about the fundamental differences between HTML and XML. In this lesson, you will learn about a relatively new Internet technology that combines some of the characteristics of both HTML and XML. It is called XHTML, which stands for *eXtensible HyperText Markup Language*. Once again, it will probably not surprise you to learn that this markup language has many things in common with the other two markup languages.

Like HTML, XHTML is a technology that is designed to instruct Web browsers how to display data on the screen. It does not attempt to describe any particular piece of data the way XML does. However, XHTML enforces the same rules of syntax that are imposed by XML. This means that Web documents that may be considered syntactically correct by HTML standards may not be acceptable to an XHTML interpreter. By completing the following exercises, you will gain valuable experience in recognizing differences between HTML and XHTML. You will also learn what is required to convert existing Web pages to the XHTML format.

Basic XHTML Document Rules

In Lesson 9 you learned that because of its extensible nature, not all XML documents can be interpreted as valid HTML Web pages. However, all HTML Web pages can be considered, or at least transitioned, into valid XML documents. *HTML transitioning* means converting a Web page into a valid XML document by locating and correcting (if necessary) all HTML elements that do not conform to the rules of XML syntax. As you learned in Lesson 9, such elements might include unmatched opening tags, unquoted attribute values, or attributes with no value at all. Once your HTML document conforms to all XML syntax rules, you essentially have an XHTML document.

Although a transitioned HTML file contains most of the requirements for a valid XHTML file, there are just a few other things you need to know to get started. For example, XHTML files are really nothing more than XML documents that contain special "instructions" for Web browsers. These instructions basically tell the browser to treat the file as though it were an HTML Web page.

The first "instruction" you need to know is the *document type tag*, which looks something like this:

```
<!DOCTYPE document type>
```

The "document type" portion of this is called a *Document Type Definition* or DTD. There are actually three different XHTML document types, but for now you only need to concern yourself with one—the "transitional" type. This specific tag looks like this:

```
<!DOCTYPE xhtml PUBLIC "-//W3C//DTD XHTML 1.0 Transitional//EN"
"http://www.w3.org/TR/xhtml1/DTD/xhtml1-transitional.dtd">
```

The second element you need to add to your transitioned HTML file is called an XML namespace URL. An *XML namespace* is simply a set of rules that define what tags and tag attributes are valid within an XML document. In this case, we want to use a namespace that defines the HTML tag set as being valid XML tags.

The way in which you specify the XML namespace for your XHTML file is to add an attribute to your opening <HTML> tag. As you should recall from Lesson 9, a valid XML attribute consists of a name-value pair. In this case, the attribute name is called xmlns and the value is the URL of the namespace you want to use. For all of the exercises in this lesson you should specify your XML namespace as follows.

```
<html xmlns="http://www.w3.org/1999/xhtml">
```

There are just a few more rules of XHTML syntax to cover, and then you can get started on your very first XHTML exercise.

First of all, the <HEAD></HEAD> section of an HTML document is optional, and the document title tags (<TITLE></TITLE>) may be placed inside the <BODY></BODY> section. This is not so in XHTML. XHTML syntax requires the presence of the header section. Title tags, if present, must be placed in the document header, not the document body.

Secondly, the header section of your XHTML documents should contain a meta tag which specifies the type of character encoding you want the browser to use. Describing all of the possible character sets that could be used in this meta tag is beyond the scope of this book.

Did You Know?

You will encounter the "W3C" acronym frequently in books and articles that relate to XML, XHTML, XSL, and other Internet technologies. This acronym identifies the *World Wide Web Consortium* which is an organization composed of industry professionals who collectively discuss and define Internet standards for the World Wide Web. (Their Web site address is *www.w3c.org*.) The Document Type Definitions (DTDs) and XML namespaces that you will use throughout this book were defined by this organization. Most industry professionals adhere to the standards defined by the W3C, but it is not strictly necessary to do so. If, for example, you wanted to write your XHTML tags in uppercase letters, you could create your own XML namespace rather than using the W3C namespace specified in this lesson's Step-by-Step exercises.

Suffice it to say that we will use UTF-8 character encoding which is the most commonly used encoding type in the United States. (It is roughly equivalent to the ASCII character set.)

Finally, all of the HTML tags in XHTML documents must appear in lowercase letters, whereas standard HTML allows any combination of upper and/or lowercase letters. The reason for this restriction is because XML is *case sensitive*. In other words, XML treats tags like <HTML> and <html> as two different tags. And since the XML namespace defines the HTML tag set in lowercase letters, the XHTML documents that use this namespace must also contain lowercase tags in order for those tags to be considered valid.

Now that you understand the basic construction of a simple XHTML document, let's get started on the first Step-by-Step.

STEP-BY-STEP 10.1

1. Open your preferred text editor and enter the XHTML code exactly as it appears in Figure 10-1.

FIGURE 10-1
An example XHTML document

```
<!DOCTYPE xhtml PUBLIC "-//W3C//DTD XHTML 1.0 Transitional//EN"
"http://www.w3.org/TR/xhtml1/DTD/xhtml1-transitional.dtd">

<html xmlns="http://www.w3.org/1999/xhtml">

<head>
    <meta http-equiv="Content-Type" content="text/html;charset=utf-8"/>
    <title>XHTML Document 1</title>
</head>

<body>
    <center>
        <h1>Hello XHTML World!</h1>
    </center>
</body>
</html>
```

2. Save this file as **one-x.html**.

3. Open your Web browser and view your *one-x.html* file. Your screen should look like Figure 10-2. Leave both your text editor and your Web browser open for the next exercise.

FIGURE 10-2
Example XHTML file when viewed in a Web browser

Analyzing the Results

As you can see, there are not too many differences between this simple XHTML document and an equivalent HTML Web page. However, let's review the various differences to make sure you have a firm grasp on the new XHTML concepts that are introduced here.

First, the code listing begins with the <!DOCTYPE> tag, which defines this Web page as a transitional XHTML document. Next, the XML namespace is identified, which determines what tags and tag attributes will, or will not, be considered valid by the XHTML parser (interpreter). As a result of the XML namespace that was identified in the <html> tag, all of the HTML tags that you entered must appear in lowercase letters rather than uppercase or mixed case letters. In addition, the header section of the Web page must be present, and the document title, if specified, must appear between the <head> and </head> tags. The <meta> tag that specifies the UTF-8 character set is technically not required, but it is a good idea to include it to make sure the user's Web browser chooses the correct character encoding method.

Finally, you should also recognize that every opening tag in this XHTML document has a matching closing tag. In addition, every closing tag must appear in the reverse order of its corresponding opening tag. These facts may not seem very significant in this simple introductory Web page, but it will become increasingly apparent as you work through the remaining exercises in this lesson that these XML rules will force you to change some of your normal HTML coding practices.

XHTML Tag Pairs and Shortcut Tags

Now that you have created an XHTML file from scratch, we will give you a chance to transition an HTML document to XHTML. Actually, you will need to transition only a portion of an HTML file that you created back in Lesson 2.

The HTML code that appears in Figure 2-3 is an example of some simple HTML tags that need to be modified in order to work properly in an XHTML environment. Consider the following snippet of HTML code from that listing.

```
<P>There are many ways to organize a Web page. This Web
page will organize text, hyperlinks, colors, and fonts.
You'll also demonstrate single spacing, double spacing,
and the use of line breaks.
<P>This Web page will display how to organize Web pages
in a number of ways using:

<BR>Powerful Lines
<BR>Hyperlinks to HTML and JavaScript Sources
<BR>Hyperlinks to Previously Created Web Pages
<BR>Fancy Fonts
<BR>Perfect Pictures
<BR>Orderly Tables
<BR>Extraordinary Extras
```

Despite the fact that this code fragment contains only a few tags, and very simple tags at that, it still does not conform to the XHTML syntax rules. It demonstrates problems with case (it contains uppercase tags), and with tag matching (no closing tags are present). Of course it is very straightforward to change the tags from uppercase to lowercase. It is also not difficult to add closing tags where they are needed. However, doing so can result in code that looks a bit strange. Consider how the bottom half of the code snippet would look after adding closing </br> tags.

```
<br></br>Powerful Lines
<br></br>Hyperlinks to HTML and JavaScript Sources
<br></br>Hyperlinks to Previously Created Web Pages
<br></br>Fancy Fonts
<br></br>Perfect Pictures
<br></br>Orderly Tables
<br></br>Extraordinary Extras
```

This is a very common situation where professional developers would most likely take advantage of the fact that XHTML, like XML, supports *shortcut tags*. As you probably recall from Lesson 9, XML shortcut tags allow you to combine the opening and closing tag whenever there is no intervening data or nested tags. So in this case, you will probably want to use the <br/> shortcut tag rather than opening and closing
</br> tags. The following exercise gives you some firsthand experience in this area.

> **Hot Tip**
>
> Nearly all of the HTML code that you will transition to XHTML in this lesson is taken from Lesson 2 and Lesson 3 exercises. Rather than spending a lot of time keying this code again, you could copy it from those previous exercises, and paste it into your current project. To copy text, simply highlight (select) the text in the old HTML file and press Ctrl+C. Then position the text cursor within your new XHTML file and press Ctrl+V to paste it.

STEP-BY-STEP 10.2

1. Switch to your text editor and, if necessary, open the **one-x.html** file you created in the previous Step-by-Step.

STEP-BY-STEP 10.2 Continued

2. Change the XHTML document number in the title from *1* to **2**.

3. Add the text shown in bold in Figure 10-3.

FIGURE 10-3
Example XHTML file containing invalid HTML tags

```
<!DOCTYPE xhtml PUBLIC "-//W3C//DTD XHTML 1.0 Transitional//EN"
  "http://www.w3.org/TR/xhtml1/DTD/xhtml1-transitional.dtd">

<html xmlns="http://www.w3.org/1999/xhtml">

<head>
    <meta http-equiv="Content-Type" content="text/html;charset=utf-8"/>
    <title>XHTML Document 2</title>
</head>

<body>
    <center>
        <h1>Hello XHTML World!</h1>
    </center>

    <P>There are many ways to organize a Web page. This Web
    page will organize text, hyperlinks, colors, and fonts.
    You'll also demonstrate single spacing, double spacing,
    and the use of line breaks.
    <P>This Web page will display how to organize Web pages
    in a number of ways using:

    <BR>Powerful Lines
    <BR>Hyperlinks to HTML and JavaScript Sources
    <BR>Hyperlinks to Previously Created Web Pages
    <BR>Fancy Fonts
    <BR>Perfect Pictures
    <BR>Orderly Tables
    <BR>Extraordinary Extras
</body>

</html>
```

STEP-BY-STEP 10.2 Continued

4. Convert all of the uppercase HTML tags to lowercase as shown in bold in Figure 10-4.

FIGURE 10-4
Example XHTML file with lowercase tags

```
<!DOCTYPE xhtml PUBLIC "-//W3C//DTD XHTML 1.0 Transitional//EN"
 "http://www.w3.org/TR/xhtml1/DTD/xhtml1-transitional.dtd">

<html xmlns="http://www.w3.org/1999/xhtml">

<head>
    <meta http-equiv="Content-Type" content="text/html;charset=utf-8"/>
    <title>XHTML Document 2</title>
</head>

<body>
    <center>
        <h1>Hello XHTML World!</h1>
    </center>


    <p>There are many ways to organize a Web page. This Web
    page will organize text, hyperlinks, colors, and fonts.
    You'll also demonstrate single spacing, double spacing,
    and the use of line breaks.
    <p>This Web page will display how to organize Web pages
    in a number of ways using:


    <br>Powerful Lines
    <br>Hyperlinks to HTML and JavaScript Sources
    <br>Hyperlinks to Previously Created Web Pages
    <br>Fancy Fonts
    <br>Perfect Pictures
    <br>Orderly Tables
    <br>Extraordinary Extras
</body>

</html>
```

STEP-BY-STEP 10.2 Continued

5. Now add the closing </p> tags, and convert the <br> tags to shortcut tags as shown in bold in Figure 10-5.

FIGURE 10-5
Example XHTML file with closing tags and shortcut tags

```
<!DOCTYPE xhtml PUBLIC "-//W3C//DTD XHTML 1.0 Transitional//EN"
"http://www.w3.org/TR/xhtml1/DTD/xhtml1-transitional.dtd">

<html xmlns="http://www.w3.org/1999/xhtml">

<head>
    <meta http-equiv="Content-Type" content="text/html;charset=utf-8"/>
    <title>XHTML Document 2</title>
</head>

<body>
    <center>
        <h1>Hello XHTML World!</h1>
    </center>
    <p>There are many ways to organize a Web page. This Web
page will organize text, hyperlinks, colors, and fonts.
You'll also demonstrate single spacing, double spacing,
and the use of line breaks.</p>
    <p>This Web page will display how to organize Web pages
in a number of ways using:</p>

    <br/>Powerful Lines
    <br/>Hyperlinks to HTML and JavaScript Sources
    <br/>Hyperlinks to Previously Created Web Pages
    <br/>Fancy Fonts
    <br/>Perfect Pictures
    <br/>Orderly Tables
    <br/>Extraordinary Extras
</body>

</html>
```

6. Save your completed XHTML file as **two-x.html**.

7. View your *two-x.html* file in your Web browser. Your screen should look very much like Figure 10-6. Leave both your text editor and your Web browser open for the next exercise.

FIGURE 10-6
Example XHTML file fully transitioned from HTML

Analyzing the Results

The unique aspect of this exercise was that it combined several HTML concepts from Lesson 2 with XML concepts from Lesson 9. The end result is your first XHTML document that was mostly transitioned from an existing HTML document.

For the sake of review, let's summarize what you did on this Web page to make it work within the syntax rules of XHTML. First, you changed the HTML tags to lowercase. Then, you added closing </p> tags to match the opening paragraph tags (<p>), and you changed the break tags (<br>) into shortcut tags. Hopefully you found these tasks to be easy, yet instructional.

XHTML Tag Attributes

Now that you have some experience with transitioning simple HTML tags to XHTML, we will take a look at transitioning tags with attributes. Another snippet of HTML code taken from Lesson 2 (Figure 2-6), shown below, will work well to illustrate the particulars of XHTML syntax with regard to tag attributes.

```
<HR>
<P><H2>Powerful Lines</H2></P>
A Horizontal Rule tag 50% wide and 10 pixels high:
<HR WIDTH=50% SIZE=10>
A Horizontal Rule tag 25% wide and 20 pixels high:
<HR WIDTH=25% SIZE=20>
A Horizontal Rule tag 10% wide and 30 pixels high:
<HR WIDTH=10% SIZE=30>
A Horizontal Rule tag without attributes:
<HR>
```

Hopefully, you will immediately recognize that the HTML tags in this code fragment need to be converted to lowercase. You should also recognize that the Horizontal Rule (<HR>) tags require the presence of matching closing tags (</HR>). Like the break (
</BR>) tags, however, the <HR></HR> tag pair looks rather strange, so this is another situation where shortcut tags would normally be used.

If you are an astute observer, and if you remember the section of Lesson 9 that discusses the rules of syntax for XML tag attributes, you should also recognize that the attributes in these example <HR> tags are not acceptable for an XHTML Web page. First, they need to be converted to lowercase like the HTML tags. (This restriction is also imposed by the XML namespace we are using.) In addition, the value part of each name-value pair needs to be enclosed in quotation marks.

The following exercise will help solidify these concepts.

STEP-BY-STEP 10.3

1. Switch to your text editor and, if necessary, open the **two-x.html** file you created in the previous exercise.

2. Change the XHTML document number in the title from *2* to **3**.

3. Add the HTML code fragment that appears in bold in Figure 10-7.

STEP-BY-STEP 10.3 Continued

FIGURE 10-7
XHTML document containing new HTML code fragment

```
<!DOCTYPE xhtml PUBLIC "-//W3C//DTD XHTML 1.0 Transitional//EN"
"http://www.w3.org/TR/xhtml1/DTD/xhtml1-transitional.dtd">

<html xmlns="http://www.w3.org/1999/xhtml">

<head>
    <meta http-equiv="Content-Type" content="text/html;charset=utf-8"/>
    <title>XHTML Document 3</title>
</head>

<body>
    <center>
        <h1>Hello XHTML World!</h1>
    </center>

    <p>There are many ways to organize a Web page. This Web
    page will organize text, hyperlinks, colors, and fonts.
    You'll also demonstrate single spacing, double spacing,
    and the use of line breaks.</p>
    <p>This Web page will display how to organize Web pages
    in a number of ways using:</p>

    <br/>Powerful Lines
    <br/>Hyperlinks to HTML and JavaScript Sources
    <br/>Hyperlinks to Previously Created Web Pages
    <br/>Fancy Fonts
    <br/>Perfect Pictures
    <br/>Orderly Tables
    <br/>Extraordinary Extras

    <HR>
    <P><H2>Powerful Lines</H2></P>
    A Horizontal Rule tag 50% wide and 10 pixels high:
    <HR WIDTH=50% SIZE=10>
    A Horizontal Rule tag 25% wide and 20 pixels high:
    <HR WIDTH=25% SIZE=20>
    A Horizontal Rule tag 10% wide and 30 pixels high:
    <HR WIDTH=10% SIZE=30>
    A Horizontal Rule tag without attributes:
    <HR>
</body>

</html>
```

STEP-BY-STEP 10.3 Continued

4. Convert all of the uppercase HTML tags and attributes to lowercase as shown in bold in Figure 10-8.

FIGURE 10-8
XHTML document with lowercase tags and attributes

```
<!DOCTYPE xhtml PUBLIC "-//W3C//DTD XHTML 1.0 Transitional//EN"
 "http://www.w3.org/TR/xhtml1/DTD/xhtml1-transitional.dtd">

<html xmlns="http://www.w3.org/1999/xhtml">

<head>
    <meta http-equiv="Content-Type" content="text/html;charset=utf-8"/>
    <title>XHTML Document 3</title>
</head>

<body>
    <center>
        <h1>Hello XHTML World!</h1>
    </center>

    <p>There are many ways to organize a Web page. This Web
page will organize text, hyperlinks, colors, and fonts.
You'll also demonstrate single spacing, double spacing,
and the use of line breaks.</p>
    <p>This Web page will display how to organize Web pages
in a number of ways using:</p>

    <br/>Powerful Lines
    <br/>Hyperlinks to HTML and JavaScript Sources
    <br/>Hyperlinks to Previously Created Web Pages
    <br/>Fancy Fonts
    <br/>Perfect Pictures
    <br/>Orderly Tables
    <br/>Extraordinary Extras

    <hr>
    <p><h2>Powerful Lines</h2></p>
A Horizontal Rule tag 50% wide and 10 pixels high:
    <hr width=50% size=10>
A Horizontal Rule tag 25% wide and 20 pixels high:
    <hr width=25% size=20>
A Horizontal Rule tag 10% wide and 30 pixels high:
    <hr width=10% size=30>
A Horizontal Rule tag without attributes:
    <hr>
</body>

</html>
```

STEP-BY-STEP 10.3 Continued

5. Now convert the <hr> tags to shortcut tags, and place double quotation marks around the attribute values as shown in bold in Figure 10-9.

FIGURE 10-9
XHTML document with shortcut tags and quoted attribute values

```
<!DOCTYPE xhtml PUBLIC "-//W3C//DTD XHTML 1.0 Transitional//EN"
 "http://www.w3.org/TR/xhtml1/DTD/xhtml1-transitional.dtd">

<html xmlns="http://www.w3.org/1999/xhtml">

<head>
    <meta http-equiv="Content-Type" content="text/html;charset=utf-8"/>
    <title>XHTML Document 3</title>
</head>

<body>
    <center>
        <h1>Hello XHTML World!</h1>
    </center>

    <p>There are many ways to organize a Web page. This Web
    page will organize text, hyperlinks, colors, and fonts.
    You'll also demonstrate single spacing, double spacing,
    and the use of line breaks.</p>
    <p>This Web page will display how to organize Web pages
    in a number of ways using:</p>

    <br/>Powerful Lines
    <br/>Hyperlinks to HTML and JavaScript Sources
    <br/>Hyperlinks to Previously Created Web Pages
    <br/>Fancy Fonts
    <br/>Perfect Pictures
    <br/>Orderly Tables
    <br/>Extraordinary Extras

    <hr/>
    <p><h2>Powerful Lines</h2></p>
    A Horizontal Rule tag 50% wide and 10 pixels high:
    <hr width="50%" size="10"/>
    A Horizontal Rule tag 25% wide and 20 pixels high:
    <hr width="25%" size="20"/>
    A Horizontal Rule tag 10% wide and 30 pixels high:
    <hr width="10%" size="30"/>
    A Horizontal Rule tag without attributes:
    <hr/>
</body>
</html>
```

STEP-BY-STEP 10.3 Continued

6. Now save your completed XHTML file as **three-x.html**.

7. View your *three-x.html* file in your Web browser. Your Web page should look similar to the one shown in Figure 10-10. Leave both your text editor and your Web browser open for the next exercise.

FIGURE 10-10
XHTML Web page for Document 3

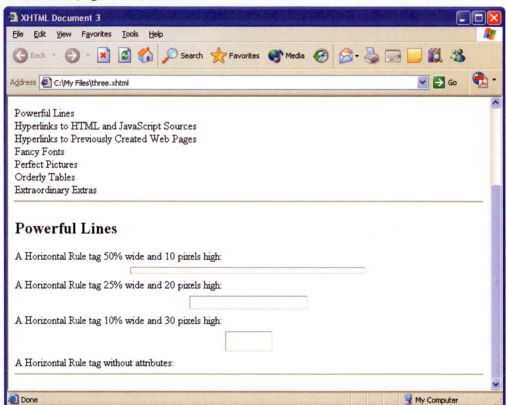

Analyzing the Results

After completing just three Step-by-Step exercises, you have already gained valuable experience with most of the syntax rules of XHTML. To be sure that you have a firm understanding of the concepts presented in Step-by-Step 10.3, let's review the important parts.

First, you had to convert the uppercase HTML tags to lowercase as you did in the previous exercise. Then you had to convert all of the tag attributes to lowercase as well. After that, you transitioned the horizontal rule (<hr>) tags into valid XHTML tags by making them shortcut tags. And finally, you placed double quotation marks around the attribute values to bring them into conformity with XML/XHTML tag attribute standards.

With just a little more effort, you will soon be able to transition most any Web page into XHTML, so let's push forward to the next section of this lesson.

More Useful Tags—XHTML Style

In Lesson 3 you learned about many useful HTML tags that can help you improve the appearance and functionality of your Web pages. For example, the HTML image (<IMG>) tag can add tremendous visual appeal and eye-catching color to an otherwise dull Web page. In addition, Web designers who need to create online forms of any kind will want to make use of the selection (<SELECT>) and option (<OPTION>) tags and/or various types of input (<INPUT>) tags.

Of course, XHTML developers can use all of these tags in their Web pages as well. However, each of these Web page components must be constructed correctly in order to work properly in an XML environment. Obviously these tags, and any associated attributes, must be converted to lowercase like all the other tags and attributes you have used so far. You must also make sure that each of these tags has a matching closing tag, since they are often not present within standard HTML files. In most cases, Web page designers will simply transition them to XHTML by adding the slash (/) character to make them shortcut tags.

As you should expect, all of the attributes that might appear in these HTML tags must have their values enclosed in double quotation marks. However, the <OPTION> and <INPUT> tags can be particularly tricky to transition, because they often contain attributes with no associated value. For example, if you wanted to indicate that a particular option within a drop-down list control (<SELECT>) should be selected by default, you would probably include a SELECTED attribute within the <OPTION> tag—and this attribute normally would not include a value.

Similarly, at times you may want a text field, a radio button, or a check box to appear on a form in a read-only or disabled state. This is easily done in HTML by adding a READONLY or DISABLED attribute to the appropriate <INPUT> tag, and no value is needed for either of these attributes. But attribute names with no associated values are not valid in XML syntax, so you need to know what to do to make them work properly within XHTML documents.

The following exercise will instruct you in this regard. To complete this exercise you will need to transition several lines of HTML code taken from Figures 3-8 and 3-12. (If you need to refresh your memory about how to download an image, please refer to Step-by-Step 3.2.)

S TEP-BY-STEP 10.4

1. Switch to your text editor and, if necessary, open the **three-x.html** file you created in the previous Step-by-Step.

2. Change the XHTML document number in the title from *3* to **4**.

3. Add the HTML code fragments that appear in bold in Figure 10-11.

FIGURE 10-11
XHTML document containing two HTML code fragments

```
<!DOCTYPE xhtml PUBLIC "-//W3C//DTD XHTML 1.0 Transitional//EN"
"http://www.w3.org/TR/xhtml1/DTD/xhtml1-transitional.dtd">
```

STEP-BY-STEP 10.4 Continued

FIGURE 10-11 (Continued)
XHTML document containing two HTML code fragments

```
<html xmlns="http://www.w3.org/1999/xhtml">

<head>
 <meta http-equiv="Content-Type" content="text/html;charset=utf-8"/>
 <title>XHTML Document 4</title>
</head>

<body>
 <center>
  <h1>Hello XHTML World!</h1>
 </center>

 <p>There are many ways to organize a Web page. This Web
 page will organize text, hyperlinks, colors, and fonts.
 You'll also demonstrate single spacing, double spacing,
 and the use of line breaks.</p>
 <p>This Web page will display how to organize Web pages
 in a number of ways using:</p>

 <br/>Powerful Lines
 <br/>Hyperlinks to HTML and JavaScript Sources
 <br/>Hyperlinks to Previously Created Web Pages
 <br/>Fancy Fonts
 <br/>Perfect Pictures
 <br/>Orderly Tables
 <br/>Extraordinary Extras

 <hr/>
 <p><h2>Powerful Lines</h2></p>
 A Horizontal Rule tag 50% wide and 10 pixels high:
 <hr width="50%" size="10"/>
 A Horizontal Rule tag 25% wide and 20 pixels high:
 <hr width="25%" size="20"/>
 A Horizontal Rule tag 10% wide and 30 pixels high:
 <hr width="10%" size="30"/>
 A Horizontal Rule tag without attributes:
 <hr/>

 <P><H2>Perfect Pictures</H2></P>
 <P><IMG SRC=levy.gif ALIGN=RIGHT HEIGHT=50 WIDTH=50></P>
 <IMG SRC=levy.gif HEIGHT=100 WIDTH=100>
 <IMG SRC=levy.gif HEIGHT=150 WIDTH=150>
```

STEP-BY-STEP 10.4 Continued

FIGURE 10-11 (Continued)
XHTML document containing two HTML code fragments

```
<IMG SRC=levy.gif HEIGHT=200 WIDTH=200>
<P><IMG SRC=levy.gif HEIGHT=150 WIDTH=150></P>
<P><IMG SRC=levy.gif HEIGHT=200 WIDTH=200></P>
<HR>

<P><H2>Extraordinary Extras</H2></P>
<FORM>
Enter your first name:
<INPUT TYPE=TEXT SIZE=25>
<BR>
Enter your last name:
<INPUT TYPE=TEXT SIZE=25>
<P>
<SELECT>
<OPTION SELECTED>Pick your favorite team from the list:
<OPTION>Chicago Bulls
<OPTION>Utah Jazz
<OPTION>Los Angeles Lakers
<OPTION>Indiana Pacers
<OPTION>New Jersey Nets
<OPTION>Phoenix Suns
</SELECT>
<P>
The best place to eat is:
<BR>
<INPUT TYPE=RADIO NAME=BEST>Wendy's<BR>
<INPUT TYPE=RADIO NAME=BEST>McDonald's<BR>
<INPUT TYPE=RADIO NAME=BEST>Taco Bell<BR>
<INPUT TYPE=RADIO NAME=BEST>Burger King<BR>
<INPUT TYPE=RADIO NAME=BEST>KFC<BR>
<P>
I like to eat:
<BR>
<INPUT TYPE=CHECKBOX>Hamburgers<BR>
<INPUT TYPE=CHECKBOX>Tacos<BR>
<INPUT TYPE=CHECKBOX>Chicken Strips<BR>
<INPUT TYPE=CHECKBOX>Fries<BR>
<INPUT TYPE=CHECKBOX>Hot Dogs<BR>
</FORM>
</body>

</html>
```

STEP-BY-STEP 10.4 Continued

4. Convert all of the uppercase HTML tags and attributes to lowercase as shown in bold in Figure 10-12.

FIGURE 10-12
XHTML document with lowercase tags and attributes

```
<!DOCTYPE xhtml PUBLIC "-//W3C//DTD XHTML 1.0 Transitional//EN"
"http://www.w3.org/TR/xhtml1/DTD/xhtml1-transitional.dtd">

<html xmlns="http://www.w3.org/1999/xhtml">

<head>
 <meta http-equiv="Content-Type" content="text/html;charset=utf-8"/>
 <title>XHTML Document 4</title>
</head>

<body>
 <center>
   <h1>Hello XHTML World!</h1>
 </center>

 <p>There are many ways to organize a Web page. This Web
page will organize text, hyperlinks, colors, and fonts.
You'll also demonstrate single spacing, double spacing,
and the use of line breaks.</p>
 <p>This Web page will display how to organize Web pages
in a number of ways using:</p>

 <br/>Powerful Lines
 <br/>Hyperlinks to HTML and JavaScript Sources
 <br/>Hyperlinks to Previously Created Web Pages
 <br/>Fancy Fonts
 <br/>Perfect Pictures
 <br/>Orderly Tables
 <br/>Extraordinary Extras

 <hr/>
 <p><h2>Powerful Lines</h2></p>
A Horizontal Rule tag 50% wide and 10 pixels high:
 <hr width="50%" size="10"/>
A Horizontal Rule tag 25% wide and 20 pixels high:
 <hr width="25%" size="20"/>
A Horizontal Rule tag 10% wide and 30 pixels high:
 <hr width="10%" size="30"/>
A Horizontal Rule tag without attributes:
 <hr/>

 <p><h2>Perfect Pictures</h2></p>
 <p><img src=levy.gif align=right height=50 width=50></p>
```

STEP-BY-STEP 10.4 Continued

FIGURE 10-12 (Continued)
XHTML document with lowercase tags and attributes

```
<img src=levy.gif height=100 width=100>
<img src=levy.gif height=150 width=150>
<img src=levy.gif height=200 width=200>
<p><img src=levy.gif height=150 width=150></p>
<p><img src=levy.gif height=200 width=200></p>
<hr>

<p><h2>Extraordinary Extras</h2></p>
<form>
Enter your first name:
<input type=text size=25>
<br>
Enter your last name:
<input type=text size=25>
<p>
<select>
<option selected>Pick your favorite team from the list:
<option>Chicago Bulls
<option>Utah Jazz
<option>Los Angeles Lakers
<option>Indiana Pacers
<option>New Jersey Nets
<option>Phoenix Suns
</select>
<p>
The best place to eat is:
<br>
<input type=radio name=best>Wendy's<br>
<input type=radio name=best>McDonald's<br>
<input type=radio name=best>Taco Bell<br>
<input type=radio name=best>Burger King<br>
<input type=radio name=best>KFC<br>
<p>
I like to eat:
<br>
<input type=checkbox>Hamburgers<br>
<input type=checkbox>Tacos<br>
<input type=checkbox>Chicken Strips<br>
<input type=checkbox>Fries<br>
<input type=checkbox>Hot Dogs<br>
</form>
</body>

</html>
```

STEP-BY-STEP 10.4 Continued

5. Now make sure that every tag has a matching closing tag, or is converted to a shortcut tag. The tags that must be transitioned to XHTML syntax include <br>, <img>, <input>, <hr>, <option>, and <p> as shown in bold in Figure 10-13.

FIGURE 10-13
XHTML document with tag pairs and shortcut tags

```
<!DOCTYPE xhtml PUBLIC "-//W3C//DTD XHTML 1.0 Transitional//EN"
 "http://www.w3.org/TR/xhtml1/DTD/xhtml1-transitional.dtd">
<html xmlns="http://www.w3.org/1999/xhtml">

<head>
 <meta http-equiv="Content-Type" content="text/html;charset=utf-8"/>
 <title>XHTML Document 4</title>
</head>

<body>
 <center>
  <h1>Hello XHTML World!</h1>
 </center>

 <p>There are many ways to organize a Web page. This Web
 page will organize text, hyperlinks, colors, and fonts.
 You'll also demonstrate single spacing, double spacing,
 and the use of line breaks.</p>
 <p>This Web page will display how to organize Web pages
 in a number of ways using:</p>

 <br/>Powerful Lines
 <br/>Hyperlinks to HTML and JavaScript Sources
 <br/>Hyperlinks to Previously Created Web Pages
 <br/>Fancy Fonts
 <br/>Perfect Pictures
 <br/>Orderly Tables
 <br/>Extraordinary Extras

 <hr/>
 <p><h2>Powerful Lines</h2></p>
 A Horizontal Rule tag 50% wide and 10 pixels high:
 <hr width="50%" size="10"/>
 A Horizontal Rule tag 25% wide and 20 pixels high:
 <hr width="25%" size="20"/>
 A Horizontal Rule tag 10% wide and 30 pixels high:
 <hr width="10%" size="30"/>
 A Horizontal Rule tag without attributes:
 <hr/>
```

STEP-BY-STEP 10.4 Continued

FIGURE 10-13 (Continued)
XHTML document with tag pairs and shortcut tags

```
<p><h2>Perfect Pictures</h2></p>
<p><img src=levy.gif align=right height=50 width=50/></p>
<img src=levy.gif height=100 width=100/>
<img src=levy.gif height=150 width=150/>
<img src=levy.gif height=200 width=200/>
<p><img src=levy.gif height=150 width=150/></p>
<p><img src=levy.gif height=200 width=200/></p>
<hr/>


<p><h2>Extraordinary Extras</h2></p>
<form>
Enter your first name:
<input type=text size=25/>
<br/>
Enter your last name:
<input type=text size=25/>
<p>
<select>
<option selected>Pick your favorite team from the list:</option>
<option>Chicago Bulls</option>
<option>Utah Jazz</option>
<option>Los Angeles Lakers</option>
<option>Indiana Pacers</option>
<option>New Jersey Nets</option>
<option>Phoenix Suns</option>
</select>
</p>
<p>
The best place to eat is:
<br/>
<input type=radio name=best/>Wendy's<br/>
<input type=radio name=best/>McDonald's<br/>
<input type=radio name=best/>Taco Bell<br/>
<input type=radio name=best/>Burger King<br/>
<input type=radio name=best/>KFC<br/>
</p>
<p>
I like to eat:
<br/>
<input type=checkbox/>Hamburgers<br/>
<input type=checkbox/>Tacos<br/>
<input type=checkbox/>Chicken Strips<br/>
<input type=checkbox/>Fries<br/>
```

STEP-BY-STEP 10.4 Continued

FIGURE 10-13 (Continued)
XHTML document with tag pairs and shortcut tags

```
    <input type=checkbox/>Hot Dogs<br/>
    </p>
    </form>
</body>

</html>
```

6. The final transitioning step is to put double quotation marks around all attribute values. For HTML attributes that have no values, you can add a "true" value as shown in bold in Figure 10-14.

FIGURE 10-14
XHTML document with double quotation marks around attributes

```
<!DOCTYPE xhtml PUBLIC "-//W3C//DTD XHTML 1.0 Transitional//EN"
"http://www.w3.org/TR/xhtml1/DTD/xhtml1-transitional.dtd">

<html xmlns="http://www.w3.org/1999/xhtml">

<head>
  <meta http-equiv="Content-Type" content="text/html;charset=utf-8"/>
  <title>XHTML Document 4</title>
</head>

<body>
  <center>
    <h1>Hello XHTML World!</h1>
  </center>

  <p>There are many ways to organize a Web page. This Web
  page will organize text, hyperlinks, colors, and fonts.
  You'll also demonstrate single spacing, double spacing,
  and the use of line breaks.</p>
  <p>This Web page will display how to organize Web pages
  in a number of ways using:</p>

  <br/>Powerful Lines
  <br/>Hyperlinks to HTML and JavaScript Sources
  <br/>Hyperlinks to Previously Created Web Pages
  <br/>Fancy Fonts
```

STEP-BY-STEP 10.4 Continued

FIGURE 10-14 (Continued)
XHTML document with double quotation marks around attributes

```
<br/>Perfect Pictures
<br/>Orderly Tables
<br/>Extraordinary Extras

<hr/>
<p><h2>Powerful Lines</h2></p>
A Horizontal Rule tag 50% wide and 10 pixels high:
<hr width="50%" size="10"/>
A Horizontal Rule tag 25% wide and 20 pixels high:
<hr width="25%" size="20"/>
A Horizontal Rule tag 10% wide and 30 pixels high:
<hr width="10%" size="30"/>
A Horizontal Rule tag without attributes:
<hr/>

<p><h2>Perfect Pictures</h2></p>
<p><img src="levy.gif" align="right" height="50" width="50"/></p>
<img src="levy.gif" height="100" width="100"/>
<img src="levy.gif" height="150" width="150"/>
<img src="levy.gif" height="200" width="200"/>
<p><img src="levy.gif" height="150" width="150"/></p>
<p><img src="levy.gif" height="200" width="200"/></p>
<hr/>

<p><h2>Extraordinary Extras</h2></p>
<form>
Enter your first name:
<input type="text" size="25"/>
<br/>
Enter your last name:
<input type="text" size="25"/>
<p>
<select>
<option selected="true">Pick your favorite team from the list:</option>
<option>Chicago Bulls</option>
<option>Utah Jazz</option>
```

STEP-BY-STEP 10.4 Continued

FIGURE 10-14 (Continued)
XHTML document with double quotation marks around attributes

```
<option>Los Angeles Lakers</option>
<option>Indiana Pacers</option>
<option>New Jersey Nets</option>
<option>Phoenix Suns</option>
</select>
</p>
<p>
The best place to eat is:
<br/>
<input type="radio" name="best"/>Wendy's<br/>
<input type="radio" name="best"/>McDonald's<br/>
<input type="radio" name="best"/>Taco Bell<br/>
<input type="radio" name="best"/>Burger King<br/>
<input type="radio" name="best"/>KFC<br/>
</p>
<p>
I like to eat:
<br/>
<input type="checkbox"/>Hamburgers<br/>
<input type="checkbox"/>Tacos<br/>
<input type="checkbox"/>Chicken Strips<br/>
<input type="checkbox"/>Fries<br/>
<input type="checkbox"/>Hot Dogs<br/>
</p>
</form>
</body>

</html>
```

7. Now save your completed XHTML file as **four-x.html**.

STEP-BY-STEP 10.4 Continued

8. View your *four-x.html* file in your Web browser. The *Perfect Pictures* portion of your Web page should look like Figure 10-15 and the *Extraordinary Extras* section like Figure 10-16. Leave both your text editor and your Web browser open for the next exercise.

FIGURE 10-15
XHTML Web page for Document 4—Perfect Pictures

STEP-BY-STEP 10.4 Continued

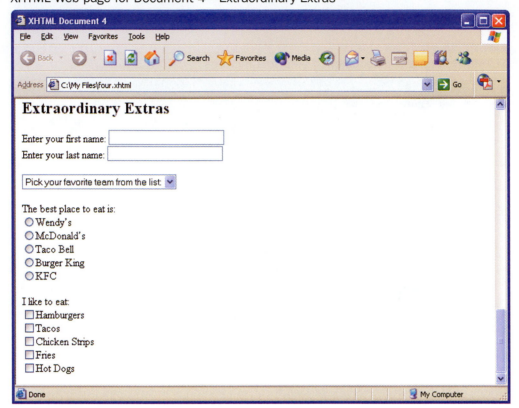

FIGURE 10-16
XHTML Web page for Document 4—Extraordinary Extras

Analyzing the Results

This exercise reinforced the concepts of converting tags and attributes to lowercase. It also gave you additional experience in making sure that every opening tag has a matching closing tag or is converted to a shortcut tag when appropriate. In addition, this exercise gave you another opportunity to transition attribute values by enclosing them in double quotation marks and introduced the concept of adding a quoted "true" value to any HTML attribute that does not have a value.

Now that you have completed your fourth Step-by-Step exercise, you should be able to transition most any HTML document to XHTML. Even if you encounter a Web page that contains many tags and attributes that are different from those you have worked with so far, the same concepts still apply.

XHTML Frame Sets

The one area of HTML Web page development that we have not yet addressed in this lesson is the construction of frame sets. Initially, you might assume that transitioning an HTML frame set document to XHTML is exactly the same as transitioning any other Web page. Well, the process is mostly the same, but there is a small difference. The document type definition that determines the correct syntax for transitional Web pages requires the presence of both <head></head> tags and <body></body> tags. But, if you recall the concepts presented in Lesson 4, you will remember that HTML frame set documents do not contain body tags. Therefore, a standard HTML frame set cannot be transitioned to XHTML unless another change is made to the XHTML document structure.

Fortunately, the way to make frame set documents work correctly in XHTML is relatively simple. This task is accomplished simply by changing the <DOCTYPE> tag to include a different Document Type Definition (DTD). (It is not even necessary to change the XML namespace URL, because the namespace URL we are using contains definitions for frame-related tags, too.) The correct DTD for an XHTML frame set document looks like this:

```
<!DOCTYPE xhtml PUBLIC "-//W3C//DTD XHTML 1.0 Frameset//EN"
"http://www.w3.org/TR/xhtml1/DTD/xhtml1-frameset.dtd">
```

Once you have included this DTD in a fully transitioned frame set document, you are good to go! The following exercise will help you get some experience with XHTML frame sets.

STEP-BY-STEP 10.5

1. Switch to your text editor, clear the contents of the editor, and enter the HTML code (taken from Figure 4-2) exactly as shown in Figure 10-17.

FIGURE 10-17
HTML frame set code

```
<HTML>
<TITLE>HTML and JavaScript</TITLE>

<FRAMESET COLS="180,*">
<FRAME NAME="LeftFrame" SRC="navbar.html">
<FRAME NAME="RightFrame" SRC="welcome.html">
</FRAMESET>
</HTML>
```

2. Add the XHTML <DOCTYPE> tag that supports frame sets. Then transition the <HTML> tag by changing it to lowercase and by adding the XML namespace attribute as shown in bold in Figure 10-18.

FIGURE 10-18
HTML frame set with XHTML <DOCTYPE> tag

```
<!DOCTYPE xhtml PUBLIC "-//W3C//DTD XHTML 1.0 Frameset//EN"
"http://www.w3.org/TR/xhtml1/DTD/xhtml1-frameset.dtd">

<html xmlns="http://www.w3.org/1999/xhtml">
```

STEP-BY-STEP 10.5 Continued

FIGURE 10-18 (Continued)
HTML frame set with XHTML <DOCTYPE> tag

```
<TITLE>HTML and JavaScript</TITLE>

<FRAMESET COLS="180,*">
<FRAME NAME="LeftFrame" SRC="navbar.html">
<FRAME NAME="RightFrame" SRC="welcome.html">
</FRAMESET>
</HTML>
```

3. Next, create an XHTML-compatible header by enclosing the document title within <head> and </head> tags. Also, change the title tags to lowercase, and change the title text as shown in bold in Figure 10-19.

FIGURE 10-19
HTML frame set with valid header

```
<!DOCTYPE xhtml PUBLIC "-//W3C//DTD XHTML 1.0 Frameset//EN"
 "http://www.w3.org/TR/xhtml1/DTD/xhtml1-frameset.dtd">

<html xmlns="http://www.w3.org/1999/xhtml">

<head>
 <meta http-equiv="Content-Type" content="text/html;charset=utf-8"/>
 <title>XHTML Document 5</title>
</head>

<FRAMESET COLS="180,*">
<FRAME NAME="LeftFrame" SRC="navbar.html">
<FRAME NAME="RightFrame" SRC="welcome.html">
</FRAMESET>
</HTML>
```

4. Now complete the transitioning of this frame set by changing the remaining tags and attributes to lowercase, and convert the frame tags to shortcut tag format. Change the name of the source file for the left frame from *navbar.html* to **navbar-x.html**. Also change the source file for the right frame from *welcome.html* to **four-x.html** as shown in bold in Figure 10-20.

FIGURE 10-20
Fully transitioned HTML frame set

```
<!DOCTYPE xhtml PUBLIC "-//W3C//DTD XHTML 1.0 Frameset//EN"
 "http://www.w3.org/TR/xhtml1/DTD/xhtml1-frameset.dtd">

<html xmlns="http://www.w3.org/1999/xhtml">
```

STEP-BY-STEP 10.5 Continued

FIGURE 10-20 (Continued)
Fully transitioned HTML frame set

```
<head>
 <meta http-equiv="Content-Type" content="text/html;charset=utf-8"/>
 <title>XHTML Document 5</title>
</head>

<frameset cols="180,*">
 <frame name="LeftFrame" src="navbar-x.html"/>
 <frame name="RightFrame" src="four-x.html"/>
</frameset>

</html>
```

5. Save your completed document as **five-x.html**.

6. Now clear the contents of your editor and enter the XHTML code as shown in Figure 10-21.

FIGURE 10-21
Sample XHTML navigation bar

```
<!DOCTYPE xhtml PUBLIC "-//W3C//DTD XHTML 1.0 Transitional//EN"
 "http://www.w3.org/TR/xhtml1/DTD/xhtml1-transitional.dtd">

<html xmlns="http://www.w3.org/1999/xhtml">

<head>
 <meta http-equiv="Content-Type" content="text/html;charset=utf-8"/>
</head>

<body>
 <center><b>Sample Links</b></center>
 <ul>
  <li>Sample Link 1</li>
  <li>Sample Link 2</li>
  <li>Sample Link 3</li>
 </ul>
</body>

</html>
```

7. Save this document as **navbar-x.html**.

8. Switch to your Web browser and view your **five-x.html** file. Your frame-based Web page should look like Figure 10-22.

STEP-BY-STEP 10.5 Continued

FIGURE 10-22
XHTML Web page for Document 5 with frames

9. Close the open files, but leave your text editor and Web browser open for the end-of-lesson exercises.

Analyzing the Results

Just to ensure that you have a firm grasp on the new concepts presented in this exercise, let's review the steps you took to transition a simple HTML frame set to XHTML.

First, you had to add a new Document Type Definition (<DOCTYPE> tag) to your file. This DTD is different from the one you used in all previous exercises because it needs to support a document structure that contains <frameset> and </frameset> tags rather than <body> and </body> tags. You also had to add the XML namespace attribute to the opening <html> tag.

Next, it was necessary for you to create a valid header section for your XHTML frame set, and then you converted the remaining tags to XHTML syntax. Don't forget that you will almost always need to transition the <frame> tags to shortcut tags since standard HTML files do not normally include closing </frame> tags.

Now that you have completed the final Step-by-Step exercise for this lesson, you should feel comfortable in transitioning virtually any HTML file to XHTML. Even if you encounter Web pages that contain tags and attributes that you have not seen in this lesson, the rules for transitioning these files to XHTML remain the same.

SUMMARY

In this lesson, you learned:

- To create simple XHTML documents.
- About common HTML tags that do not conform to XHTML syntax rules and how to recognize them.
- To transition HTML tags and attributes to XHTML format.
- To convert HTML attributes that do not include values.
- To transition HTML frame sets to XHTML.

VOCABULARY *Review*

Define the following terms:

Case sensitive	eXtensible HyperText	Shortcut tags
Document Type Definition	Markup Language	XML namespace
(DTD)	(XHTML)	
Document type tag	HTML transitioning	
(<DOCTYPE>)		

REVIEW *Questions*

TRUE/FALSE

Circle T if the statement is true or F if the statement is false.

T   F   **1.** The XHTML acronym stands for eXtensible HyperText Markup Language.

T   F   **2.** XHTML has virtually nothing in common with HTML or XML.

T   F   **3.** Like XML, XHTML does not support shortcut tags.

T   F   **4.** Like HTML, XHTML allows tag attributes with no associated value.

T   F   **5.** The Document Type Definition (DTD) tag for XHTML frame sets is different from the DTD used for other XHTML documents.

FILL IN THE BLANK

Complete the following sentences by writing the correct word or words in the blanks provided.

1. Converting an existing HTML file into a valid XHTML document is called _____.

2. A(n) _____ is a set of rules that defines the syntax for XML (and XHTML) documents.

3. Whenever an opening XHTML tag is immediately followed by its matching closing tag, the two tags can be replaced by a single _____.

4. Any language that recognizes a distinction between uppercase letters and lowercase letters is said to be _____.

5. Creating an XHTML frame set document requires the use of the appropriate _____ within its <DOCTYPE> tag.

WRITTEN QUESTIONS

Write a brief answer to each of the following questions.

1. What is a DTD, and how is it used in XHTML documents?

2. What is the purpose of an XML namespace?

3. Explain why XHTML tags must appear in lowercase letters whereas HTML tags can be in upper or lowercase letters.

4. Describe how to transition HTML attributes that have no associated values to XHTML.

5. Why is it necessary to use a special DTD for XHTML frame set documents?

PROJECTS

PROJECT 10-1

Revisit the XHTML document you saved as *four-x.html* at the end of Step-by-Step 10.4. The original HTML code on which this exercise was based (taken from Lessons 2 and 3) contains various topics at the top of the Web page, and these topics are sequentially converted into internal hyperlinks. Clicking one of these links will take the user to the location of that particular topic within the Web page.

Add this same functionality to your XHTML document for the three topics you transitioned in this lesson—Powerful Lines, Perfect Pictures, and Extraordinary Extras. (Refer to Lesson 3 if you need a refresher in creating internal hyperlinks.)

When your changes are complete, save your new XHTML document as **project10-1-x.html**. Open this file in a browser to make sure it functions correctly.

TEAMWORK PROJECT

Divide up into teams of three or four students, and briefly discuss each of the topics that are listed at the top of your *four-x.html* file but not yet implemented. These topics include:

- Hyperlinks to HTML and JavaScript Sources
- Hyperlinks to Previously Created Web Pages
- Fancy Fonts
- Orderly Tables

Each student on the team should choose one of these topics, and transition the corresponding HTML code to XHTML. (The HTML code for each topic can be found in Lesson 3.)

After each team member has completed the work for his assigned topic, he should also incorporate the transitioned HTML code that the other team members created. The end result of this team effort should be a fully functional XHTML document, which each student should save as **teamwork-x.html**.

WEB PROJECT

Review the sample navigation bar file you created as part of Step-by-Step 10.5 (and saved as *navbar-x.html*). Convert this file into an actual navigation bar by changing the bulleted list items into working hyperlinks. You are free to make these links point to other HTML or XHTML files that you created, or you can have them point to any appropriate resource on the Web. Create at least three functioning hyperlinks to make sure that you understand how to create navigational links within an XHTML document. (If you need a reminder about creating a functional navigation bar, refer to Step-by-Step 4.2 in Lesson 4.) Save your modified navigation bar as **navbar1-x.html**.

CRITICAL *Thinking*

 ACTIVITY 10-1

Create a table that identifies and explains the XHTML rules of syntax that are not necessarily enforced in standard HTML. Your table should include a brief description of the rule, and examples of XHTML and HTML code that further illustrate the differences. Your resulting work should look something like Table 10-1. Save your table as **activity10-1.doc**.

TABLE 10-1
Table of XHTML syntax rules that differ from HTML

RULE DESCRIPTION	XHTML EXAMPLES	HTML EXAMPLES
XHTML syntax rule 1	XHTML example 1	HTML example 1
XHTML syntax rule 2	XHTML example 2	HTML example 2
XHTML syntax rule 3	XHTML example 3	HTML example 3
. . .	. . .	. . .
XHTML syntax rule *N*	XHTML example *N*	HTML example *N*

 ACTIVITY 10-2

If you look through the XHTML Web page you created for Step-by-Step 10.4 (*four-x.html*) you will notice that it is almost completely black and white. (The only color is in the images of "Levy" the leviathan.) See how creative you can be and add some life and color to this Web page. Try adding in some new images that associate well with the content of the page. Experiment with new font faces, sizes, and colors to enhance the appearance of the text. Perhaps you can even add some additional input controls like text areas or buttons.

Doing all these things will allow you to further enhance your ability to create attractive Web pages that still conform to the syntax rules of XHTML.

Save your final Web page as **activity10-2-x.html**.

ACTIVITY 10-3

Reexamine the frame-based Web page you created in Step-by-Step 10.5. Consider what it would take to alter this page so that it contains three frames instead of two. Gain some additional experience with XHTML frame sets by adding a title bar frame to your previous work. (Refer to Lesson 4 if you need a reminder about what a title bar is.) You can accomplish this by adding a nested frame set to your base document, and by creating a new title bar page to display in the new frame. Your completed Web page should have the same general structure as the one shown in Figure 4-8 in Lesson 4. Save your final product as **activity10-3-x.html**.

SUMMARY *Project*

This is your chance to demonstrate that you have completely mastered the skill of XHTML development! Refer to the frame-based Web page you created in Lesson 4 that is displayed in Figure 4-8. Your assignment is to create a similar frame-based Web page that is composed of XHTML documents rather than standard HTML documents. You should begin by transitioning the four HTML Web pages that define the frame set, the title bar, the navigation bar, and the welcome page. Then make whatever changes are necessary so that your completed XHTML Web page looks like the one in Figure 10-23. Save your main frame set file as **frameset-x.html**, your title bar page as **title-x.html**, your navigation bar page as **links-x.html**, and your welcome page as **welcome-x.html**.

FIGURE 10-23
XHTML Web page with nested frames

PROJECT REQUIREMENTS

- Your base XHTML frame set document must contain a nested frame set.
- Your title bar page should display the appropriate text as shown in Figure 10-23.
- Your navigation bar page must contain at least four working hyperlinks.
- Your welcome page should display the appropriate text as shown in Figure 10-23.
- The Web pages referenced in your navigation bar should appear in the right frame (as the welcome page does in Figure 10-23).

INTRODUCTION TO XSL

OBJECTIVES

Upon completion of this lesson, you should be able to:

- Create simple XML/XSL Web pages.

- Understand what an Xpath is and how to use it.

- Use the <xsl:value-of> tag to extract and display XML data.

- Use the <xsl:attribute> tag to make Web content dynamic.

- Use the <xsl:for-each> tag to display XML data repetitively.

- Use the <xsl:if> tag for conditional XML data processing.

Estimated Time: 2.0 hours

VOCABULARY

Absolute Xpath

Node

Relative Xpath

Stylesheet

XML Stylesheet Language (XSL)

XML Stylesheet Language Transformation (XSLT)

Xpath

<xsl:attribute> tag

<xsl:for-each> tag

<xsl:if> tag

<xsl:stylesheet> tag

<xsl:template> tag

<xsl:text> tag

<xsl:value-of> tag

XSL Basics

In Lesson 9 you learned about XML, and how it differs from HTML. Specifically, you learned that the purpose of XML tags is to describe the data they contain, whereas HTML tags simply tell the Web browser how to display data without attempting to ascribe any meaning to that data.

In Lesson 10, you learned about a relatively new technology called XHTML that incorporates the syntax rules of XML while maintaining the same general purpose of HTML. Like HTML, XHTML provides instructions for Web browsers regarding the way to display data without assigning any meaning to that data.

In this lesson you will learn about another Internet technology that is specifically designed to operate as a companion to XML. The technology is called *XSL*, which is an acronym for *XML Stylesheet Language*. For the first time, you will examine a Web technology that is not simply a markup language. However, if you are expecting XSL to be significantly different from the markup languages you have been learning about, you are bound to be disappointed. The good news is, in fact, that the syntax rules of XSL are exactly the same as XML and XHTML, so you will be able to build on what you have learned. XSL does, however, contain several unique features that give it the ability to behave more like a programming language than a markup language. In addition, XSL provides the data display capabilities of HTML and XHTML without abandoning the primary purpose of XML. That is why XSL was designed to accompany XML documents rather than replace them.

Hello World—Again

In Lesson 10 you learned that even the simplest XHTML Web page requires a minimal set of tags in order to be recognized as a valid document. This is also true of XSL. But since XSL only functions as a companion technology to XML, we need to start with the fundamental requirements of the XML document on which the XSL file is based. Always keep in mind that the XML document defines a set of data, and its companion XSL file tells the Web browser how to display that data.

In Lesson 9 you learned about the basics of XML documents. In order to put an attractive "face" on your XML data, all you have to do is add a single directive tag. This is the tag that specifies which file will be used to define the XML *stylesheet*. (A stylesheet is simply a file that defines the "look" of the XML data it displays.) This tag looks something like this:

```
<?xml-stylesheet type="text/xsl" href="[URL of XSL file]"?>
```

Now that you know what the XML file requires, let's take a look at the XSL file essentials. First, an XSL file has to comply with the rules of XML syntax, so its first line is always an XML directive tag.

Next, the directive tag must be followed by a ***<xsl:stylesheet> tag***, and this tag must contain two mandatory attributes. The first attribute is called version, and it specifies the version of XSL with which this stylesheet complies. The second attribute is xmlns:xsl, and its value specifies the URL of the XML namespace that will validate the tags and attributes of the XSL stylesheet. (If you don't remember what an XML namespace is, refer to Lesson 10.) The entire XSL file is concluded with a closing </xsl:stylesheet> tag.

Another required element of a valid XSL file is the ***<xsl:template> tag***. This tag must be located inside the opening and closing stylesheet tags, and it has one mandatory attribute called match. The value of the match attribute identifies which node (data element) of the XML data set will serve as the "root" node for the XSL stylesheet. All other data elements will be located by their relationship to the root node. The end of the template is marked with a </xsl:template> tag.

Inside the <xsl:template> and </xsl:template> tags is where you will define the bulk of your XML/XSL Web page. This is where things should become more familiar to you, because most of the tags you will use within the template tags will be standard HTML tags. Or perhaps it would be more accurate to say that the tags will be XHTML tags, because they must conform to all of the syntax rules of XHTML as you learned in Lesson 10.

Now that you have covered the basics of XML and XSL documents, you may proceed to create your first XML/XSL Web page. This Web page will simply display a variation on that old familiar phrase "Hello World!"—XSL style.

S TEP-BY-STEP 11.1

1. Open your preferred text editor and enter the XML code exactly as it appears in Figure 11-1.

FIGURE 11-1
A simple XML document

```
<?xml version="1.0"?>
<?xml-stylesheet type="text/xsl" href="xsl-one.xsl"?>

<document>
  <message>Hello XSL World!</message>
</document>
```

2. Save this file as **xml-one.xml**.

3. Clear the contents of your editor, and then enter the XSL code exactly as shown in Figure 11-2.

FIGURE 11-2
A simple XSL stylesheet

```
<?xml version="1.0"?>
<xsl:stylesheet version="1.0" xmlns:xsl="http://www.w3.org/1999/XSL/Transform">
<xsl:template match="/document">

<html>

<head>
  <title>XML/XSL Web Page 1</title>
</head>

<body>
  <center>
    <h1><xsl:value-of select="message"/></h1>
  </center>
</body>

</html>

</xsl:template>
</xsl:stylesheet>
```

4. Save this file as **xsl-one.xsl**.

STEP-BY-STEP 11.1 Continued

5. Open your Web browser and view the *xml-one.xml* you saved in step 2. Your browser should display a Web page that looks like the one in Figure 11-3. Leave both your browser and your text editor open for the next exercise.

FIGURE 11-3
A simple XML/XSL Web page

Analyzing the Results

We covered the basics of XML/XSL Web page requirements previously, but let's review the code for this specific exercise to make sure you understand all of the important concepts presented here.

First, let's look at the second line of the XML file. This line consists of a directive tag that tells your browser to display the XML data with a stylesheet, and that the stylesheet is contained in the file xsl-one.xsl (as specified by the href attribute). The process of converting an XML document into a displayable format by means of an XSL file is called an *XSLT*, or *XML Stylesheet Language Transformation*.

Next, let's examine the contents of the XSL file. This document also begins with an XML directive tag that instructs the browser to parse the file in accordance with the XML 1.0 specification. This tag is then followed by an XSL stylesheet tag that includes two attributes—one to identify XSL 1.0 as the document standard (version), and the other to specify a URL for the XML namespace to be used to process this stylesheet (xmlns).

Following the opening stylesheet tag you will see an XSL template (<xsl:template>) tag. The match attribute of this tag indicates that the document tag of the base XML data set will serve as the root node for this stylesheet. This means that all data elements referenced within the XSL stylesheet will be located by their relative position to the document node in the XML data set.

You should recognize that all of the remaining tags—with one exception—are standard HTML tags with which you should be abundantly familiar. But don't forget that they must conform to XHTML syntax rules, hence they must all be lowercase, all opening tags must have matching closing tags, and so on.

The one XSL tag that we have not yet discussed is the <xsl:value-of> *tag*. The purpose of this tag is to instruct the browser to display the value of an XML data element. This tag contains a select attribute that identifies the Xpath of the specific data element to be displayed. (You will learn about Xpaths in the next section.) In this case, the XML data element is called message, and its value (as defined in the XML document) is Hello XSL World! The resulting XSLT (XSL Transformation) is the simple Web page displayed in Figure 11-3.

You should also recognize that this value-of tag is a shortcut tag. Don't forget that *every* tag, even the new XSL tags you will learn in this lesson, must have a matching closing tag or be written as a shortcut tag.

Understanding Xpaths

One of the most important concepts you can learn about creating XML/XSL Web pages is that of the *Xpath*. An Xpath is a standard convention for identifying a particular data element in an XML data set. It is intended to be similar to file paths in Windows, or Web addresses on the Internet. To understand this concept better, consider the following XML document.

```
<student>
  <name>
    <first>John</first>
    <middle>Q.</middle>
    <last>Smith</last>
  </name>
  <address>
    <street>123 Cottonwood St.</street>
    <city>Afton</city>
    <state>WY</state>
    <zip>83110</zip>
  </address>
</student>
```

The *absolute Xpath* for any given data element can be constructed by starting at the top-most level (the root node) of the XML data set, and listing each lower-level XML tag name (node) that appears between the root node and the target node. For example, the absolute Xpath for a student's last name would be /student/name/last. By the same token, the absolute Xpath for a student's city would be /student/address/city.

But, like file paths and Web addresses, Xpaths do not always have to be specified as an absolute path. For example, if the <name> tag of our simple XML document were considered to be the root node of an XSL template, then the *relative Xpath* of a student's first name would just be first. Likewise, specifying the address node as the root of an XSL template would allow a student's zip code to be identified with a relative Xpath of zip. Are you getting it? If not, don't panic yet! We will review specific examples at the end of this section following the Step-by-Step exercise.

Simple Text in XSL

Displaying text in HTML is easy—you only need to type in your text, and the browser will display it. The text will appear in the default font at its default size unless you specifically insert certain HTML tags to alter the appearance of the text.

In XSL, however, you need to be a little more conscientious about the usage of simple text. Since the syntax requirements for XML (and XSL) are more stringent than standard HTML, you will need to learn how to properly use the **<xsl:text> tag**. The purpose of this tag (and its matching closing tag) is to make sure the browser does not confuse any nonalphanumeric characters with reserved XSL symbols. In other words, these tags can help to ensure that characters like the period (.), the comma (,), the question mark (?), and so on are not misinterpreted. All you have to do is enclose your text with XSL text tags like this:

<xsl:text>This is a simple string of text.</xsl:text>

You will get a chance to practice your XSL text skills in the following exercise.

STEP-BY-STEP 11.2

1. Switch to your text editor and, if necessary, open the **xml-one.xml** file you created in the previous Step-by-Step.

2. Change the value of the href attribute in the XML stylesheet tag to **xsl-two.xsl**. Then add the text as shown in bold in Figure 11-4.

FIGURE 11-4
New data elements in your XML file

```
<?xml version="1.0"?>
<?xml-stylesheet type="text/xsl" href="xsl-two.xsl"?>

<document>
  <message>Hello XSL World!</message>

  <topic1>Powerful Lines</topic1>
  <topic2>Hyperlinks to HTML and JavaScript Sources</topic2>
  <topic3>Hyperlinks to Previously Created Web Pages</topic3>
  <topic4>Fancy Fonts</topic4>
  <topic5>Perfect Pictures</topic5>
  <topic6>Orderly Tables</topic6>
  <topic7>Extraordinary Extras</topic7>
</document>
```

3. Save this file as **xml-two.xml**.

4. Clear the contents of your editor, and then open the *xsl-one.xsl* file you created in the previous Step-by-Step.

5. Change the number of your XML/XSL Web page (in the title) from *1* to **2**. Also add the text as shown in bold in Figure 11-5. Save this file as **xsl-two.xsl**.

STEP-BY-STEP 11.2 Continued

FIGURE 11-5
New text and tags in your XSL file

```
<?xml version="1.0"?>
\xsl:stylesheet version="1.0" xmlns:xsl="http://www.w3.org/1999/XSL/Transform">
<xsl:template match="/document">

<html>

<head>
 <title>XML/XSL Web Page 2</title>
</head>

<body>
 <center>
  <h1><xsl:value-of select="message"/></h1>
 </center>

 <p>
  <xsl:text>There are many ways to organize a Web page. This Web </xsl:text>
  <xsl:text>page will organize text, hyperlinks, colors, and fonts.</xsl:text>
  <xsl:text>You will also demonstrate single spacing, double spacing, </xsl:text>
  <xsl:text>and the use of line breaks.</xsl:text>
 </p>
 <p>
  <xsl:text>This Web page will display how to organize Web pages. </xsl:text>
  <xsl:text>There are many ways to organize a Web page. </xsl:text>
 </p>

 <br/><xsl:value-of select="topic1"/>
 <br/><xsl:value-of select="topic2"/>
 <br/><xsl:value-of select="topic3"/>
 <br/><xsl:value-of select="topic4"/>
 <br/><xsl:value-of select="topic5"/>
 <br/><xsl:value-of select="topic6"/>
 <br/><xsl:value-of select="topic7"/>
</body>

</html>

</xsl:template>
</xsl:stylesheet>
```

STEP-BY-STEP 11.2 Continued

6. Open your Web browser and view the *xml-two.xml* file you saved in step 3. Your browser should display a Web page that looks like the one in Figure 11-6. Leave both your browser and your text editor open for the next exercise.

FIGURE 11-6
XML/XSL Web Page 2

Analyzing the Results

This XML/XSL Web page still does not contain anything fancy, but it does provide good examples of the topics presented in this section. You should now have a good idea about how to use the <xsl:text> and </xsl:text> tags. You simply enclose the text strings within these tags whenever you want to display static (unchanging) text on the screen.

You also should have gotten a better feel for Xpaths in this exercise, even though the Xpaths we used were quite simple. Consider, for example, the Xpath of the first topic "Powerful Lines." If we had wanted to access the value of this data element with an absolute Xpath, we could have used a tag like this:

<xsl:value-of select="/document/topic1"/>

However, we have already specified /document as the root node of our XSL template. Therefore, we can use a relative Xpath instead of an absolute one, and shorten the value of the select attribute to just topic1.

One last item worth noting is the use of </p> closing tags and <br/> shortcut tags. Never forget that the syntax of your XSL stylesheets must always conform to the rules of XHTML! If you slip into standard HTML thinking and forget to do this, your browser is certain to reprimand you.

XSL Tag Attributes

A very important part of all markup languages are the attributes, both required and optional, that their tags support. This is also true in XSL. But this is one area where XSL differs from HTML, XHTML, and even XML. XSL does support tag attributes in the same way as these markup languages, but it also offers an additional capability by means of a tag called *<xsl:attribute>*. The purpose of this tag is to allow XSL to add attributes to a tag after it has already been defined. The value of this capability may not be immediately obvious, but it gives Web designers the ability to make their Web pages dynamic. The values of dynamic attributes can be set in the stylesheet's corresponding XML document. This means that the appearance of a particular Web page can change each time a user sees it if the XML data that sets its attributes changes.

In the following Step-by-Step, you will see firsthand how to use the XSL attribute tag. The XSL stylesheet will define several horizontal line tags, but the attribute values for these <HR> tags will be specified in the XML document.

STEP-BY-STEP 11.3

1. Switch to your text editor and, if necessary, open the **xml-two.xml** file you created in the previous Step-by-Step.

2. Change the value of the href attribute in the XML stylesheet tag to **xsl-three.xsl**. Then add the text as shown in bold in Figure 11-7.

FIGURE 11-7
XML file with horizontal line attribute values

```
<?xml version="1.0"?>
<?xml-stylesheet type="text/xsl" href="xsl-three.xsl"?>

<document>
  <message>Hello XSL World!</message>

  <topic1>Powerful Lines</topic1>
  <topic2>Hyperlinks to HTML and JavaScript Sources</topic2>
  <topic3>Hyperlinks to Previously Created Web Pages</topic3>
  <topic4>Fancy Fonts</topic4>
  <topic5>Perfect Pictures</topic5>
  <topic6>Orderly Tables</topic6>
  <topic7>Extraordinary Extras</topic7>

  <hr1>
   <width>50%</width>
   <size>10</size>
  </hr1>
  <hr2>
   <width>25%</width>
```

STEP–BY–STEP 11.3 Continued

FIGURE 11-7 (Continued)
XML file with horizontal line attribute values

```
      <size>20</size>
    </hr2>
    <hr3>
      <width>10%</width>
      <size>30</size>
    </hr3>
  </document>
```

3. Save this file as **xml-three.xml**.

4. Clear the contents of your editor, and then retrieve the *xsl-two.xsl* file you created in the previous Step-by-Step.

5. Change the number of your XML/XSL Web page (in the title) from 2 to **3**. Also add the text as shown in bold in Figure 11-8.

FIGURE 11-8
XSL stylesheet with <xsl:attribute> tags

```
<?xml version="1.0"?>
<xsl:stylesheet version="1.0" xmlns:xsl="http://www.w3.org/1999/XSL/Transform">
<xsl:template match="/document">

<html>

<head>
  <title>XML/XSL Web Page 3</title>
</head>

<body>
  <center>
    <h1><xsl:value-of select="message"/></h1>
  </center>

  <p>
    <xsl:text>There are many ways to organize a Web page. This Web </xsl:text>
    <xsl:text>page will organize text, hyperlinks, colors, and fonts.</xsl:text>
    <xsl:text>You will also demonstrate single spacing, double spacing, </xsl:text>
    <xsl:text>and the use of line breaks.</xsl:text>
  </p>
  <p>
    <xsl:text>This Web page will display how to organize Web pages. </xsl:text>
    <xsl:text>There are many ways to organize a Web page. </xsl:text>
  </p>
```

STEP-BY-STEP 11.3 Continued

FIGURE 11-8 (Continued)
XSL stylesheet with <xsl:attribute> tags

```
<br/><xsl:value-of select="topic1"/>
<br/><xsl:value-of select="topic2"/>
<br/><xsl:value-of select="topic3"/>
<br/><xsl:value-of select="topic4"/>
<br/><xsl:value-of select="topic5"/>
<br/><xsl:value-of select="topic6"/>
<br/><xsl:value-of select="topic7"/>

<hr/>
<p><h2><xsl:value-of select="topic1"/></h2></p>
<xsl:text>A Horizontal Rule tag </xsl:text>
  <xsl:value-of select="hr1/width"/>
<xsl:text> wide and </xsl:text>
  <xsl:value-of select="hr1/size"/>
<xsl:text> pixels high. </xsl:text>
<hr>
  <xsl:attribute name="width">
    <xsl:value-of select="hr1/width"/>
  </xsl:attribute>
  <xsl:attribute name="size">
    <xsl:value-of select="hr1/size"/>
  </xsl:attribute>
</hr>
<xsl:text>A Horizontal Rule tag </xsl:text>
  <xsl:value-of select="hr2/width"/>
<xsl:text> wide and </xsl:text>
  <xsl:value-of select="hr2/size"/>
<xsl:text> pixels high. </xsl:text>
<hr>
  <xsl:attribute name="width">
    <xsl:value-of select="hr2/width"/>
  </xsl:attribute>
  <xsl:attribute name="size">
    <xsl:value-of select="hr2/size"/>
  </xsl:attribute>
</hr>
<xsl:text>A Horizontal Rule tag </xsl:text>
  <xsl:value-of select="hr3/width"/>
<xsl:text> wide and </xsl:text>
  <xsl:value-of select="hr3/size"/>
<xsl:text> pixels high. </xsl:text>
<hr>
  <xsl:attribute name="width">
```

STEP-BY-STEP 11.3 Continued

FIGURE 11-8 (Continued)
XSL stylesheet with <xsl:attribute> tags

```
      <xsl:value-of select="hr3/width"/>
    </xsl:attribute>
    <xsl:attribute name="size">
      <xsl:value-of select="hr3/size"/>
    </xsl:attribute>
  </hr>
  <xsl:text>A Horizontal Rule tag without attributes and values.</xsl:text>
  <hr/>
</body>

</html>

</xsl:template>
</xsl:stylesheet>
```

6. Save this file as **xsl-three.xsl**.

7. Switch to your Web browser and view the *xml-three.xml* file you saved in step 3. Your browser should display a Web page that, when you scroll down, looks like the one in Figure 11-9. Leave both your browser and your text editor open for the next exercise.

FIGURE 11-9
XML/XSL Web Page 3

Analyzing the Results

This Step-by-Step not only introduced you to the <xsl:attribute> tag, it also gave you a good review of some concepts that were presented in the previous two exercises. Therefore, let's begin our analysis by reviewing those earlier topics.

First, we used the <xsl:value-of> tag to display the "Powerful Lines" header for this section of our Web page. This is beneficial because if we changed the value of the topic1 data element in our XML file, the XSL stylesheet would display the new value in the topic list above *and* as the topic header below. This coding style ensures that the topic list and the topic headers will always match, and if they ever need to be changed, the change can be made in a single place in the XML file.

Next, we made ample use of the <xsl:text> tag to mark those parts of the stylesheet that should be displayed as static text on the screen. But the parts of the screen that are dynamic—that is, the parts that can change from one viewing to the next—are extracted from the XML document. Notice that the horizontal line description, and the horizontal line itself, both get their values from the XML data set. Once again this ensures that the description of the line and the actual line will always stay in sync.

It is also worthwhile to take note of the Xpaths used in this new section of the Web page. If, for instance, we had wanted to use an absolute Xpath for the width of the second horizontal line, we could have specified it in the select attribute as /document/hr2/width. But since /document is already specified as the root node of our XML data set, we can shorten the reference by using the relative Xpath hr2/width.

And finally, you should take special note of the newly introduced <xsl:attribute> tags. Notice that these appear inside the opening <hr> and the closing </hr> tags. This indicates that we are adding an attribute to the <hr> tag. Notice also that the name attribute of the <xsl:attribute> tag determines the name of the attribute we are adding. The value that appears between the opening <xsl:attribute> tag and the closing </xsl:attribute> tag will be used as the value of the new attribute we are adding to the <hr> tag. This value could be a constant that is simply typed into the stylesheet, but in this case the value is being extracted from the XML data set by means of the <xsl:value-of> tag.

Concept Review

This is actually one of the most complex concepts in XSL, so let's go through it one more time to make sure you understand everything that is happening here. First, we specify a simple horizontal line (<hr>) tag. Then, we instruct the browser that we want to add two new attributes to this tag by including two <xsl:attribute> tags inside the <hr> and </hr> tags. The name attribute of these two attribute tags indicates that the names of the two attributes we are adding to the <hr> tag are width and size. The values of the width and size attributes are then extracted from the XML file by means of the <xsl:value-of> tags that appear inside of the two <xsl:attribute> tags.

XSL for Loops

Every programming language (Pascal, C++, Java, etc.) includes the ability to repeat a set of instructions multiple times. None of the markup languages you have studied up to now have this ability. In HTML, for example, if you want a table to contain ten rows, you have to type ten sets of <tr> and </tr> tags. There is no way in this markup language to tell the browser that you would like to repeat a particular set of tags ten times.

In most respects, the XML Stylesheet Language (XSL) is more like a markup language than it is a programming language. However, it can behave like a programming language in this regard, because it does provide a way to repeat specific tags multiple times. The XSL tag that allows you to accomplish this is called *<xsl:for-each> tag*. This tag is similar to the <xsl:value-of> tag in that it also requires the presence of an attribute called select. The select attribute identifies the Xpath of the XML data element (or elements) that will control the looping process.

A for Loop Example

Let's take a look at a specific example. Suppose that an XML document contains a list of 101 students who attained the honor roll for a given semester. This XML file might look something like this:

```
<honor_roll>
  <student1>John Q. Smith</student1>
  <student2>Mary Anderson</student2>
  <student3>Pedro Martinez</student3>
     .
     .
     .
  <student101>Laura Turner</student101>
</honor_roll>
```

If the honor roll data were indeed structured this way, you could easily display it in an XSL stylesheet, right? Unfortunately, you would have to use 101 different <xsl:value-of> tags to specify the 101 different Xpaths for the 101 different students. But thanks to XSL's ability to eliminate repetitive tags, there is a much better way to accomplish the same goal.

The first step is to make a minor change to the XML data file so that it looks something like this:

```
<honor_roll>
  <student>John Q. Smith</student>
  <student>Mary Anderson</student>
  <student>Pedro Martinez</student>
     .
     .
     .
  <student>Laura Turner</student>
</honor_roll>
```

Now that the numbers have been removed from the student XML data tags, you can treat the students as one group of 101 data elements instead of 101 groups of one data element. The XSL code that allows you to process all of the students in a repetitive manner looks like this:

```
<xsl:for-each select="student">
     .
     .   (repeated tags)
     .
</xsl:for-each>
```

So now that you have been introduced to the <xsl:for-each> tag, you should gain some experience in using it. If you refer to Step-by-Step 3.3 (in Lesson 3) you may recall creating some HTML code that displays six images of "Levy" the leviathan. In this exercise, you will do the same thing, but in a more efficient XSL way. The attributes for each image will be stored in an XML file, and your XSL code will display each image in a for-each loop.

STEP-BY-STEP 11.4

1. Switch to your text editor and, if necessary, open the **xml-three.xml** file you created in the previous Step-by-Step.

2. Change the value of the href attribute in the XML stylesheet tag to **xsl-four.xsl**. Then add the text as shown in bold in Figure 11-10.

FIGURE 11-10
XML file with image attribute values

```
<?xml version="1.0"?>
<?xml-stylesheet type="text/xsl" href="xsl-four.xsl"?>

<document>
 <message>Hello XSL World!</message>

 <topic1>Powerful Lines</topic1>
 <topic2>Hyperlinks to HTML and JavaScript Sources</topic2>
 <topic3>Hyperlinks to Previously Created Web Pages</topic3>
 <topic4>Fancy Fonts</topic4>
 <topic5>Perfect Pictures</topic5>
 <topic6>Orderly Tables</topic6>
 <topic7>Extraordinary Extras</topic7>

 <hr1>
  <width>50%</width>
  <size>10</size>
 </hr1>
 <hr2>
  <width>25%</width>
  <size>20</size>
 </hr2>
 <hr3>
  <width>10%</width>
  <size>30</size>
 </hr3>

 <img>
  <height>50</height>
  <width>50</width>
 </img>
 <img>
  <height>100</height>
  <width>100</width>
 </img>
 <img>
  <height>150</height>
```

STEP-BY-STEP 11.4 Continued

FIGURE 11-10 (Continued)
XML file with image attribute values

```
      <width>150</width>
    </img>
    <img>
      <height>200</height>
      <width>200</width>
    </img>
    <img>
      <height>150</height>
      <width>150</width>
    </img>
    <img>
      <height>200</height>
      <width>200</width>
    </img>
  </document>
```

3. Save this file as **xml-four.xml**.

4. Clear the contents of your editor, and then retrieve the *xsl-three.xsl* file you created in the previous Step-by-Step.

5. Change the number of your XML/XSL Web page (in the title) from *3* to **4**. Also add the text as shown in bold in Figure 11-11.

FIGURE 11-11
XSL stylesheet with <xsl:for-each> tag

```
<?xml version="1.0"?>
<xsl:stylesheet version="1.0" xmlns:xsl="http://www.w3.org/1999/XSL/Transform">
<xsl:template match="/document">

<html>

<head>
  <title>XML/XSL Web Page 4</title>
</head>

<body>
  <center>
    <h1><xsl:value-of select="message"/></h1>
  </center>

  <p>
    <xsl:text>There are many ways to organize a Web page. This Web </xsl:text>
```

STEP-BY-STEP 11.4 Continued

FIGURE 11-11 (Continued)
XSL stylesheet with <xsl:for-each> tag

```
    <xsl:text>page will organize text, hyperlinks, colors, and fonts.</xsl:text>
    <xsl:text>You will also demonstrate single spacing, double spacing, </xsl:text>
    <xsl:text>and the use of line breaks.</xsl:text>
</p>
<p>
    <xsl:text>This Web page will display how to organize Web pages. </xsl:text>
    <xsl:text>There are many ways to organize a Web page. </xsl:text>
</p>

<br/><xsl:value-of select="topic1"/>
<br/><xsl:value-of select="topic2"/>
<br/><xsl:value-of select="topic3"/>
<br/><xsl:value-of select="topic4"/>
<br/><xsl:value-of select="topic5"/>
<br/><xsl:value-of select="topic6"/>
<br/><xsl:value-of select="topic7"/>

<hr/>
<p><h2><xsl:value-of select="topic1"/></h2></p>
<xsl:text>A Horizontal Rule tag </xsl:text>
    <xsl:value-of select="hr1/width"/>
<xsl:text> wide and </xsl:text>
    <xsl:value-of select="hr1/size"/>
<xsl:text> pixels high. </xsl:text>
<hr>
    <xsl:attribute name="width">
      <xsl:value-of select="hr1/width"/>
    </xsl:attribute>
    <xsl:attribute name="size">
      <xsl:value-of select="hr1/size"/>
    </xsl:attribute>
</hr>
<xsl:text>A Horizontal Rule tag </xsl:text>
    <xsl:value-of select="hr2/width"/>
<xsl:text> wide and </xsl:text>
    <xsl:value-of select="hr2/size"/>
<xsl:text> pixels high. </xsl:text>
<hr>
    <xsl:attribute name="width">
      <xsl:value-of select="hr2/width"/>
    </xsl:attribute>
    <xsl:attribute name="size">
      <xsl:value-of select="hr2/size"/>
```

STEP-BY-STEP 11.4 Continued

FIGURE 11-11 (Continued)
XSL stylesheet with <xsl:for-each> tag

```
      </xsl:attribute>
    </hr>
    <xsl:text>A Horizontal Rule tag </xsl:text>
      <xsl:value-of select="hr3/width"/>
    <xsl:text> wide and </xsl:text>
      <xsl:value-of select="hr3/size"/>
    <xsl:text> pixels high. </xsl:text>
    <hr>
      <xsl:attribute name="width">
        <xsl:value-of select="hr3/width"/>
      </xsl:attribute>
      <xsl:attribute name="size">
        <xsl:value-of select="hr3/size"/>
      </xsl:attribute>
    </hr>
    <xsl:text>A Horizontal Rule tag without attributes and values.</xsl:text>
    <hr/>

    <p><h2><xsl:value-of select="topic5"/></h2></p>
    <xsl:for-each select="img">
      <img src="levy.gif">
        <xsl:attribute name="height">
          <xsl:value-of select="height"/>
        </xsl:attribute>
        <xsl:attribute name="width">
          <xsl:value-of select="height"/>
        </xsl:attribute>
      </img>
    </xsl:for-each>
  </body>

</html>

</xsl:template>
</xsl:stylesheet>
```

6. Save this file as **xsl-four.xsl**.

7. Open your Web browser and view the *xml-four.xml* file you saved in step 3. Your browser should display a Web page that looks like the one in Figure 11-12. Leave both your browser and your text editor open for the next exercise.

STEP-BY-STEP 11.4 Continued

FIGURE 11-12
XML/XSL Web Page 4

Analyzing the Results

Several parts of this exercise reinforce the concepts presented in Step-by-Step 11.3. The attributes of the images are set in the XML file in precisely the same way as the attributes of the horizontal lines were set in the previous exercise. There is one difference, however. The six image tags in the latter XML file all share a common name (<img>). The three horizontal line tags in the former XML file, on the other hand, all had unique names (<hr1>, <hr2>, <hr3>, etc.). It is this small difference that allowed you to use the <xsl:for-each> tag in this exercise rather than having to use six separate sets of image tags.

Another important item to take note of here is the way in which the data Xpaths are referenced within <xsl:for-each> loops. If we wanted to access the width value of the first image with an absolute Xpath, this Xpath would be something like /document/img/width. And, since the XSL template tag specifies /document as the root node for this stylesheet, you might expect to see a relative Xpath to the width attribute appear as img/width. But instead you can see that the width attribute is referenced simply as width. Why is this? Well, it turns out that the <xsl:for-each> tag temporarily changes the XML document root node to include the data element referenced in its select attribute. In this case, the select attribute specifies the img data element, so each relative Xpath inside the for-each loop will use /document/img as its root node.

This is what allows us to access the width and height attribute values as simply width and height, respectively.

Benefits of for Loops

One of the benefits of using the <xsl:for-each> tag is that the number of iterations (times) it is performed is determined by the number of matching data items in the XML file. Whether we wanted to display two images or twenty, the XSL code will operate correctly without requiring any changes. You should make a mental note that it will also operate correctly if there are no matching data elements in the XML file. This means that the tags within the <xsl:for-each> loop will not be applied at all if there is no corresponding data to display.

XSL Conditional Tags

Another standard feature of programming languages that is not found in markup languages is the conditional statement. In programming languages such as C++ and Java, conditional statements are commonly referred to as if statements because the programming keyword that controls the evaluation of a condition is "if." The purpose of a conditional statement is to determine the state of a particular condition, and then react accordingly. In its simplest form, a conditional statement will cause a set of instructions to execute if a condition is true, but not if the condition is false.

Since markup languages do not possess this capability, they do not give Web designers the ability to specify a set of tags that will only be applied if a particular condition is true. But once again, XSL more closely resembles a programming language than a markup language in this regard. XSL supports a tag called the *<xsl:if> tag* that allows you to evaluate a condition, and then apply a set of tags if the condition is true. The condition to be evaluated will appear as the value of a mandatory attribute called test.

The <xsl:if> tag can be used in many ways to enhance the appearance or behavior of an XSL stylesheet. But one of the most useful ways it can be used is to determine whether a particular XML data element is present or not. In the following Step-by-Step, you will use the <xsl:if> tag to determine which of a list of options should be selected in a drop-down list. If the XML data item that indicates an option should be selected is present, the XSL stylesheet will add an appropriate attribute to the <option> tag. Otherwise, the attribute will not be added.

STEP-BY-STEP 11.5

1. Switch to your text editor and, if necessary, open the **xml-four.xml** file you created in the previous Step-by-Step.

2. Change the value of the href attribute in the XML stylesheet tag to **xsl-five.xsl**. Then add the text as shown in bold in Figure 11-13.

STEP-BY-STEP 11.5 Continued

FIGURE 11-13
XML file with interactive control attribute values

```
<?xml version="1.0"?>
<?xml-stylesheet type="text/xsl" href="xsl-five.xsl"?>

<document>
 <message>Hello XSL World!</message>

 <topic1>Powerful Lines</topic1>
 <topic2>Hyperlinks to HTML and JavaScript Sources</topic2>
 <topic3>Hyperlinks to Previously Created Web Pages</topic3>
 <topic4>Fancy Fonts</topic4>
 <topic5>Perfect Pictures</topic5>
 <topic6>Orderly Tables</topic6>
 <topic7>Extraordinary Extras</topic7>

 <hr1>
  <width>50%</width>
  <size>10</size>
 </hr1>
 <hr2>
  <width>25%</width>
  <size>20</size>
 </hr2>
 <hr3>
  <width>10%</width>
  <size>30</size>
 </hr3>

 <img>
  <height>50</height>
  <width>50</width>
 </img>
 <img>
  <height>100</height>
  <width>100</width>
 </img>
 <img>
  <height>150</height>
  <width>150</width>
 </img>
 <img>
  <height>200</height>
  <width>200</width>
 </img>
```

STEP-BY-STEP 11.5 Continued

FIGURE 11-13 (Continued)
XML file with interactive control attribute values

```
<img>
  <height>150</height>
  <width>150</width>
</img>
<img>
  <height>200</height>
  <width>200</width>
</img>
<favorite-team>
  <option>
    <selected>true</selected>
    <team>Boston Celtics</team>
  </option>
  <option>
    <team>Chicago Bulls</team>
  </option>
  <option>
    <team>Los Angeles Lakers</team>
  </option>
  <option>
    <team>New York Knicks</team>
  </option>
  <option>
    <team>Utah Jazz</team>
  </option>
</favorite-team>
<best-place-to-eat>
  <option>
    <place>Arbys</place>
  </option>
  <option>
    <selected>true</selected>
    <place>Burger King</place>
  </option>
  <option>
    <place>McDonalds</place>
  </option>
  <option>
    <place>Taco Bell</place>
  </option>
  <option>
    <place>Wendys</place>
  </option>
```

STEP-BY-STEP 11.5 Continued

FIGURE 11-13 (Continued)
XML file with interactive control attribute values

```
    </best-place-to-eat>
    <like-to-eat>
     <option>
       <food>Chicken Nuggets</food>
     </option>
     <option>
       <food>French Fries</food>
     </option>
     <option>
       <selected>true</selected>
       <food>Hamburgers</food>
     </option>
     <option>
       <selected>true</selected>
       <food>Roast Beef</food>
     </option>
     <option>
       <selected>true</selected>
       <food>Tacos</food>
     </option>
    </like-to-eat>
   </document>
```

3. Save this file as **xml-five.xml**.

4. Clear the contents of your editor, and then retrieve the *xsl-four.xsl* file you created in the previous Step-by-Step.

5. Change the number of your XML/XSL Web page (in the title) from *4* to **5**. Also add the text as shown in bold in Figure 11-14.

FIGURE 11-14
XSL stylesheet with <xsl:if> tags

```
<?xml version="1.0"?>
<xsl:stylesheet version="1.0" xmlns:xsl="http://www.w3.org/1999/XSL/Transform">
<xsl:template match="/document">

<html>

<head>
 <title>XML/XSL Web Page 5</title>
</head>
```

STEP-BY-STEP 11.5 Continued

FIGURE 11-14 (Continued)
XSL stylesheet with <xsl:if> tags

```
<body>
 <center>
   <h1><xsl:value-of select="message"/></h1>
 </center>

 <p>
   <xsl:text>There are many ways to organize a Web page. This Web </xsl:text>
   <xsl:text>page will organize text, hyperlinks, colors, and fonts.</xsl:text>
   <xsl:text>You will also demonstrate single spacing, double spacing, </xsl:text>
   <xsl:text>and the use of line breaks.</xsl:text>
 </p>
 <p>
   <xsl:text>This Web page will display how to organize Web pages. </xsl:text>
   <xsl:text>There are many ways to organize a Web page. </xsl:text>
 </p>

 <br/><xsl:value-of select="topic1"/>
 <br/><xsl:value-of select="topic2"/>
 <br/><xsl:value-of select="topic3"/>
 <br/><xsl:value-of select="topic4"/>
 <br/><xsl:value-of select="topic5"/>
 <br/><xsl:value-of select="topic6"/>
 <br/><xsl:value-of select="topic7"/>

 <hr/>
 <p><h2><xsl:value-of select="topic1"/></h2></p>
 <xsl:text>A Horizontal Rule tag </xsl:text>
   <xsl:value-of select="hr1/width"/>
 <xsl:text> wide and </xsl:text>
   <xsl:value-of select="hr1/size"/>
 <xsl:text> pixels high. </xsl:text>
 <hr>
   <xsl:attribute name="width">
     <xsl:value-of select="hr1/width"/>
   </xsl:attribute>
   <xsl:attribute name="size">
     <xsl:value-of select="hr1/size"/>
   </xsl:attribute>
 </hr>
 <xsl:text>A Horizontal Rule tag </xsl:text>
   <xsl:value-of select="hr2/width"/>
 <xsl:text> wide and </xsl:text>
   <xsl:value-of select="hr2/size"/>
```

STEP–BY–STEP 11.5 Continued

FIGURE 11-14 (Continued)
XSL stylesheet with <xsl:if> tags

```
<xsl:text> pixels high. </xsl:text>
<hr>
 <xsl:attribute name="width">
  <xsl:value-of select="hr2/width"/>
 </xsl:attribute>
 <xsl:attribute name="size">
  <xsl:value-of select="hr2/size"/>
 </xsl:attribute>
</hr>
<xsl:text>A Horizontal Rule tag </xsl:text>
 <xsl:value-of select="hr3/width"/>
<xsl:text> wide and </xsl:text>
 <xsl:value-of select="hr3/size"/>
<xsl:text> pixels high. </xsl:text>
<hr>
 <xsl:attribute name="width">
  <xsl:value-of select="hr3/width"/>
 </xsl:attribute>
 <xsl:attribute name="size">
  <xsl:value-of select="hr3/size"/>
 </xsl:attribute>
</hr>
<xsl:text>A Horizontal Rule tag without attributes and values.</xsl:text>
<hr/>

<p><h2><xsl:value-of select="topic5"/></h2></p>
<xsl:for-each select="img">
 <img src="levy.gif">
  <xsl:attribute name="height">
   <xsl:value-of select="height"/>
  </xsl:attribute>
  <xsl:attribute name="width">
   <xsl:value-of select="height"/>
  </xsl:attribute>
 </img>
</xsl:for-each>

<hr/>
<p><h2><xsl:value-of select="topic7"/></h2></p>
<form>
 <p>
 <xsl:text>Pick your favorite team from the list:</xsl:text><br/>
 <select>
```

STEP-BY-STEP 11.5 Continued

FIGURE 11-14 (Continued)
XSL stylesheet with <xsl:if> tags

```
       <option>- select -</option>
       <xsl:for-each select="favorite-team/option">
         <option>
           <xsl:if test="selected = 'true'">
             <xsl:attribute name="selected">true</xsl:attribute>
           </xsl:if>
           <xsl:value-of select="team"/>
         </option>
       </xsl:for-each>
     </select>
     </p>
     <p>
     <xsl:text>The best place to eat is:</xsl:text><br/>
     <xsl:for-each select="best-place-to-eat/option">
       <input type="radio" name="best">
         <xsl:if test="selected = 'true'">
           <xsl:attribute name="checked">true</xsl:attribute>
         </xsl:if>
       </input>
       <xsl:value-of select="place"/><br/>
     </xsl:for-each>
     </p>
     <p>
     <xsl:text>I like to eat:</xsl:text><br/>
     <xsl:for-each select="like-to-eat/option">
       <input type="checkbox">
         <xsl:if test="selected = 'true'">
           <xsl:attribute name="checked">true</xsl:attribute>
         </xsl:if>
       </input>
       <xsl:value-of select="food"/><br/>
     </xsl:for-each>
     </p>
   </form>
 </body>

 </html>

 </xsl:template>
 </xsl:stylesheet>
```

6. Save this file as **xsl-five.xsl**.

STEP-BY-STEP 11.5 Continued

7. Open your Web browser and view the *xml-five.xml* file you saved in step 3. Your browser should display a Web page that looks like the one in Figure 11-15. Leave both your browser and your text editor open for the next exercise.

FIGURE 11-15
XML/XSL Web Page 5

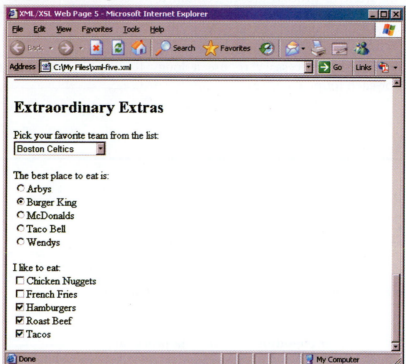

Analyzing the Results

Once again you have learned some valuable XSL concepts, so let's review this most recent XML/XSL Web page to make sure you have a firm grasp of everything in it.

First, we added three new sections of data to the XML file called <favorite-team>, <best-place-to-eat>, and <like-to-eat>. Within each of these three sections we added five <option> tags—one for each option we wanted to include on our Web page. Each option tag contains the text that corresponds with that option, and some of the options contain a <selected> tag. This latter tag indicates which, if any, of the available options should appear as being selected on the resulting Web page.

The corresponding XSL stylesheet displays the first set of options in a drop-down list box. The second set appears as a group of radio buttons, and the third set forms a group of check boxes. Since all of the options in each set of data share a common XML tag name (<option>), we can use the <xsl:for-each> tag to process the data more efficiently. But the <selected> tag does not appear with every option in each group, so it is necessary to apply conditional logic to construct the Web page properly. We use the <xsl:if> tag inside of each <xsl:for-each> loop to make sure that the selected option (or options) are processed differently from the other options. In the first section we add a selected attribute to the appropriate <option> tag within the select control. For the second and third sections we add a checked attribute to the appropriate radio button and check boxes.

As a final note, let's also make sure that you completely understand the relative Xpaths used in this exercise. Within the <xsl:for-each> tags, the select attribute specifies a relative Xpath to the options contained within each section of data. It is important for you to recognize that the relative Xpath for the drop-down list box, for example, is not simply option. It is favorite-team/option because the five options we want to process are all contained within the <favorite-team> tag. The same concept applies to the second and third for-each loop also. But once the target set of options has been selected by the <xsl:for-each> tag, it is not necessary to use a long Xpath inside the for-each loop.

> **Hot Tip**
>
> Remember that the <xsl:for-each> tag temporarily changes the document root node to allow for shorter relative Xpaths within the loop.

SUMMARY

In this lesson you learned:

- To create simple XML/XSL Web pages.

- To understand what an Xpath is and how to use it.

- To use the <xsl:value-of> tag to extract and display XML data.

- To use the <xsl:attribute> tag to make Web content dynamic.

- To use the <xsl:for-each> tag to display XML data repetitively.

- To use the <xsl:if> tag for conditional XML data processing.

VOCABULARY *Review*

Define the following terms:

Absolute Xpath	XML Stylesheet Language	<xsl:if> tag
Node	Transformation (XSLT)	<xsl:stylesheet> tag
Relative Xpath	Xpath	<xsl:template> tag
Stylesheet	<xsl:attribute> tag	<xsl:text> tag
XML Stylesheet	<xsl:for-each> tag	<xsl:value-of> tag
Language (XSL)		

REVIEW *Questions*

TRUE/FALSE

Circle T if the statement is true or F if the statement is false.

T F **1.** The XSL acronym stands for XML Stylesheet Language.

T F **2.** The XSL and XSLT acronyms mean the same thing, and can be used interchangeably.

T F **3.** XSL incorporates some characteristics of both programming languages and markup languages.

T F **4.** Xpaths must always be specified as absolute paths, never as relative paths.

T F **5.** XSL is not able to detect whether a particular XML data element is present or not.

FILL IN THE BLANK

Complete the following sentences by writing the correct word or words in the blanks provided.

1. The results of an XML document that has been processed by an XSL stylesheet is called a(n) _____.

2. A(n) _____ is a convention used to identify a particular data element in an XML data set.

3. The purpose of the _____ tag is to specify the root node of an XML document.

4. The XSL tag that allows a set of tags to be applied repetitively is called _____.

5. The _____ tag allows XSL to implement conditional logic.

WRITTEN QUESTIONS

Write a brief answer to each of the following questions.

1. What is XSL and what is XSLT? How do these terms relate to each other?

2. Explain the difference between an absolute Xpath and a relative Xpath.

3. Describe the purpose of the <xsl:attribute> tag. What benefit does it afford Web developers?

4. How is an XSL "for loop" defined, and how does it work?

5. Explain what conditional logic is and how it is implemented in XSL.

PROJECTS

 PROJECT 11-1

In Step-by-Step 11.3 you created an XSL Web page that displays three types of horizontal lines. In Step-by-Step 11.4 you learned how to handle repetitive tasks more efficiently with the XSL "for" loop. Revisit the final XSL code you created for XML/XSL Web Page 4, and make the third section more efficient by adding an <xsl:for-each> tag. In order to do this, you will have to revisit your XML data file first and change the names of three tag pairs. Specifically, change the horizontal line tags so that they share the common name <hr>. After completing these XML changes, it should be very straightforward to change the XSL stylesheet to use an <xsl:for-each> tag to display these lines. Save your completed XML and XSL files as **xml-project.xml** and **xsl-project.xsl**.

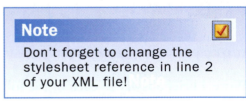

Note

Don't forget to change the stylesheet reference in line 2 of your XML file!

  TEAMWORK PROJECT

Divide into teams of three or four students, and briefly discuss each of the topics that are listed at the top of your XML/XSL Web Page 5 but not yet implemented. These topics include:

- Hyperlinks to HTML and JavaScript Sources
- Hyperlinks to Previously Created Web Pages
- Fancy Fonts
- Orderly Tables

Each student on the team should choose one of these topics and add the appropriate XML and XSL code to implement the topic.

After each team member has completed the work for his assigned topic, he should also incorporate the XML/XSL code that the other team members created. The end result of this team effort should be a fully functional XML/XSL Web page, which each student should save as **xml-teamwork.xml**, and **xsl-teamwork.xsl**.

  ## WEB PROJECT

Review the XML/XSL Web page that resulted from your work in Step-by-Step 11.4. Notice that the src attribute of each <img> tag is static. That is, it is constant for every image generated by the XSL for-each loop. The height and width attributes, on the other hand, are dynamic rather than static. Their values are determined by the data elements in the base XML file.

Under appropriate instructor supervision, surf the Web and locate five images that relate in some way to the image of "Levy" the leviathan. Download these images to your workstation, and then use them to change the appearance of the "Perfect Pictures" section of your Web page. To do this, you will first need to add a new data element to each <img> tag of your XML file. Call this data element src, and type the name of each image between the <src> and </src> tags. These new <src> tags should appear very much like the <height> and <width> tags that each <img> tag already contains. Save your resulting file as **xml-web.xml**.

After you have modified the XML file, you will also need to modify the corresponding XSL file. Remove the static reference to levy.gif from the <img> tag. Then add a new set of <xsl:attribute> tags that will extract its value from the XML file, and use this data element for the value of the src attribute. After you have completed your modifications to the stylesheet, save it as **xsl-web.xsl**.

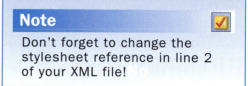

Note ✓

Don't forget to change the stylesheet reference in line 2 of your XML file!

CRITICAL *Thinking*

 ## ACTIVITY 11-1

If you look through the XML/XSL Web page you created for this lesson (**xsl-five.xsl**) you will notice that it is almost completely black and white. (The only color is in the images of "Levy" the leviathan.) See how creative you can be in adding some color and life to this Web page. First, try adding some foreground and background colors to the XSL stylesheet. If you are feeling sufficiently adventurous, try adding some tasteful images to the stylesheet to enhance the Web page's overall appearance. Save your stylesheet as **xsl-act1.xsl**.

Once you have finalized a stylesheet that pleases you, try to identify those elements that could be made dynamic by adding attribute values to the base XML file. For example, you could add XML tags to define the primary foreground and background colors of your Web page. You could also add other pieces of data such as image filenames and dimensions (width and height). After you have made any changes you feel are appropriate, save the resulting XML file as **xml-act1.xml**, and re-save the revised stylesheet as **xsl-act1.xsl**.

ACTIVITY 11-2

To help ensure that you feel comfortable working with XSL stylesheets, return to the **xsl-teamwork.xsl** file you created for the teamwork project. Modify this file so that all seven of the topics listed in the first section become hyperlinks. Also modify the header text of each section so that they become the target of the corresponding hyperlink in the topic list. Completing this task will help ensure that you can add content to XML/XSL Web pages that conforms to XSL (XHTML) syntax rules without corrupting the content that is already there. Once you have completed this task, save your new stylesheet as **xsl-act2.xsl**.

ACTIVITY 11-3

One of the most important concepts you can learn from this lesson is the appropriate use of Xpaths. To make sure you understand this concept fully, return to the **xsl-five.xsl** file you created in Step-by-Step 11.5. Identify all of the relative Xpaths this stylesheet contains, and then try replacing them one at a time with an absolute Xpath. If you perform this function correctly, your stylesheet should continue to display a proper Web page. But if you make a mistake, you will either receive an unpleasant error message from your browser, or you will see one or more elements of your original Web page disappear. For each attempt you make at changing an Xpath, save your stylesheet as **xsl-act3.xsl**.

Note ✅

Don't forget to change the stylesheet reference in line 2 of your **xml-five.xml** file!

SUMMARY *Project*

This is your chance to demonstrate that you have completely mastered the ability to create XML/XSL Web pages! In this project you will create a table that is filled with information about your classmates. Your table should contain each student's last name, first name, favorite NBA team (if any), favorite place to eat, and favorite foods. In order to complete this project, you will need to use every specialized XSL tag you have learned in this lesson.

Each row in your student information table will contain two columns of text (for last and first names), a drop-down list box (for favorite team), a list of radio buttons (for favorite place to eat), and a list of check boxes (for favorite foods). (In order to keep the number of options more manageable, each drop-down list, radio button list, and check box list should only contain between four and six options.) Refer to Figure 11-16 for an example of what your completed Web page should look like.

FIGURE 11-16

XML/XSL student information Web page

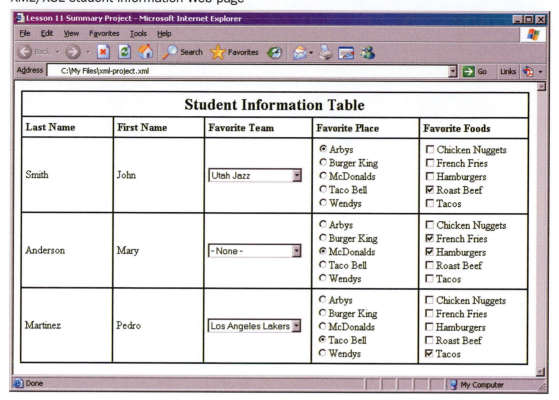

PROJECT REQUIREMENTS

- Your student information table must have an appropriate title.

- Your table must have appropriate column headings.

- The third column must contain a drop-down list.

- The fourth column must contain a list of radio buttons.

- The fifth column must contain a list of check boxes.

- Your stylesheet must use XSL value-of, attribute, for-each, and if tags.

- Name your XML and XSL files **xml-summary.xml** and **xsl-summary.xsl**.

ADVANCED XSL WITH JAVASCRIPT

OBJECTIVES

Upon completion of this lesson, you should be able to:

- Construct an XSL stylesheet that sorts XML data.
- Define and use an XSL variable.
- Recognize and use XSL intrinsic functions.
- Integrate JavaScript functions into an XML/XSL Web page.
- Use JavaScript to access other XML documents.

Estimated Time: 2.0 hours

VOCABULARY

Data sorting

Intrinsic functions

name() function

position() function

Variables

XSL modulus (mod) operator

<xsl:sort> tag

<xsl:variable> tag

Data Sorting with XSL

In Lesson 11 you learned a lot about the basic capabilities of the XML Stylesheet Language (XSL). You also learned a little about the features of XSL that give it some of the capabilities of advanced programming languages. In this lesson, you will learn more about XSL's features including various advanced tags and some of its intrinsic functions. Once you have mastered these features, you will be able to create XSL stylesheets that are capable of some fairly sophisticated XML data processing.

The <xsl:sort> Tag

Whenever a Web page needs to display a list of data, it is often desirable to display that data in a particular order. Manipulating information so that it appears in a specific order is called *data sorting*. For example, many Web-based applications will display a list of names, and it is often beneficial to display these names in alphabetical order. In fact, the longer a list of data gets, the more important it becomes to display it in some predictable order. Otherwise, it becomes increasingly difficult to find any useful information that may be in the data set.

Several different ways are available to sort lists of data—whatever that data may be. But if the Web developer has to sort the data manually, the task can become very tedious. In addition, it is also common for Web pages to allow users to sort data in various ways. This means that going through the trouble of manually sorting it by one criterion may not be very useful if the user wants to see the data in a different order. For instance, if the Web developer sorted a list of people by last name, it would not be beneficial to anyone who wanted or needed the list sorted by first name.

Fortunately, XSL provides the means to sort information in an easy, efficient manner. The **<xsl:sort> tag** is designed to be used in conjunction with the <xsl:for-each> tag you learned about in Lesson 11. The <xsl:for-each> tag will select all of the information that matches a specific Xpath, and then the sort tag will order that information before it is displayed. This means that there is no need to manually sort your XML data files in order to get the data set to display in a particular order.

Let's look at a specific example. Suppose you have a list of student information that consists of student name (first and last), grade, and GPA. Suppose also that this information exists in an unsorted XML data file, and this file needs to be displayed alphabetically by last name. The following exercise will teach you how to use the XSL sort tag to accomplish this task.

S TEP-BY-STEP 12.1

1. Open your preferred text editor and enter the XML code exactly as it appears in Figure 12-1.

FIGURE 12-1
An XML document containing student information

```
<?xml version="1.0"?>
<?xml-stylesheet type="text/xsl" href="xsl-six.xsl"?>

<document>
 <student>
  <last>Smith</last>
  <first>John</first>
  <grade>12</grade>
  <gpa>3.85</gpa>
 </student>
 <student>
  <last>Anderson</last>
  <first>Mary</first>
  <grade>10</grade>
  <gpa>3.03</gpa>
 </student>
 <student>
  <last>Martinez</last>
  <first>Pedro</first>
  <grade>11</grade>
  <gpa>3.55</gpa>
 </student>
 <student>
  <last>DeSisto</last>
  <first>Natalie</first>
  <grade>12</grade>
  <gpa>3.90</gpa>
 </student>
 <student>
  <last>Rosenberg</last>
```

STEP-BY-STEP 12.1 Continued

FIGURE 12-1
An XML document containing student information

```
    <first>Clayton</first>
    <grade>10</grade>
    <gpa>2.67</gpa>
  </student>
</document>
```

2. Save this file as **xml-six.xml**.

3. Clear the contents of your editor, and then enter the XSL code exactly as shown in Figure 12-2.

FIGURE 12-2
An XSL stylesheet to display student information

```
<?xml version="1.0"?>
<xsl:stylesheet version="1.0" xmlns:xsl="http://www.w3.org/1999/XSL/Transform">
<xsl:template match="/document">

<html>

<head>
  <title>XML/XSL Web Page 6</title>
</head>

<body>
  <center>
    <h1>Student Information List</h1>
    <table border="1" bordercolor="#000000" cellpadding="5" cellspacing="0">
      <tr>
        <td>
          <table cellpadding="1" cellspacing="0">
            <tr>
              <td width="125">
                <b>Last Name</b>
              </td>
              <td width="125">
                <b>First Name</b>
              </td>
              <td width="75">
                <b>Grade</b>
              </td>
              <td width="75">
                <b>GPA</b>
              </td>
            </tr>
```

STEP-BY-STEP 12.1 Continued

FIGURE 12-2 (Continued)
An XSL stylesheet to display student information

```
        <xsl:for-each select="student">
         <tr>
          <td>
            <xsl:value-of select="last"/>
          </td>
          <td>
            <xsl:value-of select="first"/>
          </td>
          <td>
            <xsl:value-of select="grade"/>
          </td>
          <td>
            <xsl:value-of select="gpa"/>
          </td>
         </tr>
        </xsl:for-each>
       </table>
      </td>
     </tr>
    </table>
   </center>
  </body>

 </html>

 </xsl:template>
 </xsl:stylesheet>
```

4. Save this file as **xsl-six.xsl**.

5. Open your Web browser and view the **xml-six.xml** file you saved in step 2. Your browser should display a Web page that looks like the one in Figure 12-3. Notice that the student information appears in the same order as your unsorted XML file.

STEP-BY-STEP 12.1 Continued

FIGURE 12-3
XML/XSL Web Page 6 unsorted

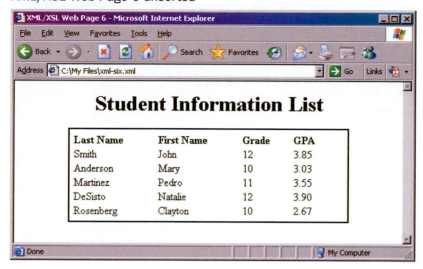

6. Return to your text editor and enter the <xsl:sort> tag as shown in bold in Figure 12-4.

FIGURE 12-4
XSL stylesheet with <xsl:sort> tag included

```
<?xml version="1.0"?>
<xsl:stylesheet version="1.0" xmlns:xsl="http://www.w3.org/1999/XSL/Transform">
<xsl:template match="/document">

<html>

<head>
  <title>XML/XSL Web Page 6</title>
</head>

<body>
  <center>
    <h1>Student Information List</h1>
    <table border="1" bordercolor="#000000" cellpadding="5" cellspacing="0">
      <tr>
        <td>
          <table cellpadding="1" cellspacing="0">
            <tr>
              <td width="125">
                <b>Last Name</b>
              </td>
              <td width="125">
                <b>First Name</b>
              </td>
```

STEP-BY-STEP 12.1 Continued

FIGURE 12-4 (Continued)
XSL stylesheet with <xsl:sort> tag included

```
            <td width="75">
             <b>Grade</b>
            </td>
            <td width="75">
             <b>GPA</b>
            </td>
           </tr>
           <xsl:for-each select="student"><xsl:sort select="last"/>
            <tr>
             <td>
               <xsl:value-of select="last"/>
             </td>
             <td>
               <xsl:value-of select="first"/>
             </td>
             <td>
               <xsl:value-of select="grade"/>
             </td>
             <td>
               <xsl:value-of select="gpa"/>
             </td>
            </tr>
           </xsl:for-each>
          </table>
         </td>
        </tr>
       </table>
      </center>
     </body>

    </html>

    </xsl:template>
    </xsl:stylesheet>
```

7. Re-save this file as **xsl-six.xsl**.

STEP-BY-STEP 12.1 Continued

8. Switch to your Web browser and refresh the **xml-six.xml** file you are currently viewing. Your browser should now display the student information list sorted alphabetically by last name as shown in Figure 12-5. Leave your browser and your text editor open for the next exercise.

FIGURE 12-5
XML/XSL Web Page 6 sorted by last name

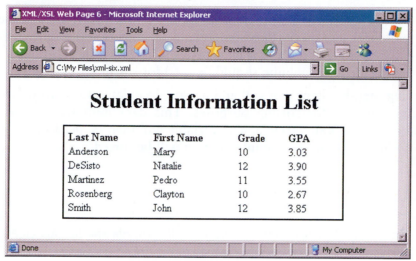

Analyzing the Results

Most of the tasks you performed in this Step-by-Step are not new. They simply reinforce some of the concepts you learned in Lesson 11. There is nothing new about the structure of the XML data file you created. There is also nothing new about the first version of your XSL stylesheet. This XSL code simply extracts the student information from the XML data set, and then displays it by means of a for-each loop.

However, after viewing your XML/XSL Web page once, you were asked to add an XSL tag that you had not seen previously. The <xsl:sort> shortcut tag simply instructs your browser to sort the data extracted by the for-each loop, according to the value of the data stored at the specified Xpath, before it displays it. You should recognize that this is a simple but powerful feature of XSL.

XSL Variables

Another standard feature of programming languages that is not found in markup languages is support for *variables*. A variable is basically just a name that is assigned to a specific location in a computer's memory. The value (or values) stored at that location can then be referenced by a meaningful name rather than a cryptic memory address.

Support for variables is another way in which XSL is more like a programming language than a markup language. There are times when it can be very useful for an XSL stylesheet to store a value in a variable, and then retrieve that value at some later point. For this reason, the language definition for XSL includes an *<xsl:variable> tag*. This tag allows you to retrieve a value from an XML data file and save it with a meaningful name. You may then use this variable name as often as you wish throughout your stylesheet whenever you need to access this stored value.

Sorting By the Data File

To give you a more specific example, consider the stylesheet you created in the previous Step-by-Step. In this stylesheet you used a specific name to identify the column by which the student information should be sorted. However, it may be desirable to let the XML data file, rather than the XSL stylesheet, decide what column should be used for sorting.

In the following Step-by-Step, you will add a <sort-by> data tag to your XML file that will identify the column to use for sorting purposes. This data item will be extracted by your stylesheet and stored in an XSL variable. The variable will then be used in the <xsl:sort> tag to determine the way in which the student information will be sorted.

S TEP-BY-STEP 12.2

1. Switch to your text editor and, if necessary, open the **xml-six.xml** file you created in the previous Step-by-Step.

2. Change the value of the href attribute in the XML stylesheet tag to **xsl-seven.xsl**. Then add the text as shown in bold in Figure 12-6.

FIGURE 12-6
XML file with <sort-by> tag

```
<?xml version="1.0"?>
<?xml-stylesheet type="text/xsl" href="xsl-seven.xsl"?>
<document>

<sort-by>last</sort-by>
<student>
 <last>Smith</last>
 <first>John</first>
 <grade>12</grade>
 <gpa>3.85</gpa>
</student>
<student>
  <last>Anderson</last>
  <first>Mary</first>
  <grade>10</grade>
  <gpa>3.03</gpa>
</student>
<student>
  <last>Martinez</last>
```

STEP-BY-STEP 12.2 Continued

FIGURE 12-6 (Continued)
XML file with <sort-by> tag

```
      <first>Pedro</first>
      <grade>11</grade>
      <gpa>3.55</gpa>
    </student>
    <student>
      <last>DeSisto</last>
      <first>Natalie</first>
      <grade>9</grade>
      <gpa>3.90</gpa>
    </student>
    <student>
      <last>Rosenberg</last>
      <first>Clayton</first>
      <grade>10</grade>
      <gpa>2.67</gpa>
    </student>
</document>
```

3. Save this file as **xml-seven.xml**.

4. Clear the contents of your editor, and then retrieve the **xsl-six.xsl** file you created in the previous Step-by-Step.

5. Change the number of your XML/XSL Web page (in the title) from 6 to **7**. Then add the XSL variable tag and change the sort tag as shown in bold in Figure 12-7.

FIGURE 12-7
XSL stylesheet with variable

```
<?xml version="1.0"?>
<xsl:stylesheet version="1.0" xmlns:xsl="http://www.w3.org/1999/XSL/Transform">
<xsl:template match="/document">

<html>

<head>
 <title>XML/XSL Web Page 7</title>
</head>

<body>
 <center>
  <h1>Student Information List</h1>
  <table border="1" bordercolor="#000000" cellpadding="5" cellspacing="0">
   <tr>
```

STEP-BY-STEP 12.2 Continued

FIGURE 12-7 (Continued)
XSL stylesheet with variable

```
   <td>
    <table cellpadding="1" cellspacing="0">
     <tr>
      <td width="125">
       <b>Last Name</b>
      </td>
      <td width="125">
       <b>First Name</b>
      </td>
      <td width="75">
       <b>Grade</b>
      </td>
      <td width="75">
       <b>GPA</b>
      </td>
     </tr>
     <xsl:variable name="column" select="sort-by"/>
     <xsl:for-each select="student"><xsl:sort select="*[name()=$column]"/>
      <tr>
       <td>
        <xsl:value-of select="last"/>
       </td>
       <td>
        <xsl:value-of select="first"/>
       </td>
       <td>
        <xsl:value-of select="grade"/>
       </td>
       <td>
        <xsl:value-of select="gpa"/>
       </td>
      </tr>
     </xsl:for-each>
    </table>
   </td>
  </tr>
 </table>
</center>
</body>

</html>

</xsl:template>
</xsl:stylesheet>
```

STEP-BY-STEP 12.2 Continued

6. Save this file as **xsl-seven.xsl**.

7. Switch to your Web browser and view the **xml-seven.xml** file you saved in step 3. Your browser should display a Web page that looks like the one in Figure 12-8. Notice that the student information appears sorted by last name.

FIGURE 12-8
XML/XSL Web Page 7 sorted by last name

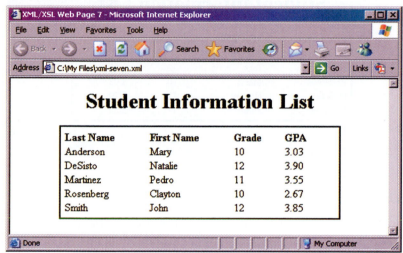

8. Now, return to your text editor and open the **xml-seven.xml** file you saved in step 3.

9. Change the value of the <sort-by> tag from *last* to **first**, and then save the file using the same name (**xml-seven.xml**).

10. Switch to your Web browser and refresh the **xml-seven.xml** file to view the edits you made to the file you saved in step 9. Your browser should now display a Web page that looks like the one in Figure 12-9. Notice that the student information appears sorted by first name. Leave your browser and your text editor open for the next exercise.

FIGURE 12-9
XML/XSL Web Page 7 sorted by first name

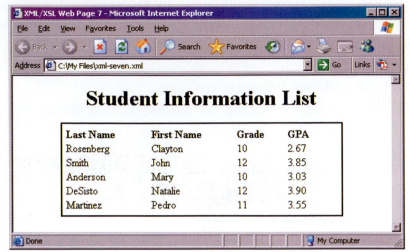

Analyzing the Results

This Step-by-Step was fairly simple but it shows the power and versatility of XSL. Let's step through this exercise again to make sure you grasp this new concept.

First, we added a new data element to your XML file. The value of the <sort-by> tag identifies which column of the student information will be used by the XSL stylesheet to order the display. This is significant because it allows the XML data file to determine the sort order rather than a fixed value in the stylesheet.

Next, we made two simple, but important, changes to the stylesheet. The first change was to add an <xsl:variable> tag that defines an XSL variable named column. The value of this variable will be extracted from the <sort-by> node of the XML file. The second change was to modify the value of the select attribute in the <xsl:sort> tag. The new value probably looks fairly complex and cryptic to you. However, all you really need to understand is that the <xsl:sort> tag will order the student information using the node name that is equal to the value of the column variable. The **name()** part of this expression is just one of many intrinsic functions that XSL supports, which will be explained in greater detail in the next section.

Using XSL Intrinsic Functions

One of the features of XSL that distinguishes it from markup languages is its *intrinsic functions*. These are functions that are built into the XSL processor that can be invoked from within XSL tags. Their purpose is to return information about XML data values, rather than the value itself. For example, one XSL intrinsic function can return the length of an XML data string, rather than the string itself.

The XSL intrinsic function library can be divided into several different groups. Some of these groups include string functions, numeric functions, Boolean functions, date/time functions, and so on. A detailed analysis of all the XSL intrinsic functions is far beyond the scope of this book.

However, you will gain experience with one of the most commonly used functions that XSL has to offer in following exercise. You will gain experience with other intrinsic functions through the exercises at the end of this lesson.

The position() Function

In the following Step-by-Step, you will be introduced to the intrinsic function called position(). This function returns the position of a node within a group of nodes. This value is typically used in conjunction with an <xsl:for-each> tag to determine which iteration of the loop is currently being processed. We will make use of this function to improve the appearance of our student information list. For each iteration of our loop we will alter the background color for each student's information from white to light gray, and back to white again.

STEP-BY-STEP 12.3

1. Switch to your text editor and, if necessary, open the **xml-seven.xml** file you created in the previous Step-by-Step.

2. Change the value of the href attribute in the XML stylesheet tag to **xsl-eight.xsl** as shown in bold in Figure 12-10.

FIGURE 12-10
XML file for Web Page 8

```
<?xml version="1.0"?>
<?xml-stylesheet type="text/xsl" href="xsl-eight.xsl"?>

<document>
  <sort-by>first</sort-by>
  <student>
    <last>Smith</last>
    <first>John</first>
    <grade>12</grade>
    <gpa>3.85</gpa>
  </student>
  <student>
    <last>Anderson</last>
    <first>Mary</first>
    <grade>10</grade>
    <gpa>3.03</gpa>
  </student>
  <student>
    <last>Martinez</last>
    <first>Pedro</first>
    <grade>11</grade>
    <gpa>3.55</gpa>
  </student>
  <student>
```

STEP-BY-STEP 12.3 Continued

FIGURE 12-10 (Continued)
XML file for Web Page 8

```
        <last>DeSisto</last>
        <first>Natalie</first>
        <grade>12</grade>
        <gpa>3.90</gpa>
    </student>
    <student>
        <last>Rosenberg</last>
        <first>Clayton</first>
        <grade>10</grade>
        <gpa>2.67</gpa>
    </student>
</document>
```

3. Save this file as **xml-eight.xml**.

4. Clear the contents of your editor, and then open the **xsl-seven.xsl** file you created in the previous Step-by-Step.

5. Change the number of your XML/XSL Web page (in the title) from 7 to **8**. Also add the text as shown in bold in Figure 12-11.

FIGURE 12-11
XSL stylesheet with position() function

```
<?xml version="1.0"?>
<xsl:stylesheet version="1.0" xmlns:xsl="http://www.w3.org/1999/XSL/Transform">
<xsl:template match="/document">

<html>

<head>
  <title>XML/XSL Web Page 8</title>
</head>

<body>
  <center>
   <h1>Student Information List</h1>
   <table border="1" bordercolor="#000000" cellpadding="5" cellspacing="0">
    <tr>
     <td>
```

STEP-BY-STEP 12.3 Continued

FIGURE 12-11 (Continued)
XSL stylesheet with position() function

```xml
<table cellpadding="1" cellspacing="0">
 <tr>
  <td width="25">
   <br/>
  </td>
  <td width="125">
   <b>Last Name</b>
  </td>
  <td width="125">
   <b>First Name</b>
  </td>
  <td width="75">
   <b>Grade</b>
  </td>
  <td width="75">
   <b>GPA</b>
  </td>
 </tr>
 <xsl:variable name="column" select="sort-by"/>
 <xsl:for-each select="student"><xsl:sort select="*[name()=$column]"/>
  <xsl:if test="(position() mod 2) = 0">
   <tr>
    <td bgcolor="#BFBFBF">
     <xsl:value-of select="position()"/>
    </td>
    <td bgcolor="#BFBFBF">
     <xsl:value-of select="last"/>
    </td>
    <td bgcolor="#BFBFBF">
     <xsl:value-of select="first"/>
    </td>
    <td bgcolor="#BFBFBF">
     <xsl:value-of select="grade"/>
    </td>
    <td bgcolor="#BFBFBF">
```

STEP-BY-STEP 12.3 Continued

FIGURE 12-11 (Continued)
XSL stylesheet with position() function

```
                  <xsl:value-of select="gpa"/>
               </td>
            </tr>
         </xsl:if>
         <xsl:if test="(position() mod 2) = 1">
            <tr>
               <td bgcolor="#FFFFFF">
                  <xsl:value-of select="position()"/>
               </td>
               <td bgcolor="#FFFFFF">
                  <xsl:value-of select="last"/>
               </td>
               <td bgcolor="#FFFFFF">
                  <xsl:value-of select="first"/>
               </td>
               <td bgcolor="#FFFFFF">
                  <xsl:value-of select="grade"/>
               </td>
               <td bgcolor="#FFFFFF">
                  <xsl:value-of select="gpa"/>
               </td>
            </tr>
         </xsl:if>
      </xsl:for-each>
    </table>
   </td>
  </tr>
 </table>
</center>
</body>

</html>

</xsl:template>
</xsl:stylesheet>
```

6. Save this file as **xsl-eight.xsl**.

STEP-BY-STEP 12.3 Continued

7. Switch to your Web browser and view the **xml-eight.xml** file you saved in step 3. Your browser should display a Web page that looks like the one in Figure 12-12. Leave your browser and the text editor open for the next exercise.

FIGURE 12-12
XML/XSL Web Page 8

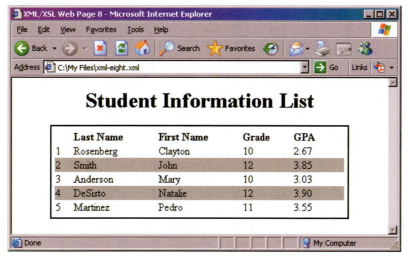

Analyzing the Results

Your XML/XSL Web page continues to grow in size and complexity, so let's make sure you understand the new concepts presented in this section. The only change that you made to the XML file was the name of the stylesheet, so let's move straight into the XSL changes.

First, we added a new column to our student information table. Then we used the value returned by the position() function to fill this column with numbers. We also used the position function to help us determine the background color of each row in the table. The way we accomplished this was by means of the <xsl:if> tag and the *XSL modulus (mod) operator*. This operator divides one number by another, and then returns the remainder. Dividing any number by 2 will always return a remainder of 0 if the number is even and a remainder of 1 if the number is odd. We use these two possible values (inside the test attribute of the <xsl:if> tags) to decide if the row of student information should be displayed with a white background or a gray one. The result is an alternating display pattern that enhances the readability of tabular data.

Adding JavaScript to XSL

Despite the many advantages that XSL offers over simple markup languages, it still has its limitations. For this reason, XSL also supports the inclusion of JavaScript functions into its Web pages as does HTML. However, integrating JavaScript code into an XSL stylesheet is not quite as simple as with markup languages. It is important for you to understand the reason for this difference.

JavaScript in HTML

If you wanted to add one or more JavaScript functions to a standard HTML file, all you need to do is insert <script> and </script> tags into the document header, and then write as many functions as you wish between these two tags. Your browser will simply ignore anything it finds within script tags, and this text will be interpreted as JavaScript code.

JavaScript in XML

In the case of XSL, however, the entire stylesheet is parsed and interpreted as an XML document, and no special consideration is given for <script> or </script> tags. To understand the significance of this fact, consider the following JavaScript function.

```
function maximum(a, b)
{
 max = a;
 if (b > a) max = b;
 return max;
}
```

This function is very simple to a JavaScript interpreter. But consider the problems it would cause for an XML parser. This small snippet of code contains many symbols that an XML interpreter is not prepared to handle, such as parentheses, semicolons, and "curly" braces. In addition, the XML parser would recognize the "greater than" symbol (>) and incorrectly interpret it as part of an incomplete XML tag. Obviously, the end-result of this would be chaos and an ugly error message from your browser.

JavaScript in XSL

Fortunately, there is a way around this dilemma. XSL supports the inclusion of a <script> tag that identifies the location of an external JavaScript file. This approach allows you to create as much JavaScript code as you wish in a separate file, and then access that code within your XML/XSL Web page. The JavaScript events that invoke these functions (such as onClick, onMouseOver, onMouseOut, and so forth) are included within the XHTML tags just as they are in standard HTML. The following exercise will show you exactly how this is done.

STEP-BY-STEP 12.4

1. Switch to your text editor and, if necessary, open the **xml-eight.xml** file you created in the previous Step-by-Step.

STEP-BY-STEP 12.4 Continued

2. Change the value of the href attribute in the XML stylesheet tag to **xsl-nine.xsl** as shown in bold in Figure 12-13.

FIGURE 12-13
XML file for Web Page 9

```
<?xml version="1.0"?>
<?xml-stylesheet type="text/xsl" href="xsl-nine.xsl"?>

<document>
  <sort-by>first</sort-by>
  <student>
    <last>Smith</last>
    <first>John</first>
    <grade>12</grade>
    <gpa>3.85</gpa>
  </student>
  <student>
    <last>Anderson</last>
    <first>Mary</first>
    <grade>10</grade>
    <gpa>3.03</gpa>
  </student>
  <student>
    <last>Martinez</last>
    <first>Pedro</first>
    <grade>11</grade>
    <gpa>3.55</gpa>
  </student>
  <student>
    <last>DeSisto</last>
    <first>Natalie</first>
    <grade>12</grade>
    <gpa>3.90</gpa>
  </student>
  <student>
    <last>Rosenberg</last>
    <first>Clayton</first>
    <grade>10</grade>
    <gpa>2.67</gpa>
  </student>
</document>
```

3. Save this file as **xml-nine.xml**.

4. Clear the contents of your editor, and then open the **xsl-eight.xsl** file you created in the previous Step-by-Step exercise.

STEP-BY-STEP 12.4 Continued

5. Change the number of your XML/XSL Web page (in the title) from 8 to **9**. Also add the <script> tag and the hyperlinks as shown in bold in Figure 12-14.

FIGURE 12-14
XSL stylesheet with <script> tag and hyperlinks

```
<?xml version="1.0"?>
<xsl:stylesheet version="1.0" xmlns:xsl="http://www.w3.org/1999/XSL/Transform">
<xsl:template match="/document">

<html>

<head>
  <title>XML/XSL Web Page 9</title>
  <script src="js-nine.js"/>
</head>

<body>
  <center>
    <h1>Student Information List</h1>
    <table border="1" bordercolor="#000000" cellpadding="5" cellspacing="0">
      <tr>
        <td>
          <table cellpadding="1" cellspacing="0">
            <tr>
              <td width="25">
                <br/>
              </td>
              <td width="125">
                <a href="javascript:sort(1)"><b>Last Name</b></a>
              </td>
              <td width="125">
                <a href="javascript:sort(2)"><b>First Name</b></a>
              </td>
              <td width="75">
                <a href="javascript:sort(3)"><b>Grade</b></a>
              </td>
              <td width="75">
                <a href="javascript:sort(4)"><b>GPA</b></a>
              </td>
            </tr>
            <xsl:variable name="column" select="sort-by"/>
            <xsl:for-each select="student"><xsl:sort select="*[name()=$column]"/>
            <xsl:if test="(position() mod 2) = 0">
              <tr>
                <td bgcolor="#BFBFBF">
```

STEP-BY-STEP 12.4 Continued

FIGURE 12-14 (Continued)
XSL stylesheet with <script> tag and hyperlinks

```
                    <xsl:value-of select="position()"/>
                  </td>
                  <td bgcolor="#BFBFBF">
                    <xsl:value-of select="last"/>
                  </td>
                  <td bgcolor="#BFBFBF">
                    <xsl:value-of select="first"/>
                  </td>
                  <td bgcolor="#BFBFBF">
                    <xsl:value-of select="grade"/>
                  </td>
                  <td bgcolor="#BFBFBF">
                    <xsl:value-of select="gpa"/>
                  </td>
                </tr>
              </xsl:if>
              <xsl:if test="(position() mod 2) = 1">
                <tr>
                  <td bgcolor="#FFFFFF">
                    <xsl:value-of select="position()"/>
                  </td>
                  <td bgcolor="#FFFFFF">
                    <xsl:value-of select="last"/>
                  </td>
                  <td bgcolor="#FFFFFF">
                    <xsl:value-of select="first"/>
                  </td>
                  <td bgcolor="#FFFFFF">
                    <xsl:value-of select="grade"/>
                  </td>
                  <td bgcolor="#FFFFFF">
                    <xsl:value-of select="gpa"/>
                  </td>
                </tr>
              </xsl:if>
            </xsl:for-each>
          </table>
        </td>
      </tr>
    </table>
```

STEP-BY-STEP 12.4 Continued

FIGURE 12-14 (Continued)
XSL stylesheet with <script> tag and hyperlinks

```
    </center>
  </body>

</html>

</xsl:template>
</xsl:stylesheet>
```

6. Save this file as **xsl-nine.xsl**.

7. Clear the contents of your text editor, and then enter the text exactly as shown in Figure 12-15.

FIGURE 12-15
JavaScript file containing one function

```
function sort(index)
{
  if (index == 1) column = "last name";
  if (index == 2) column = "first name";
  if (index == 3) column = "grade";
  if (index == 4) column = "GPA";
  message = "This function will sort the student\n";
  message += "information list by " + column + ".";
  alert(message);
  return;
}
```

STEP-BY-STEP 12.4 Continued

8. Save this file as **js-nine.js**.

9. Switch to your Web browser and view the **xml-nine.xml** file you saved in step 3. Your browser should display a Web page that looks like the one in Figure 12-16.

> **Warning**
>
> When you open the *xml-nine.xml* file in Internet Explore 6.0 you may see an Information Bar and its dialog box. Click **OK** to close the dialog box.

FIGURE 12-16
XML/XSL Web Page 9

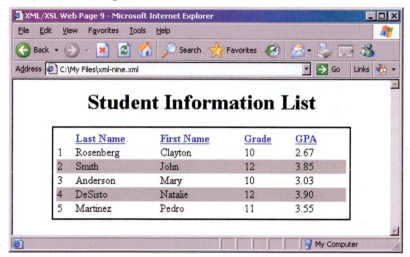

10. Click on any of the column headers and observe the JavaScript alert message that is displayed. Leave your browser and your text editor open for the next exercise.

Analyzing the Results

Let's review the concepts presented in this Step-by-Step to make sure there are no misunderstandings. The changes to the XML data file are negligible, so we will move directly to the additions we made in the XSL file.

First, we added a <script> tag to the header section of the document, and the src attribute of this tag identifies the *js-nine.js* file as the source for the JavaScript code. Next, we added four anchor (<a>) tags to convert the column headers into hyperlinks. All four of these hyperlinks invoke the same JavaScript function (called sort()), but they each pass a different numeric parameter to the function. The sort() function then uses this value to determine which column header invoked it, and displays an appropriate alert message.

As you can see, integrating JavaScript functions into your XML/XSL Web pages is not terribly difficult. However, it does have the drawback of requiring you to create an additional file (js-nine.js in this case). This particular JavaScript source file only contains a single function, but it is common for JS files to contain many functions. The important concept to remember is the way in which JavaScript code can be included in XML/XSL Web pages without corrupting the syntax of the XSL stylesheet.

XSL Data Sorting with JavaScript

In the previous section you learned how to define, integrate, and call a JavaScript function from an XSL stylesheet. However, the JavaScript function only displays a message about what it is about to do, but then it does not actually do it. In this section you will complete the JavaScript function so that it will actually sort our student information list by whatever column the user clicks.

Altering the XML Data File for Sorting

Before we can complete the JavaScript sort() function, we need to do a little work with our XML data file. Remember that our XSL stylesheet will order the data according to the value of the <sort-by> tag in the XML file. But if we want to order the list in four different ways, we need four different data XML files, one for each possible column. In the following Step-by-Step, you will create these four files, and then you will see how the JavaScript sort() function can instruct the browser to load the appropriate XML file to obtain the requested sort order.

S TEP-BY-STEP 12.5

1. Switch to your text editor and, if necessary, open the **xml-nine.xml** file you created in the previous Step-by-Step.

2. Change the value of the href attribute in the XML stylesheet tag to **xsl-ten.xsl**. Then set the value of the <sort-by> tag as shown in bold in Figure 12-17.

FIGURE 12-17
XML file with <sort-by> tag set to last

```
<?xml version="1.0"?>
<?xml-stylesheet type="text/xsl" href="xsl-ten.xsl"?>

<document>
 <sort-by>last</sort-by>
 <student>
  <last>Smith</last>
  <first>John</first>
  <grade>12</grade>
  <gpa>3.85</gpa>
 </student>
 <student>
  <last>Anderson</last>
  <first>Mary</first>
  <grade>10</grade>
  <gpa>3.03</gpa>
 </student>
 <student>
  <last>Martinez</last>
  <first>Pedro</first>
```

STEP-BY-STEP 12.5 Continued

FIGURE 12-17 (Continued)
XML file with <sort-by> tag set to last

```
        <grade>11</grade>
        <gpa>3.55</gpa>
      </student>
      <student>
        <last>DeSisto</last>
        <first>Natalie</first>
        <grade>12</grade>
        <gpa>3.90</gpa>
      </student>
      <student>
        <last>Rosenberg</last>
        <first>Clayton</first>
        <grade>10</grade>
        <gpa>2.67</gpa>
      </student>
    </document>
```

3. Save this file as **xml-ten-1.xml**.

4. Change the value of the <sort-by> tag from *last* to **first**, and then save the file again as **xml-ten-2.xml**.

5. Now change the value of the <sort-by> tag from *first* to **grade**, and then save the file again as **xml-ten-3.xml**.

6. Finally, change the value of the <sort-by> tag from *grade* to **gpa**, and then save the file again as **xml-ten-4.xml**.

7. Clear the contents of your editor, and then retrieve the **xsl-nine.xsl** file you created in the previous Step-by-Step.

8. Change the number of your XML/XSL Web page (in the title) from 9 to **10**. Also change the src attribute in the <script> tag as shown in bold in Figure 12-18.

FIGURE 12-18
XSL stylesheet for Web Page 10

```
<?xml version="1.0"?>
<xsl:stylesheet version="1.0" xmlns:xsl="http://www.w3.org/1999/XSL/Transform">
<xsl:template match="/document">

<html>

<head>
  <title>XML/XSL Web Page 10</title>
```

STEP-BY-STEP 12.5 Continued

FIGURE 12-18 (Continued)
XSL stylesheet for Web Page 10

```
    <script src="js-ten.js"/>
  </head>

<body>
 <center>
  <h1>Student Information List</h1>
  <table border="1" bordercolor="#000000" cellpadding="5" cellspacing="0">
   <tr>
    <td>
     <table cellpadding="1" cellspacing="0">
      <tr>
       <td width="25">
        <br/>
       </td>
       <td width="125">
        <a href="javascript:sort(1)"><b>Last Name</b></a>
       </td>
       <td width="125">
        <a href="javascript:sort(2)"><b>First Name</b></a>
       </td>
       <td width="75">
        <a href="javascript:sort(3)"><b>Grade</b></a>
       </td>
       <td width="75">
        <a href="javascript:sort(4)"><b>GPA</b></a>
       </td>
      </tr>
      <xsl:variable name="column" select="sort-by"/>
      <xsl:for-each select="student"><xsl:sort select="*[name()=$column]"/>
       <xsl:if test="(position() mod 2) = 0">
        <tr>
         <td bgcolor="#BFBFBF">
          <xsl:value-of select="position()"/>
         </td>
         <td bgcolor="#BFBFBF">
          <xsl:value-of select="last"/>
         </td>
         <td bgcolor="#BFBFBF">
          <xsl:value-of select="first"/>
         </td>
         <td bgcolor="#BFBFBF">
          <xsl:value-of select="grade"/>
         </td>
```

STEP-BY-STEP 12.5 Continued

FIGURE 12-18 (Continued)
XSL stylesheet for Web Page 10

```
                    <td bgcolor="#BFBFBF">
                      <xsl:value-of select="gpa"/>
                    </td>
                  </tr>
                </xsl:if>
                <xsl:if test="(position() mod 2) = 1">
                  <tr>
                    <td bgcolor="#FFFFFF">
                      <xsl:value-of select="position()"/>
                    </td>
                    <td bgcolor="#FFFFFF">
                      <xsl:value-of select="last"/>
                    </td>
                    <td bgcolor="#FFFFFF">
                      <xsl:value-of select="first"/>
                    </td>
                    <td bgcolor="#FFFFFF">
                      <xsl:value-of select="grade"/>
                    </td>
                    <td bgcolor="#FFFFFF">
                      <xsl:value-of select="gpa"/>
                    </td>
                  </tr>
                </xsl:if>
              </xsl:for-each>
            </table>
          </td>
        </tr>
      </table>
    </center>
  </body>

</html>

</xsl:template>
</xsl:stylesheet>
```

9. Save this file as **xsl-ten.xsl**.

10. Clear the contents of your editor, and then retrieve the **js-nine.js** file you created in the previous Step-by-Step.

11. Add the JavaScript code as shown in bold in Figure 12-19.

STEP-BY-STEP 12.5 Continued

FIGURE 12-19
JavaScript file containing updated sort() function

```
function sort(index)
{
  if (index == 1) column = "last name";
  if (index == 2) column = "first name";
  if (index == 3) column = "grade";
  if (index == 4) column = "GPA";
  message = "This function will sort the student\n";
  message += "information list by " + column + ".";
  alert(message);
  window.location = "xml-ten-" + index + ".xml";
  return;
}
```

12. Save this file as **js-ten.js**.

13. Switch to your Web browser and view the **xml-ten-1.xml** file you saved in step 3. Your browser should display a Web page that looks like the one in Figure 12-20.

FIGURE 12-20
XML/XSL Web Page 10

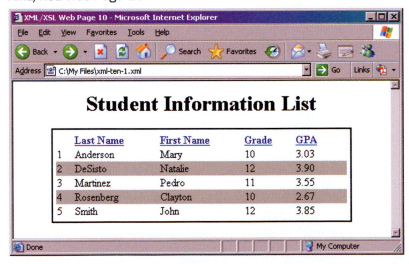

14. Click on any column header and notice the results. The JavaScript function will display an alert message, and then the student information list will be redisplayed in the appropriate order. Leave your browser and text editor open for the end-of-lesson exercises.

Analyzing the Results

Once again you have learned some valuable concepts, so let's review this final XML/XSL Web page to make sure all the elements are clear to you.

First, you created four XML data files that are nearly identical. The only difference is the value of the <sort-by> tag at the top of the file. Take note of the fact that these four files do not reference four different XSL stylesheets. They all reference the same one, and this stylesheet contains sufficient information to respond correctly to all four XML files.

Next, you updated your XSL stylesheet to display the proper Web page title, and you updated its reference to a new JavaScript source file. This task was very simple to perform.

Lastly, you added a new instruction to your JavaScript sort() function. This new line of code simply uses the index parameter that is passed in by the column header hyperlink to construct an XML filename. The browser then updates its location property, which causes it to load the designated XML file.

SUMMARY

In this lesson you learned:

- To construct an XSL stylesheet that sorts XML data.
- To define and use an XSL variable.
- To recognize and use XSL intrinsic functions.
- To integrate JavaScript functions into an XML/XSL Web page.
- To use JavaScript to access other XML documents.

VOCABULARY *Review*

Define the following terms:

Data sorting	position() function	<xsl:sort> tag
Intrinsic functions	Variables	<xsl:variable> tag
name() function	XSL modulus (mod) operator	

REVIEW *Questions*

TRUE/FALSE

Circle T if the statement is true or F if the statement is false.

T   F   **1.** An XSL stylesheet can sort XML data before it displays the data.

T   F   **2.** Like programming languages, XSL supports the ability to define and use variables.

T   F   **3.** Unlike JavaScript, XSL is composed entirely of tags, and contains no intrinsic functions.

T   F   **4.** Because of the conflicts in syntax it causes, it is not possible to integrate JavaScript into an XML/XSL Web page.

T   F   **5.** It is not possible for JavaScript functions to instruct Web browsers to load and process XML files.

FILL IN THE BLANK

Complete the following sentences by writing the correct word or words in the blanks provided.

1. The process of reorganizing the information in a list into a particular order is called _____.

2. _____ are basically names that are assigned to specific locations in a computer's memory space.

3. The XSL operator _____ returns the remainder of an integer division operation.

4. An XSL stylesheet can use the _____ tag to identify a JavaScript module to use.

5. The intrinsic function _____ returns the current iteration of an XSL for-each loop.

WRITTEN QUESTIONS

Write a brief answer to each of the following questions.

1. Describe the proper use of the <xsl:sort> tag.

2. What are XSL variables? How are they defined and accessed?

3. What are XSL intrinsic functions?

4. Explain why JavaScript code cannot be embedded directly in XSL stylesheets.

5. Describe the process of integrating a JavaScript source file with an XSL stylesheet.

PROJECTS

 PROJECT 12-1

Revisit the XML/XSL Web page you created in Step-by-Step 12.3, and consider what the final Web page would look like if the XML file contained no student information. The <xsl:for-each> tag would not execute, so the resulting Web page would look rather strange because it would display the column headers with no data beneath them. In this situation, professional Web page developers will usually include logic in their stylesheet to display a message that confirms to the user that there was no data available to display.

This may seem to be an easy issue to address, but there is one major question to answer: "How do you know whether or not the XML file contains student data?" Fortunately, XSL includes an intrinsic function called count() that can answer this question for you. Here is an example of its use:

```
<xsl:if test="count(student) = 0">
```

Using this example, modify your **xsl-eight.xsl** stylesheet so that it will display an appropriate message if the XML data file contains no student information. Save your changes as **xsl-project.xsl**. Test your new stylesheet by creating a new XML file that references *xsl-project.xsl* as its XSL stylesheet, and that contains no student data.

  TEAMWORK PROJECT

Divide your class into teams of three to four students, and discuss the following question: "What changes must be made to the XML, XSL, and JavaScript files you created for Step-by-Step 12.5 in order to add a new column of student data, and to allow the student information list to be sorted by this new column?"

Once you have identified the changes that must be made, add a new column called "City." As you might expect, this data item identifies the city in which each student lives. (This may be helpful in rural areas, for example, where students from several neighboring towns might attend a common school.) Save your new project files as **xml-team.xml**, **xsl-team.xsl**, and **js-team.js**.

> **Note**
>
> There will be one XML file created for each of the columns that is created or modified. If you need to create more than one XML file, name them sequentially as **xml-team-1.xml**, **xml-team-2.xml**, and so on.

WEB PROJECT

Under appropriate instructor supervision, use your favorite search engine to identify several Web sites that can help beginners learn how to create Web pages with XSL. Take a few minutes to examine a few of these sites, and determine what type (or types) of information these sites contain. To be more specific, determine if these sites contain information about XSL tags, XSL intrinsic functions, XSL/JavaScript integration, or some combination of these topics. Based on your findings, complete a table like the one shown in Table 12-1 that contains at least five entries.

TABLE 12-1
XSL reference Web sites

WEB SITE ADDRESS	XSL TAGS?	XSL FUNCTIONS?	XSL/JAVASCRIPT?
www.website1.com	yes/no	yes/no	yes/no
www.website2.com	yes/no	yes/no	yes/no
www.website3.com	yes/no	yes/no	yes/no
www.website4.com	yes/no	yes/no	yes/no
www.website5.com	yes/no	yes/no	yes/no

CRITICAL *Thinking*

 ## ACTIVITY 12-1

Essentially all programming languages have the ability to evaluate a condition, and then perform certain instructions if the condition is true. This is commonly referred to as a simple "if" statement. The XSL equivalent of the simple "if" statement is the <xsl:if> tag.

However, programming languages also support compound "if" statements (also known as "if-else" statements), and "case" statements. The former statement allows a program to take one action if a condition is true and a different action if the condition is false. The latter statement allows a program to test for multiple conditions, and take a different action for each possible case. As it turns out, XSL also gives stylesheets the ability to behave in a similar fashion. This is accomplished with the <xsl:choose> tag.

The syntax of the <xsl:choose> tag is as follows:

```
<xsl:choose>
  <xsl:when test="[condition 1]">
  </xsl:when>
  <xsl:when test="[condition 2]">
  </xsl:when>
  <xsl:when test="[condition 3]">
```

```
  </xsl:when>
      .
      .
      .
  <xsl:otherwise>
  </xsl:otherwise>
</xsl:choose>
```

Use this XSL tag to enhance the appearance of your student information list by color coding each student's GPA. If the GPA is above 3.0, display it in green text. If the GPA falls in the range 2.0 to 3.0, display it in yellow, and display it in red if it is lower than 2.0. Prepare an appropriate XML file to test your new logic, and save your final XSL stylesheet as **xsl-activity1.xsl**.

Hot Tip

You can not use the traditional greater than (>) and less than symbols (<) symbols to complete this activity since these symbols are part of the XML tagging. You need to use &gt for greater than and &lt for less than.

SCANS **ACTIVITY 12-2**

Suppose you had an XML data file containing the names of several (*N*) students, and the structure of this file is as follows.

```
<student>[student name 1]</student>
<student>[student name 2]</student>
<student>[student name 3]</student>
              .
              .
              .
<student>[student name N]</student>
```

Now assume that you need to create an XSL stylesheet that will display these *N* names. At first this may seem easy to do with an <xsl:for-each> tag. But examine the following XSL code snippet carefully:

```
<xsl:for-each select="student">
  <xsl:value-of select="???"/><br/>
</xsl:for-each>
```

The important problem to resolve here is what value to use in the select attribute of the <xsl:value-of> tag. If the <student> tag contained an inner tag, you would simply use the name of that inner tag. But in this case there are no inner tags. The value we want to display is the value of the XML tag we already selected in the for-each tag! Fortunately, XSL provides an intrinsic function called current() to handle this situation. Simply insert the current() function as the value of the select attribute, and you are good to go.

To ensure that you understand this concept, create a simple XML file containing the names of ten or more students. Then create a simple XSL stylesheet that uses the current() function to display these names. Save your resulting files as **xml-activity2.xml** and **xsl-activity2.xsl**.

SCANS **ACTIVITY 12-3**

The Step-by-Step exercises throughout Unit 2 and Unit 3 contain numerous examples of how to use the JavaScript alert() method. This method is very useful for telling the user that something has happened, or in some cases, that something is about to happen. In Step-by-Step 12.4 and 12.5, you used the alert() method to notify the user that the student information list is about to be sorted.

You should note, however, that the alert() method only gives users the ability to acknowledge the message. It does not give them the ability to cancel the operation that is about to take place. For this reason, JavaScript also provides a confirm() method that does provide users with this ability. Its usage is as follows.

ok = confirm("[message text]");

When the confirm dialog box appears, it will display a message, just like the alert dialog box. However, the confirm dialog box includes an OK button and a Cancel button, whereas the alert dialog box displays only an OK button. The value returned from the confirm() method is *true* if the user clicks the OK button and *false* if the user clicks the Cancel button.

Use this new information to modify the behavior of the JavaScript module you created in Step-by-Step 12.5. Replace the call to the alert() method with a call to the confirm() method. Then add logic to ensure that the student information list is sorted only if the user clicks the OK button. If the user clicks Cancel, no action should be taken. Save the results of your changes in a new JavaScript source file called **js-activity3.js**.

> **Note**
>
> Don't forget to update the src attribute in the <script> tag of your corresponding XSL stylesheet.

SUMMARY *Project*

In Lesson 7 you learned about the importance of data validation for electronic forms, and how to implement it with JavaScript. In this project you will have the opportunity to show that you can also implement JavaScript data validation functions within XML/XSL Web pages.

Review the electronic "JavaScript Pizza Parlor" form you created in Lesson 7, and re-create it with an XML data file and an XSL stylesheet. After you get the form looking the way it should (see Figure 12-21), create a JavaScript source file that contains all of the functions you need to validate the pizza order form. Save your three solution files as **xml-pizza.xml, xsl-pizza.xsl,** and **js-pizza.js**.

> **Note**
>
> The   entities used in the XSL stylesheet can cause some browsers to display a strange A character instead of a space. You may simply delete these entities if necessary.

FIGURE 12-21
Lesson 12 summary project Web page

PROJECT REQUIREMENTS

- Your pizza order form should have an appropriate title.

- The pizza sizes and pizza toppings that are displayed on your form must be data elements within your XML file.

- Your XSL stylesheet must be able to adapt to any reasonable number of pizza sizes and pizza toppings.

- Your JavaScript functions must validate the form correctly regardless of the number of pizza toppings that appear on the form.

ADVANCED INTERNET TECHNOLOGIES

ADVANCED INTERNET TECHNOLOGIES VOCABULARY

TAGS AND TERMS	DESCRIPTION	LESSON
absolute Xpath	The term for the path to a data element that is constructed by starting at the top-most level (the root node) of the XML data set, and listing each lower-level XML tag name (node) that appears between the root node and the target node.	11
case sensitive	Term applied to any computer language that makes a distinction between upper and lowercase letters.	10
data sorting	The process of reorganizing a list of information into a specific order.	12
directive tag	A markup language tag that provides instructions to the Web browser.	9
<DOCTYPE> tag	Document type tag. This tag informs the Web browser what type of document it is about to process.	10
Document Type Definition (DTD)	A specialized XML file that determines the proper syntax of tags and attributes for a particular markup language.	10
extensible	Term applied to a markup language that has no predetermined limit to the number of tags that it can support.	9
XHTML	(eXtensible HyperText Markup Language) A form of HTML that conforms to the syntax rules of XML.	10
XML	(eXtensible Markup Language) A generalized markup language that describes the meaning of data rather than how the data should be displayed.	9
HTML transitioning	The process of converting a standard HTML file into a format that conforms to the syntax rules of XHTML.	10
intrinsic functions	Internal functions that can be invoked from XSL tags.	12
mod operator	The XSL modulus operator. This operator returns the remainder of an integer division operation rather than the quotient.	12
name() function	XSL intrinsic function that returns the name of an XML node.	12
name-value pair	The format of all tag attributes in XML.	9
node	A data element.	11
platform neutral	Term applied to all computer languages that can operate in many computing environments.	9

TAGS AND TERMS	DESCRIPTION	LESSON
position() function	XSL intrinsic function that returns the current iteration of a for-each loop.	12
relative Xpath	The term for the path to a data element that is constructed by designating a specific node as the root node of an XSL template. Then the path starts at that level, rather than the top-most level, of the XML data set, and list each lower-level XML tag name (node) that appears between the designated root node and the target node.	11
shortcut tag	An XML tag that combines an opening tag and its matching closing tag into a single tag.	9
stylesheet	An XSL document that describes how XML data should be displayed in a Web browser.	11
tag nesting	Place one or more tags inside of an opening-closing tag pair.	9
variables	Names within computer languages that are assigned to specific locations in memory.	12
XML namespace	An XML document that defines a set of acceptable tags and attributes.	10
XSL	(XML Stylesheet Language) A language definition that defines the set of XML tags and attributes that can be used to describe how XML data should be displayed.	11
XSLT	(XML Stylesheet Language Transformation) The resulting output when an XML document has been processed by an XSL stylesheet.	11
Xpath	Notational convention used to identify a particular data element in an XML document.	11
<xsl:attribute> tag	XSL tag that adds an attribute to a previously defined tag.	11
<xsl:for-each> tag	XSL tag that can repetitively process multiple XML data elements.	11
<xsl:if> tag	XSL tag that allows conditional processing of one or more tags.	11
<xsl:sort> tag	XSL tag that is used in conjunction with the for-each tag to sort a list of XML data.	12
<xsl:stylesheet> tag	XSL tag that specifies the XML namespace to be used for the current stylesheet.	11
<xsl:template> tag	XSL tag that identifies the relative root node of an XML data file.	11
<xsl:text> tag	XSL tag that defines static text to be displayed in an XML/XSL Web page.	11
<xsl:value-of> tag	XSL tag that extracts a data value from an XML document.	11
<xsl:variable> tag	XSL tag that defines the name and value of an XSL variable.	12

REVIEW *Questions*

MATCHING

Match the correct term in the right column to its description in the left column.

_____ **1.** Provides instructions to the Web browser rather than a description of a data element.

_____ **2.** Combines an opening tag and its matching closing tag into a single tag.

_____ **3.** Notational convention used to identify a specific data element in an XML document.

_____ **4.** XSL operator that returns the remainder of an integer division operation.

_____ **5.** Composition of an XML tag attribute.

_____ **6.** Computer language that distinguishes between upper and lowercase letters.

_____ **7.** XSL tag that specifies the relative root node of an XML data file.

_____ **8.** XSL tag that defines the name and value of an XSL variable.

_____ **9.** Tag used to specify the type of document the Web browser is about to process.

_____ **10.** XSL function used to obtain the current iteration of a for-each loop.

A. Xpath

B. case sensitive

C. <DOCTYPE>

D. shortcut tag

E. name-value pair

F. <xsl:variable>

G. directive tag

H. mod

I. <xsl:template>

J. position()

WRITTEN QUESTIONS

Write a brief answer to each of the following questions.

1. Describe the purpose and characteristics of XML.

2. Identify the primary differences between HTML and XHTML.

3. Describe the characteristics of XSL that distinguish it from a simple markup language.

4. Explain how JavaScript code is integrated with XSL stylesheets.

5. Explain the relationship that exists between XML, XHTML, and XSL.

CROSS-CURRICULAR *Projects*

In this exercise, you will use XML and XSL to create a Web page that will help users locate books that can be used to find information on a variety of subjects.

Your first task will be to create an XML document called cc-project.xml that will contain information about 20 to 25 books. This XML file will contain five sections, and each section will contain information for 4 to 5 books. The book information should consist of title, author, copyright date, and publisher. The XML format of the book data should look like this:

```
<book>
  <title>HTML and JavaScript</title>
  <author>E. Shane Turner</author>
  <copyright>2005</copyright>
  <publisher>Course Technology</publisher>
</book>
```

The five sections should include the following topics and be designated in the XML file as described here:

LANGUAGE ARTS 3

Include a section in your XML data file that is delimited by the XML tags <language-arts> and </language-arts>.

SCIENCE 3

Include a section in your XML data file that is delimited by the XML tags <science> and </science>.

SOCIAL STUDIES 3

Include a section in your XML data file that is delimited by the XML tags <social-studies> and </social-studies>.

MATH 3

Include a section in your XML data file that is delimited by the XML tags and.

YOUR CHOICE OF SUBJECT 3

Include a section in your XML data file that is delimited by the XML tags <my-choice> and </my-choice>.

Your next task will be to create an XSL stylesheet called **cc-project.xsl** that will display the book information in an organized way. Your final Web page should display the information in a tabular format grouped by topic. A sample Web page is shown in Figure U3-1.

FIGURE U3-1
Book information Web page

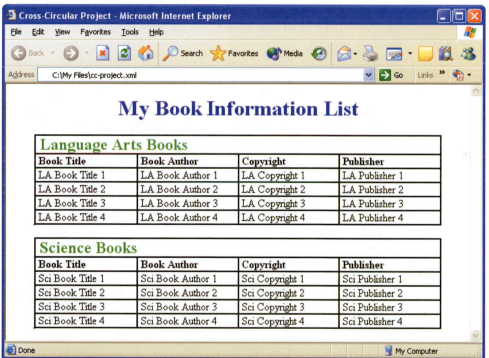

REVIEW*Projects*

PROJECT 3-1

Review the requirements for the Unit 2 Summary Project found at the end of the Unit 2 Review. In this project you were asked to create a JavaScript-enabled form for ordering computer systems. Demonstrate that you have mastered the ability to create XML/XSL Web pages by converting this project to XML and XSL with JavaScript.

You should begin this project by creating an XML document (called **project3-1.xml**) that contains the names and prices of the various computer components. Next, create an XSL stylesheet (called **project3-1.xsl**) that will display the order form as shown in Figure U2-1. And finally, create a JavaScript source file (called **project3-1.js**) that will implement all of the appropriate JavaScript functions.

PROJECT 3-2

Revisit the Web page you created for Step-by-Step 12.5 in Lesson 12. This Web page displays a list of student information, and allows the user to sort this list in various ways. Demonstrate your mastery of XML/XSL Web pages by adding a new column to this list. This additional column will contain a small photo (thumbnail) of each student. (Note that it is not necessary to allow the user to sort the list by this new column.)

To accomplish this task, add the name of the image file to each student node in the XML data file. Then add some new tags to your XSL stylesheet to display the image in a 64 × 64 pixel box next to each student's name. Make sure that the images move as they should whenever the user changes the sort order of the student list. When you are finished, save your modified files with the names **project3-2.xml**, **project3-2.xsl**, and **project3-2.js**.

SIMULATION

JOB 3-1

Make a list of the top 10 Web sites that you like to visit. Use your browser's View Source menu option to view the source code for several Web pages on each site. Based on what you see, create a table like the one below that indicates if the creators of each site used any of the advanced Internet technologies you have been studying in Unit 3. You will need to think carefully about what to look for to determine what technologies a particular Web site may be using. Save your completed table as **job3-1.doc** or **job3-1.txt**.

TABLE U3-1
Web sites that use advanced Internet technologies

WEB SITE ADDRESS	XML?	XHTML?	XSL?	JAVASCRIPT?
www.website1.com	no	no	no	yes
www.website2.com	no	yes	no	no
www.website3.com	yes	no	yes	yes
...	...	...	...	...
www.website10.com	no	yes	no	yes

JOB 3-2

Several national Web sites are available to help people find all sorts of jobs. (Such sites include *monster.com*, *careerbuilder.com*, *jobweb.com*, and so forth.) Choose a variety of these sites, and do some job searches to get an idea of how many employers are looking to hire people with advanced Internet technology skills. (Search for positions such as Web designer, Web developer, Software Engineer, and so forth.) Based on the results of your search, create a table like the one below to determine how many positions are available that list an advanced Internet technology skill in the job requirements. Save your completed table as **job3-2.doc** or **job3-2.txt**.

TABLE U3-2
Positions available that require advanced Internet technology skills

JOB SEARCH WEB SITE	XML?	XHTML?	XSL?	JAVASCRIPT?
www.monster.com	38	6	12	29
www.careerbuilder.com	41	9	4	17
www.jobweb.com	16	3	8	11
...	...	...	...	...

SUMMARY *Project*

This is your opportunity to demonstrate your mastery of creating XML/XSL Web pages and your ability to combine these skills with previously learned concepts.

For this project, you will create an HTML frame set that will display multiple XML/XSL Web pages. The left-hand frame will contain an XML-based navigation array, and the right-hand frame will initially display a simple HTML welcome screen. When the user clicks on a hyperlink in the left frame, however, the right frame will display the appropriate XML/XSL Web page. An example Web page is shown in Figure U3-2.

FIGURE U3-2
Unit 3 Summary Project Web page

PROJECT REQUIREMENTS

■ Your frame set should be built as a standard HTML file called **unit3-summary.html** or **unit3-summary.htm**.

■ Your left-hand navigation bar must be an XML/XSL Web page. The Web page names and addresses must be contained within an XML document called **navbar.xml**, and displayed by a stylesheet called **navbar.xsl**.

■ The initial welcome screen in the right frame should be a simple HTML document called **welcome.html** or **welcome.htm**.

■ The right-hand Web pages that appear in response to hyperlink clicks in the left frame should be the XML/XSL Web pages you created for Lessons 11 and 12.

PORTFOLIO *Checklist*

Include the following files from this unit in your student portfolio:

___ Advanced Internet Technologies summary questions

___ Cross-Curricular Project

___ Project 3-1

___ Project 3-2

___ Job 3-1

___ Job 3-2

___ Unit 3 Summary Project

GLOSSARY

A

Absolute Xpath The term for the path to a data element that is constructed by starting at the top-most level (the root node) of the XML data set, and listing each lower-level XML tag name (node) that appears between the root node and the target node.

Ad banner *See* Cycling banner.

Angle brackets HTML tags appear in pairs and are enclosed in angle brackets. The brackets can be found on the comma (,) and period (.) keys on the keyboard.

Array A collection of similar objects that are accessed by a variable name and an index. When you give several controls the same name, they are considered an array of objects. The array is required to have an index value that will always start with zero and increase for each element in the array.

Attribute Attribute tags are used to enhance an HTML tag. The <BODY> tag is considered an attribute tag because many different types of values are used to change the appearance of the Web page's body or background.

B

Binary code After JavaScript code has been translated by interpretation, it becomes binary code, or machine-readable code.

Buttons Input controls that are defined with the TYPE attribute instead of the INPUT tag.

C

Case sensitive Making a distinction between upper and lower case letters.

Check boxes An input control that allows the user to select any or all of the listed options from a set of options.

Compiler A highly specialized piece of software that takes a programming language that humans can understand and converts it into a language computers can understand.

Components *See* Controls.

Condition Made up of two tokens and a relational operator. A conditional statement tells the browser that if this condition is met, perform this function; if not (ELSE), perform a different function.

Controls/components An interactive object with a JavaScript form. Controls or components must be given a name so they can be referenced within the JavaScript code.

Cross-frame interaction Action performed when an action in one frame affects the appearance of a different frame. All of the frames that make up a Web page can communicate with each other by means of JavaScript functions.

Cycling banner Several graphics are displayed one after another with a pause between images. The graphics scroll on either a fixed or random order.

D

Data sorting The process of reorganizing a list of information into a specific order.

Data validation The process of checking user input data to make sure it is complete and accurate.

Decrement To subtract one member from a value.

Directive tag XML tag used to give instructions to the XML interpreter.

Document Type Definition (DTD) A special file that defines the type of file being processed.

document type tag (<DOCTYPE>) A special tag that identifies the DTD to use for the current file.

E

Event The operating system's response to the occurrence of a specific condition.

Extensible Allows the addition of tags (no predefined set).

eXtensible HyperText Markup Language What the acronym XHTML stands for.

eXtensible Markup Language What the acronym XML stands for.

F

Flash A high-impact multimedia creation tool for the creation of Web page content.

Fonts Also known as the style of letters, fonts determine the appearance of text in Web documents. Fonts have three attributes that can be changed: size, style, and color of text.

Frame A rectangular area, a subset of a browser's screen, capable of displaying a Web page that is separate from other frames on the screen.

Frame set Allows the definition of a set of rectangular areas on a Web page called frames where each frame is capable of displaying a different Web page.

Function A piece of JavaScript that can be called upon to perform certain tasks. Functions are written by the programmer and can contain any number of JavaScript statements, including calls to other functions or methods.

Function parameter An efficient way to pass a parameter to a function, especially if there are ten, twenty, or a hundred different parameters.

G

.gif An acronym for Graphics Interchange Format. GIF files are compact in size and are one of two popular graphic formats used in Web documents. The extension, .gif, helps to tell the Web browser that these files are pictures, not Web documents.

Graphics Pictures that can be placed in Web documents.

Graphics Interchange Format Compact graphics, also called .gifs, that are small enough in size to use in Web documents.

H

Hexadecimal Hexadecimal digits operate on a base-16 number system rather than the base-10 number system most people use. Hexadecimal numbers use the letters A, B, C, D, E, and F along with the numbers 0 to 9 to create 16 different digits.

Home page The main Web page for a corporation, individual, or organization. A home page is often the first page you see when you start your Web browser.

HTML An acronym for Hypertext Markup Language.

HTML page An HTML page, or HTML document, is any document created in HTML that can be displayed on the World Wide Web.

HTML transitioning Converting a standard HTML file into an XHTML file.

HTTP An acronym that stands for Hypertext Transfer Protocol. On the location line in your Web browser, this is often seen in the following format: *http://www.course.com.*

Hyperlink rollover An image that changes when the mouse pointer clicks on or moves over a hyperlink graphic.

Hyperlinks Allows users to click on a specific spot in a Web document and have it link to another page they've created, to another Web page on the World Wide Web, or to another spot within the current document.

Hypertext links Links that transport Web visitors to selected information. Links can be made to information within a document, in another document on the same computer, or to a document residing on any Web server on the Internet. Links are often used to make Web pages more interesting and easier to navigate.

Hypertext Markup Language Tags created within a Web document that give instructions to a Web browser. These instructions determine the look and feel of a Web document on the Internet.

Hypertext Transfer Protocol The type of digital language that Web servers use to communicate with Web browsers. A protocol is a communications system that is used to transfer data over networks.

I

Image A term used to refer to a graphic in a Web document. The letters IMG of the word are part of the HTML tag used to determine attributes of an image on the World Wide Web.

Image rollover The appearance of an image changes when the mouse pointer moves over the image.

Increment To add one number to a value.

Index A variable that usually has the value of zero assigned to it. The index variable is used to access information about the array.

Instantiate The process of creating a new object and assigning it a value.

Internet Explorer One of two major Web browsers used to view information on the World Wide Web. Internet Explorer was created by Microsoft Corporation.

Interpretation A term used by programmers to describe the line-by-line conversion process that occurs automatically at run time or when the Web browser launches the JavaScript commands that are enabled in the Web document.

Intrinsic Functions Functions built into the XSL processor that return information about XML values rather than the values themselves.

J

Java A programming language that creates programs called applets. Applets can be added to Web documents using tags similar to HTML text.

JavaScript More powerful than HTML, JavaScript allows Web page developers to add programming features to a Web document without having to know a programming language.

Joint Photographic Experts Group Compact graphics called JPEGs that are small enough in size to use in Web documents.

.jpg or .jpeg An acronym for Joint Photographic Experts Group. .Jpg or .jpeg files are compact in size and are one of two popular graphic formats used in Web documents. The extensions, .jpg and .jpeg, tell the Web browser that these files are pictures.

K

Keywords A word that is recognized by the programming language as part of its language. A keyword, like IF, ELSE, or RETURN, cannot be used as a variable.

L

Left-hand navigation A narrow left-hand frame that contains hyperlinks that can be used to navigate a Web site.

M

Methods Specialized functions within the object that call upon the services of the object. A method is invoked after you enter the name of the object, followed by a period.

mod operator XSL operator that returns the remainder of a division operation rather than the quotient.

Mosaic The first Web browser that allowed pictures and sound to accompany text on a Web page. Mosaic was created in 1992 at the University of Illinois.

N

name( ) function XSL intrinsic function that returns the name of an XML node.

Name-value pair The name of an XML attribute and its associated value.

Navigation bar A series of hypertext links, usually organized horizontally or vertically on a Web page or in a frame. Used to navigate a Web site.

Nested frame set A term programmers use to describe a structure, keyword, or tag that contains one or more additional instances of the same item.

Netscape Navigator One of two major Web browsers used on the Internet today. Navigator, created in 1994, added to the powerful features of Mosaic, allowing additional features like animated graphics into a Web document.

Node A data element.

O

Objects Invisible entities that have a defined set of capabilities.

Operators Placed between two tokens in a conditional statement.

P

Parameter list A list of information that provides a programming method what it needs to perform a specific function correctly.

Parent object In order for a JavaScript function to access an object in a different file, the two files must be linked. The "parent" frame set can be referenced via a JavaScript object. The frame set file defines "child" frames, and these frames are given names.

Pixel An individual tiny dot of light inside a computer monitor.

Platform neutral A technology that will operate with many types of computers.

position( ) function XSL intrinsic function that returns the current iteration of a for-each loop.

Programming language A language that has to be converted from a human-readable format into machine-readable format. This process is accomplished by using a compiler to complete the operation.

Properties Objects that programmers access to obtain information about the object.

R

Radio button An input control that allows the user to select just one option from a set of options.

Real number (floating-point number) A real number that has a decimal portion.

Relative Xpath The term for the path to a data element that is constructed by designating a specific node as the root node of an XSL template. Then the path would just start at that level, rather than the top-most level, of the XML data set, and list each lower-level XML tag name (node) that appears between the designated root node and the target node.

Return value Whenever a function is called, its name is replaced by the value it returns.

S

<SCRIPT> and </SCRIPT> tags The beginning and end tags that are necessary in a Web document for a JavaScript statement to be executed. All JavaScript code must be placed within the beginning and ending tag.

Scripting language A language that does not have to be run through a compiler for it to be understood. Web browsers take the human-readable format and convert it into machine-readable format "on-the-fly."

Shortcut tags XML tag that combines opening and closing tags.

Slide show A collection of images that change when the user clicks on the image.

Status line The area of the screen that displays various messages at the bottom of the browser's window that can be accessed from within a JavaScript program.

Stylesheet An XSL document.

Syntax The rules of grammar for a scripting language.

T

Table cells Boxes in which you can place things to keep your Web document organized. Each table box, or cell, can have different attributes applied to text, can have a different background color, or can contain a different graphic.

Tag nesting Placing XML tags inside of other tags.

Text field An input control that allows someone to type a string value into a specific location on a Web page.

Title bar The topmost bar in an open window or a frame used at the top of the Web page.

Token Either a variable name or a literal constant, which is followed by a relational operator. A JavaScript condition will always consist of two tokens.

Top object JavaScript functions can be defined in the top-level frame set file, no matter how deeply it is nested within the Web page framework. These functions can be accessed by using a JavaScript "top" object.

U

Uniform Resource Locator Abbreviated as URL, the Internet addressing scheme that defines the route, or path, to a file or program. The URL is used as the initial access to an online resource.

V

Value Used to define attributes. Values are used in conjunction with attributes. For example, in the tag <BODY BGCOLOR = RED> Red is a value used to define the background color attribute in a body tag. The value can be changed to a hexadecimal number such as #0000ff, or words such as BLUE.

Variable A name that is assigned to a literal value or to an object. Once assigned, that name can be used throughout the HTML document referred to that particular value or object.

Variables User-friendly names that refer to specific locations in memory.

VRML An acronym for Virtual Reality Markup Language. A language used on the World Wide Web that allows people to view and search three-dimensional landscapes and models.

W

Web browser Often referred to as a Web client, it allows users to interface with different operating systems and view information on the World Wide Web. It allows Web page developers to have JavaScript compiled and interpreted "on-the-fly."

Web page Any page created in HTML that can be placed on the World Wide Web.

Web site Includes a series of Web pages that can be linked to other Web sites on the Internet. Web sites are stored on Web servers.

Webmaster A person assigned to maintain Web pages for a Web site.

Welcome page An introduction page to a Web site. A welcome page often includes the Web page owner's e-mail address and name.

X

XML namespace A set of naming rules that determines which tags are valid and which are not.

XML Stylesheet Language (XSL) Companion language to XML that determines how data elements should be displayed.

XML Stylesheet Language Transformation (XSLT) The resulting output after an XML file has been processed by an XSL stylesheet.

Xpath Naming convention used to identify a particular XML data element.

<xsl:attribute> tag XSL tag used to add an attribute to a previously defined HTML tag.

<xsl:for-each> tag XSL tag used to process multiple XML data items that share a common name.

<xsl:if> tag XSL tag used to process HTML tags conditionally.

<xsl:sort> tag XSL tag that orders the data within a for-each loop before it is displayed.

<xsl:stylesheet> tag Identifies the XML namespace to be used by the current stylesheet.

<xsl:template> tag Identifies the "relative root" node of the corresponding XML document.

<xsl:text> tag Allows stylesheets to display static text in Web pages.

<xsl:value-of> tag Extracts a data value from an XML document.

<xsl:variable> tag XSL tag that defines a variable.

INDEX